Hitler's Heroes During Operation Barbarossa

Hitler's Heroes During Operation Barbarossa

Knight's Cross Generals on the Eastern Front, 22 June–5 December 1941

Jeremy Dixon

Frontline Books

First published in Great Britain in 2024 by
Frontline Books
An imprint of Pen & Sword Books Limited
Yorkshire – Philadelphia

ISBN 978 1 03610 153 4

A CIP catalogue record for this book is
available from the British Library

Typeset by Mac Style
Printed in the UK by CPI Group (UK) Ltd, Croydon, CR0 4YY.

FSC
www.fsc.org
MIX
Paper | Supporting
responsible forestry
FSC® C013604

Pen & Sword Books Limited incorporates the imprints of After
the Battle, Atlas, Archaeology, Aviation, Discovery, Family History,
Fiction, History, Maritime, Military, Military Classics, Politics,
Select, Transport, True Crime, Air World, Frontline Publishing, Leo
Cooper, Remember When, Seaforth Publishing, The Praetorian Press,
Wharncliffe Local History, Wharncliffe Transport, Wharncliffe True
Crime and White Owl.

For a complete list of Pen & Sword titles please contact

PEN & SWORD BOOKS LIMITED
47 Church Street, Barnsley, South Yorkshire, S70 2AS, England
E-mail: enquiries@pen-and-sword.co.uk
Website: www.pen-and-sword.co.uk
or
PEN AND SWORD BOOKS
1950 Lawrence Road, Havertown, PA 19083, USA
E-mail: uspen-and-sword@casematepublishers.com
Website: www.penandswordbooks.com

Dedicated to Wendy and Richard – my Mum and Dad

Contents

Acknowledgements

I would like to thank Paul Budden for proof-reading the book and offering advice and assistance, and I must also thank my mum and dad, sister and nephew for their continued support. I would also like to thank my friends for their help and interest. My thanks go out to Ann Driscoll, Anne Taylor, Jo Robinson, Jo Jeffrey, Angela Axton-Green, Nick Isles, Hazel Kirby, Jackie Snowling, Carol Ryan, Laura Fisher, Lisa Hunt, Liz Ross, Jane Budgen, Lois Farnie, Bev Drew, Gemma Ross, Vanessa Gardner, Lois Farnie, Lauretta Kelly, Linda Hurd, Colin Harris, Alex Curran, Nathan Pearce, and Debra and Dave Mills.

Introduction

This is the first of a four-volume work that describes how 554 German officers who held the rank of general were awarded the highest award for bravery and command, the Knight's Cross. This, the first of those volumes, describes how the 172 generals – twenty-five *Generalmajor*, fifty-five *Generalleutnant*, eighty-three full *Generals*, eight *Generaloberst* and one *Generalfeldmarschall* – gained the award during the first six months of the German invasion of the Soviet Union.

On 22 June 1941 Germany invaded its former ally. Code-named Operation Barbarossa after a twelfth-century Holy Roman emperor and German king, it was the largest land offensive in history, one in which more than 3 million troops took part. Germany had begun massing personnel near the Soviet border from February 1941, with about 680,000 soldiers gathered in an area on the Romanian–Soviet frontier. In preparation Hitler had secretly moved about 3 million German troops and 690,000 Axis soldiers to the Soviet border. Taking part in the invasion were 600,000 vehicles, 750,000 horses, 3,580 tanks and 1,830 aircraft. Hitler's aim was to conqueror the western Soviet Union and to repopulate it with Germans – his intention was to use Soviet prisoners as forced labour for the war effort.

The Soviet defenders were 4½ million strong along the frontier but were caught off guard by the Germans. There was no deception; at 0300 hours, when the guard was changed at the International Bridge at Brest-Litovsk, the German sentries simply gunned down their Soviet counterparts instead of saluting them. The Soviet–German Pact that had been agreed and signed by Vyacheslav Molotov and German Foreign Minister Joachim von Ribbentrop on 23 August 1939 was forgotten. Germany declared war on the Soviet Union and Hitler's immediate objectives were to direct an Army Group at the key Soviet cities of Leningrad, Moscow and Kiev.

On 23 June, day two of the invasion, German troops crossed the Bug River using rubber dinghies until a bridge could be built. The Soviets lost 500 aircraft while only destroying about twelve German aircraft. The next day Vilnius and Lithuania fell to the Germans and it was reported that in just seventy-two hours they had virtually destroyed the world's largest air force. Three days later

German forces began an assault and crossed the Dvina River, capturing Brest-Litovsk and Daugavpils. In the north the Germans had pushed on 190 miles and *General der Infanterie* Erich von Manstein's LVI. Motorised Army Corps had been ordered to halt by Hitler to let the infantry catch up. Manstein had lost an opportunity to strike at Leningrad.

Heinz Guderian began his military career as an officer candidate with *Jäger* Battalion 10 in 1907 and later served during the First World War with the cavalry and later as a general staff officer. He was awarded the Iron Cross 2nd Class in September 1914 and two years later he was awarded the Iron Cross 1st Class and ended the war with the rank of *Hauptmann.* (*Deutsches Wehrkundearchiv*)

From 27 to 29 June, Panzer Group 2 under *Generaloberst* Heinz Guderian began the drive to link up near Minsk in an effort to trap three Soviet armies. On the 28th, German forces captured Minsk, and Lvov fell to the Germans on 30 June; they took 7,000 prisoners, but had lost 8,886 troops. Panzer units under Guderian crossed the Berezina River on the central Russian front on 1 July, while German forces in the north captured Riga, the capital of Latvia. A few days' later German troops encountered the Soviet T-34 tank for the first time and on 9 July the Minsk Pocket and Vitebsk were overrun by German troops. A total of 290,000 Soviet troops surrendered and almost 2,500 Soviet tanks were lost. German Army Group Centre captured Smolensk during the Battle of Uman

At the beginning of the Second World War Guderian was serving as *General der Panzertruppe* and Commanding General of the XIX. Army Corps and was awarded the Bar to the Iron Cross 1st and 2nd Class during September 1939. He later took part in the Western campaign, the Battle of Sedan and later joined the attack on the Allied armies in Belgium and France along the Maginot Line. With the Western campaign over, Guderian was promoted to the rank of *Generaloberst* in July 1940. (*Author's Collection*)

Hermann Hoth with Georg Pfeiffer. Hoth was a cadet at Potsdam from 1896 and from 1904 he was assigned to the War School in Danzig. He was commissioned as a *Leutnant* in January 1905 and was adjutant of II. Battalion of Infantry Regiment 72 until September 1913. He was attached to the General Staff at the beginning of the First World War and was promoted to *Hauptmann* in November 1914. From August 1918 he served as Chief of Operations in the General Staff of the 30th Infantry Division and he remained in the Army after the war. (*Author's Collection*)

on 15 July and 600,000 Soviet troops were trapped. It was a military disaster, but Soviet resistance began to strengthen for the first time since the invasion.

On 17 July *Generaloberst* Hermann Hoth and *Generaloberst* Guderian's panzer armies encircled more than 300,000 Soviet troops east of Smolensk – almost 1 million Soviet troops had now become trapped! Five days later, and for the first time in their Soviet offensive, German forces came to a temporary halt. A month after the beginning of the campaign, the Axis forces had conquered around 720,000 square miles of Soviet territory.

On 30 July Hitler ordered *Generalfeldmarschall* Fedor von Bock to halt his drive on Moscow and direct Army Group Centre to concentrate on the Ukraine and to capture Leningrad. A few days later German units crushed resistance in the Smolensk Pocket and fighting continued in the area for the next few days. On 13 August, the Siege of Odessa began; the Germans calculated they had lost 30,000 dead in the first six weeks of the Soviet campaign. Within the next few days, the Germans cleared Novgorod and Kiev, and Dnepropetrovsk fell.

On 21 August Hitler issued a strategic directive in which he stated: 'The most important objective to be achieved before the onset of winter is not the capture of Moscow but the seizure of the Crimea.' Hitler felt the need for Crimean wheat and the industrial facilities of the Donet's Basin were more important.

Hermann Hoth with Heinz Guderian (left) and Hans von Greiffenberg, later his chief of staff, to his right. Hoth served with various infantry regiments, was attached to the Reich Defence Ministry from 1925 and promoted to *Oberstleutnant* four years later. He attended various courses and was promoted to *Oberst* in February 1932, when he became Commander of Infantry Regiment 17. He was promoted to *Generalmajor* in October 1934 and the following year he was named Commander of the 18th Division. By November 1938 he was Commanding General of the XV. Army Corps with the rank of *General der Infanterie* and saw action during the invasion of Poland. (*Author's Collection*)

During the next few days Tallinn, the capital of Estonia, fell to the Germans and by 2 September they were within 20 miles of Leningrad. Five days later Guderian's Panzer Group 2 was 100 miles east of Kiev and together with Panzer Group 1 under the command of *Generaloberst* Ewald von Kleist, had surrounded the Soviets at Kiev. On 8 September German tank columns had encircled Leningrad and were 150 rail miles from Moscow, and just two days later the Battle of Smolensk ended with a German victory and Kiev was close to being encircled. On the 16th, in the greatest capitulation of the war so far, more than 500,000 Soviet soldiers in the area around Kiev surrendered to the Germans. Around 665,000 Soviet soldiers were captured, although the Russians disputed the figure and would only admit to 527,000 men captured or wounded. Russian troops were trapped in the Kiev Pocket and on 19 September Kiev fell to the Germans. The battle for the city was disastrous for the Soviets, who suffered 350,000 casualties and lost 3,718 guns together with 884 armoured vehicles, and five armies were eliminated.

By 21 September the Germans had reached the Sea of Azov and cut off the Crimea, and on the 26th Hitler ordered a halt in the offensive directed at Moscow. He refused his generals permission to concentrate on a drive towards the Soviet capital, preferring to take the Ukraine. The 2nd Panzer Army began an offensive directed at Orel and Bryansk, the 1st Panzer Group reached the

Dnieper River in the Ukraine and on 2 October the 3rd and 4th Panzer Groups launched a massive offensive directed towards Vyazma. The Soviet 9th and 10th Armies suffered heavy casualties and more than 100,000 troops were captured in Ukrainian pockets. In fact, the Germans enjoyed a two-to-one advantage in men and tanks over the encircled Soviet defenders.

On 8 October the Germans captured Orel and the heavy rain made most of the front a quagmire; the Soviets lost 50,000 troops taken prisoner. Three days later Soviet T-34 tanks went into action against the German XXIV. Panzer Corps and inflicted severe losses. However, on the 13th the Germans managed to take 673,000 Soviet prisoners in the Vyazma Pocket and all resistance ended. Panzer units captured Kalinin, which was 93 miles north-west of Moscow, and two days later the Soviet government left the capital for Kuibyshev, 525 miles to the east. However, Stalin remained in the city. Odessa fell to the Germans on 16 October and the Soviets suffered another military disaster as the battles of Bryansk and Vyazma ended. The Germans took 663,000 prisoners and destroyed or captured 1,240 tanks and more than 5,400 artillery guns.

A state of siege was declared in Moscow, with German forces only 60 miles away. Kharkov, the industrial centre of the Ukraine, fell to the LV. Army Corps under the command of *General der Infanterie* Erwin Vierow and *Generalmajor* Anton Dostler, the Commander of the 57th Infantry Division. However, the German advance towards Moscow became stalled on 25 October, and two days later the Soviets launched a counter-attack from the capital. On the 30th, German Army Group Centre, under *Generalfeldmarschall* von Bock, launched an attack on Moscow and the Siege of Sevastopol began, which would last for nine months.

On 1 November the German 1st Panzer Group under *Generaloberst* Ewald von Kleist began a major attack aimed at Rostock and the Caucasus. Two days later the Germans attacked Kursk and that same day the Soviets admitted they had lost 350,000 troops with 378,000 missing and a total of 1,020,000 troops wounded since the German invasion. However, Hitler claimed that the Soviet losses were much higher – as high as 8 to 10 million! In reality, by the end of 1941 the Soviets had lost 566,852 troops, of which 101,471 died in hospital from wounds and 235,339 died from non-combat causes.

On 13 November *Generaloberst* Franz Halder, Chief of the German General Staff of the Army, summoned the Chiefs of Staff of all the major units in Russia for a secret conference in Orscha, a city in occupied Belarus. The advance on Moscow was discussed. The senior Army Group commanders, *Generalfeldmarschalls* von Rundstedt and von Leeb both wanted to switch to a solid defence line, and rest on the territorial gains against the Soviet Union until mid-November 1941.

Generalfeldmarschall von Bock, the Commander of Army Group Centre had a different opinion, he wanted to capture Moscow. Bock insisted that the march towards Moscow should continue, ignoring the terrible weather and weakened state of his army. Hitler supported this stance, as did the High Command. So it was agreed the advance on Moscow should continue. With temperatures at -20 degrees centigrade the winter was to be the coldest in 140 years!

The Germans launched the Autumn Offensive, directed at Moscow, on 19 November, and the following day the 1st Panzer Army under the command of *Generaloberst* Ewald von Kleist captured Rostov-on-Don. On 27 November the Germans were stopped just 19 miles from Moscow and the following day the Soviets forced the Germans out of Rostov. It was the first setback for the Germans on the Soviet Front – not their last. *Generalfeldmarschall* Gerd von Rundstedt, commander of Army Group South resigned, rather than issue the order to retreat! On 2 December, due to a Soviet counter-attack, von Kleist was forced to issue a retreat order to his Panzer Army.

German units had suffered 40 per cent frostbite casualties and began to pull back from the suburbs of Moscow. On 5 December the Soviet counter-attack began and Hitler ordered a halt to German offensive operations aimed at Moscow. Of the 3½ million German soldiers committed to the Soviet Union, 750,000 had been killed or wounded, or were listed as missing. It was against this backdrop that Operation *Barbarossa* was finally terminated on 7 January 1942.

Knight's Cross Recipients

NB: Underlined Christian names are those the subject chose to be known by.

Erich MARCKS

General der Artillerie

* (born) 6 June 1891, Berlin-Schöneberg, Brandenburg
+ (died) 12 June 1944, near Hébécrevon, South Normandy, France

Knight's Cross: Awarded on 26 June 1941 as *Generalleutnant* and Commander of 101st Light Infantry Division while attached to the LVII. Army Corps for his leadership and for the success of his division during the invasion of the Soviet Union. Throughout four days of battle while crossing the San River north-east of Przemyśl, Marcks was a great example for his men, always present among them and personally directing the fire against enemy bunkers from very close range. On the day he was notified of his award he was seriously wounded near Medyka on the Eastern Front and had to have his left leg amputated. He was away from active duty until 25 March 1942.

He returned to duty as Commander of the

Erich Marcks was described as a highly capable staff officer who drew up the plans for the invasion of the Soviet Union. His plan was to encircle the Soviet armies close to the frontier and then most of the industrial regions would be occupied – Leningrad, Moscow and the Donez areas. He had proposed that two army groups, North and South, be created, but he did not believe that the Soviet Union could be conquered in a single campaign and he expressed his fear of an Anglo-Soviet coalition to the high command. However, *Generalfeldmarschall* Walter von Brauchitsch and *Generaloberst* Franz Halder disagreed. The whole planning operation was turned over to the new Deputy Chief of the General Staff for Operations, *Generalleutnant* Friedrich Paulus. (*Deutsches Wehrkundearchiv*)

337th Infantry Division, which was stationed in Brittany, France, on garrison duty. On 20 September he was appointed Commanding General of the LXVI. Army Corps, which was also based in Brittany, and on 1 October he was promoted to *Generalleutnant* and took over as Commanding General of the LXXXIV. Army Corps, stationed in Saint-Lô, France. On 6 June 1944, Marcks' 53rd birthday, his staff presented him with a cake, but he couldn't concentrate on the celebrations as he was convinced the Allies were about to strike. He couldn't get anyone to believe his suspicions and was the only German general on D-Day who believed the Allies were coming.

Knight's Cross with Oakleaves: He became the 503rd recipient, posthumously, on 24 June 1944 as *General der Artillerie* and Commanding General of LXXXIV. Army Corps while attached to the 7th Army in France. It was awarded for his role in the containing of the Allied invasion of Normandy during the first vital weeks. On 12 June, during a daily inspection, his staff car was attacked by an American fighter-bomber near Hébécrevon, a few miles north-west of Saint-Lô. A 20mm projectile struck Marcks to the upper groin of his left leg, which ruptured an artery, and his driver carried him to a nearby ditch to protect him from further attacks. However, in under an hour Marcks had died from loss of blood. He is buried today in the Marigny War Cemetery in Block 2, Row 38, Grave No: 1478 and he shares a headstone with *Gefreiter* Gerhardt Eberhard, his long-time Orderly, who had been killed in an air raid on the same day.

Gustav HÖHNE

General der Infanterie

* 17 February 1893, Kruschwitz, Strelno in Posen
+ 1 July 1951, Oberursel, Frankfurt Rhein-Main

Knight's Cross: Awarded on 30 June 1941 as *Generalmajor* and Commander of the 8th Infantry Division while attached to the VIII. Army Corps for the swift capture of fortress Grodno in Belarus, using a bridge over the Niemen River on 23 June. The advance of the division and the capture of Grodno by his division were of great importance and were largely due to his own planning and strategy. He later took part in the campaign at Bryansk and the Battle of Moscow, where the division suffered heavy losses. Höhne headed to France with the division in late 1941, where it was converted to a Light Division and returned to the Soviet Union in early 1942.

Gustav Höhne entered Army service as a *Fahnenjunker* with Infantry Regiment 150 in March 1911 and was commissioned as a *Leutnant* in August 1912. He was Company Leader from January 1915 and was wounded a month later. He was promoted to *Oberleutnant* in January the following year, after being awarded the Iron Cross 1st and 2nd Classes. He served much of the war assigned to Infantry Regiment 150 and he was wounded twice again in March 1918. He was serving with Infantry brigade 73 when the war ended. He remained in the Army after the war and by August 1935 he had been promoted to the rank of *Oberstleutnant* and was serving as Commander of the III. Battalion of Infantry Regiment 6. He was promoted to *Oberst* in March 1938 and during the invasion of Poland he commanded Infantry Regiment 28. (*Author's Collection*)

Knight's Cross with Oakleaves: He became the 238th recipient on 17 May 1943 as *Generalleutnant* and Commanding General of Corps Group '*Höhne*' as part of the 16th Army for his continued actions on the Russian Front. On 28 November 1942, Höhne positioned his forces in the Demyansk area and was tasked with holding the area against a new Soviet offensive, which he succeeded in doing. He continued to distinguish himself as a commander until the area was finally evacuated early the following year. The Oakleaves were presented to him by a grateful Hitler at *Führer* Headquarters, the Wolf's Lair in East Prussia on 28 August 1943. With his promotion to *General der Infanterie* in May 1943 Höhne was appointed Commanding General of the VIII. Army Corps two months later. He took command of the LXXXIX. Army Corps in December 1944 and saw action on the Western Front where he was taken prisoner by US troops on 8 May 1945, and was released two years later.

Helmut Karl Georg THÜMM

General der Infanterie

* 25 August 1895, Ravensburg, Württemberg
+ 13 July 1977, Welzheim, Baden-Württemberg

Knight's Cross: Awarded on 30 June 1941 as *Oberstleutnant* and Commander of Infantry Regiment 56 part of the 5th Infantry Division for actions during the invasion of the Soviet Union. On the very first day of the invasion he contributed decisively to the breakthrough of the Soviet border positions along the front and which permitted the entire corps to advance rapidly across the Niemen

Helmut Thümm entered the war as a volunteer in August 1914 and saw action with Infantry Regiment 125 from May 1915. He was commissioned as a *Leutnant* three months later. He served with the Assault Company of the 54th Reserve Division from August 1916 and was captured by the British in August 1918. He remained in the Army after the war. He was promoted to *Oberleutnant* in July 1925, serving with various machine gun units, and was promoted to *Hauptmann* in March 1930. He served as adjutant of Infantry Regiment 13 from October 1934 and from January 1937, now with the rank of *Major*, he was named as Commander of I. Battalion of Infantry Regiment 75. He was promoted to *Oberstleutnant* in 1938 and awarded the Bar to the Iron Cross 1st and 2nd Classes during the French campaign of 1940. (*Deutsches Wehrkundearchiv*)

Horst Niemack entered the Army in June 1927 as an officer candidate and trained with the 18th Mounted Regiment in Stuttgart from July 1928. In February 1932 he was commissioned as a *Leutnant* and from October the following year he was assigned to a special section of the Cavalry School in Hannover. He was promoted to *Oberleutnant* in February 1934 and served with the Cavalry School in Hannover from 1936 until October 1939, when he held the rank of *Rittmeister*. From April 1940 he was Commander of Reconnaissance Battalion 5 and saw action during the invasion of France. (*Deutsches Wehrkundearchiv*)

River. He made an independent decision to commit his Reserve Battalion to the fighting at Lazdijai in Lithuania, this resulted in the fall of the town enabling the Reconnaissance Battalion under *Rittmeister* Horst Niemack to advance towards the Niemen River. Thümm was presented with the Knight's Cross by the Commander of the 5th Infantry Division *Generalmajor* Karl Allmendinger.

Knight's Cross with Oakleaves: He became the 166th recipient on 23 December 1942 as *Oberst* and Commander of *Jäger* Regiment 56 part of the 5th *Jäger* Division, awarded for his successful leadership during the important battles on the Eastern Front. He saw action during the German push towards the Demyansk Pocket and during the battles around Staraya Russa. He was presented with the Oakleaves personally by Hitler at *Führer* Headquarters at Rastenburg in early

Oberst Horst Niemack as Commander of the 130th Panzer Lehr Division together with *General der Panzertruppe* Hasso von Manteuffel, the Commander-in-Chief of the 5th Panzer Army, in early 1945. (*Deutsches Wehrkundearchiv*)

1943. Thümm was appointed Commander of the 5th *Jäger* Division in February and the following month was promoted to *Generalmajor.* Just six months later he was promoted to *Generalleutnant*. He took part in the defensive fighting between Vitebsk and Orscha and after the collapse of Army Group Centre his division was sent west to aid in the defence of Poland. On 29 September he was delegated with the leadership of the LXIV. Army Corps. By the end of December 1944 the German 1st Army launched Operation North Wind, an offence aimed at destroying the Allied forces in Alsace. In January 1945 he was promoted to *General der Infanterie* and Commanding General of the LXIV. Army Corps. On 5 January, when it became obvious that Operation North Wind had failed, *Reichsführer-SS* Himmler's Army Group Upper Rhine began its attack north of Strasbourg, seizing a 10-mile bridgehead. Thümm now led an attack with infantry and panzer forces north from the Colmar Pocket along the western bank of the Rhine Canal to link up with the Gamsheim Bridgehead and encircle Strasbourg. However, the attack failed and Thümm was blamed and dismissed by Himmler. He was to face court martial but the war ended before it could begin, and he was captured by the Allies on 19 April 1945.

Johann SINNHUBER

General der Artillerie

* 27 March 1887, Wilkoschen, East Prussia
\+ 23 October 1979, Augsburg

Knight's Cross: Awarded on 5 July 1941 as *Generalleutnant* and Commander of 28th Infantry Division while attached to the VIII. Army Corps for his part in the fighting near Smolensk on the Russian Front. Sinnhuber was transferred together with his division to France in November 1941, where the division was converted into a *Jäger* Division. In early 1942 his division returned to the Soviet Union, this time on the southern sector, where it fought on the Kerch

Peninsula and during the final assault on the naval forces of Sevastopol in the Crimea. Later his division was transferred to the northern sector while attached to Manstein's 11th Army, ready for attachment to Finland but this was cancelled and the unit saw action as part of Army Group North near Demyansk in late 1942. In early 1943 he saw action during the Second Battle of Lake Ladoga before being rested and assigned to the Reserves in May. On 10 July he took command of the LXXXII. Army Corps and was used for coastal protection at the Pas-de-Calais and then in Bruges. In October Sinnhuber was promoted to *General der Artillerie* and by June 1944 his Corps patrolled the French–Belgian border to the south of Étaples. From April 1945 he was the Commanding General of the Defensive Sector of Hamburg-Bremen and surrendered to the Allies in May 1945. He was released from captivity two years later.

Hans BERGEN
Generalleutnant

* 5 March 1890, Munich, Bavaria
+ 17 February 1957, Landshut, Bavaria

Hans Bergen was wounded just four weeks into the start of the First World War, and from January 1917 was attached to the Recruit Depot of the III. Bavarian Army Corps, and for the rest of the war he served with Bavarian Infantry Regiment 10. From December 1923 he served with the Landespolizei in Bavaria and was appointed chief of the Schutzpolizei in Zweibrücken in July 1930, and from August 1933 he was Chief of Staff of the Inspector of Police in the Ministry of the Interior in Bavaria. On 15 October 1935 Bergen transferred into the Army as an *Oberstleutnant* and became Commander of I. Battalion of Infantry Regiment 62. From August 1939 he became Commander of Infantry Regiment 179, part of the 7th Infantry Division, and saw heavy fighting during the Polish campaign. He then took part in the Western campaign and was wounded and hospitalised in June 1940, and on release spent time with Replacement Battalion 179. (*Deutsches Wehrkundearchiv*)

Knight's Cross: Awarded on 9 July 1941 as *Oberst* and Commander of Infantry Regiment 187 as part of the 87th Infantry Division for his success during the first days of Operation Barbarossa. On 22 June 1941 he demonstrated outstanding leadership during an attack on high ground north-east of Novgorod and three days after his regiment formed a bridgehead over the Biebrza River south of the Osowiec Fortress. In doing so he managed to tie down strong Soviet forces ,which forced them to ultimately give up the fight for the fortress. He saw action at Bialystok in Smolensk and Vyazma, and took part in the opening phase of the Battle of Moscow. In January 1942 he was delegated with the leadership of the 32nd Infantry Division, and from February he commanded the 323rd Infantry Division. He then served in France on occupation duty until May 1942, when he led his division at the southern sector of the Eastern Front. On 5 November he was transferred as Commander of the 290th Infantry Division, still fighting on the Eastern Front just east of Orel. From early May 1943 Bergen was named as Commander of the 390th Field Training Division and was promoted to *Generalleutnant* in October. From 10 December he fought during the Battle of Aachen as Commander of Division Nr. 526, a replacement and training division. In March 1945 he was on the Western Front as part of the 15th Army on the Lower Rhine as Commander of Replacement Division 476. Bergen surrendered to American troops on 29 March and remained in Allied custody until 11 June 1947.

Kuno-Hans Paul Hermann Viktor Ludwig von BOTH

General der Infanterie

* 9 April 1884, Zabern, Alsace
+ 22 May 1955, Eheln in Habichtswald, Hesse

Both was commissioned as a *Leutnant* in August 1904 and at the beginning of the First World War he was an *Oberleutnant* and Leader of the 8th Company of Reserve Infantry Regiment 90. In April 1918 he was awarded the Pour le Mérite, one of the highest awards from the First World War, and soon after was appointed adjutant to the Staff of the 226th Infantry Division. He remained in the Army after the war and served in various regiments, mainly the 90th and 6th, and was promoted to *Major* in January 1928. He served as an instructor at the Infantry School in Dresden from February 1930, and just two years later he had been promoted to *Oberst* and was Battalion Commander with Infantry Regiment 5. He was promoted to *Generalmajor* in October 1938 and saw action during the Polish campaign. He was appointed Commanding General of the I. Army Corps in October 1939 and promoted to *General der Infanterie* in June 1940. Both was awarded the Blood Order by Hitler for the part he played in the 9 November 1923 failed Munich Putsch. (*Author's Collection*)

Knight's Cross: Awarded on 9 July 1941 as *General der Infanterie* and Commanding General of the I. Army Corps as part of the 16th Army for actions on the Russian Front. It was thanks to his clear leadership that his corps was able to thrust out of the vicinity of Žemaičių Naumiestis in the region of Lithuania and over a period of five days managed to advance despite fierce Soviet resistance and difficult terrain. Despite the great difficulties involved, Both took key positions away from the Soviets and he always fought at the front with his men. He was awarded the German Cross in Gold on 9 September 1942 and continued to serve on the Eastern Front as part of Army Group North until April 1943, when he was appointed Commanding General of Security Troops and Commander in Army Area North. A year later he took over as German Commander in Operations Area East Hungary. On 23 June 1944 his son, *Hauptmann* Hans-Kuno von Both, was killed in action and from July General Kuno was appointed Commander of German troops in the rear operations area of Army Group South Ukraine. On 8 April 1945 he was transferred to the Reserve and on 2 May he was taken prisoner by Western forces. He was released in April 1947.

Leo Dietrich Franz *Freiherr* GEYR VON SCHWEPPENBURG

General der Panzertruppe

* 2 March 1886, Potsdam, Brandenburg
+ 27 January 1974, Irchenhausen, Bavaria

Knight's Cross: Awarded on 9 July 1941 as *General der Panzertruppe* and Commanding General of the XXIV. Motorised Army Corps while attached to Panzer Group 2 in recognition of his outstanding planned attack across the Bug River and his drive through Polesia through difficult terrain. He led an attack across the Bug River and directed an unstoppable advance across the Soviet Union and during this time his command captured or destroyed 150 enemy tanks and a similar number of artillery pieces. From November 1941 Geyr von Schweppenberg's Corps, now a Panzer Corps, consisted of the 3rd, 4th and 17th Panzer Divisions, as well as the Infantry Regiment *Grossdeutschland*, which spearheaded the advance of Army Group Centre during the Battle of Moscow. From July 1942 he took over from Georg Stumme, who had been court martialled, to command the XXXX. Panzer Corps in the Caucasus. At the end of September Geyr lost his command after a general shake-up and was placed on the Reserves. He was, however, recalled in February 1943 as Acting Commanding General of LXXXXVI. Army Corps and from April was attached

Leo Geyr von Schweppenburg entered Army service in June 1904 with Dragoon Regiment 26, and from January 1905 attended the War School in Potsdam. When the First World War began he held the rank of *Oberleutnant* from November 1914 and served as an Orderly and Translation Officer with the Staff of the 9th Cavalry Division. Promoted to *Hauptmann* in January 1915, he served as a staff officer for the rest of the war. He remained in the Army after the war and was transferred into the General Staff in March 1919. He was an instructor at the Infantry School in Munich from October. Promoted to *Major* in April 1925, he attended various courses and from April 1933, now with the rank of *Oberst*, he was Military Attaché in London, Brussels and the Hague until October 1937. (*Author's Collection*)

to the General Staff of Army Group D. On 20 May *Generalfeldmarschall* Gerd von Rundstedt ordered Geyr to prepare a force of ten panzer and motorised infantry divisions and named him General of Panzer Troops with Commander-in-Chief West – responsible for training. At the same time, between August 1943 and January 1944 he was Commanding General of the LVII. Reserve Panzer Corps in France. On 6 June, D-Day, the Allied invasion of Normandy, he moved three panzer divisions north against British and Canadian troops that were advancing on Caen. Four days later his headquarters at La Caine, Normandy, was attacked by RAF bombers. He was wounded and many of his staff were killed. Geyr was relieved of his command on 2 July by Hitler, after agreeing with Rundstedt that his troops should withdraw from Caen. However, in August he was named as successor to *General der Panzertruppe* Heinrich Eberbach as Inspector of Panzer Troops with the Replacement Army. Geyr surrendered to US troops on 9 May 1945 and remained in captivity until his release in July 1947.

Gerhard KAUFFMANN

Generalleutnant

* 29 June 1887, Mariendorf, Teltow
+ 16 June 1969, Berlin

Knight's Cross: Awarded on 9 July 1941 as *Generalleutnant* and Commander of the 256th Infantry Division, part of the XX. Army Corps, for actions at Bialystok, Nevel, Vekikije and various other locations on the Russian Front. During the

Gerhard Kauffmann entered Army service in August 1908 with Infantry Regiment 68, and was commissioned as a *Leutnant* in January 1910. At the beginning of the war in August 1914 he was serving as an Orderly Officer with the I. Battalion of his Regiment and from early 1915 he served as a Company Leader. He was promoted to *Oberleutnant* in September 1915 and continued serving as a staff officer until the end of the war. He stayed in the Army and was promoted to *Hauptmann* in October 1918 and served as a General staff officer with the 16th Infantry Division, and from 1920 he served as a regimental adjutant. In November 1927 he was Company Chief with Infantry Regiment 17 and joined the *Wehrmacht* in October 1935 with the rank of *Oberst*. He was appointed Commander of Infantry Regiment 59 and from October 1936 he was Commander of Infantry Regiment 73. At the beginning of the Second World War he was serving as Office Chief of Army matters, attached to the High Command and with the rank of *Generalmajor*. (*Deutsches Wehrkundearchiv*)

last days of December 1941 his command held its line near Moscow against all odds, and a month later managed to play an important role in the saving of the XXIII. Army Corps when the Soviets surrounded it west of Rzhev. He was relieved of his command in January 1942 and entered the Reserves until 30 September 1943, when he retired from the Army after a rift with Hitler.

Otto Moritz Walter MODEL

Generalfeldmarschall

* 24 January 1891, Genthin, Saxony
+ 21 April 1945, woods near Ratingen, Rhine Province

Knight's Cross: Awarded on 9 July 1941 as *Generalleutnant* and Commander of 3rd Panzer Division while attached to XXIV. Army Corps for his leadership during the opening stages of the invasion of the Soviet Union. Despite the very difficult terrain and fierce Soviet resistance, his division was very successful along the road from the Bug River to Brest-Litovsk, and despite difficult terrain and fierce resistance he was able to push through with just minor losses. By the fourth day of the invasion his division had advanced 186 miles, further than any other division of the XXIX. Army Corps. Model led his division across the Bug River, then across the Dnieper River, captured Bobruisk and played a vital role in the encirclement at Bialystok, Minsk and Smolensk. Model excelled as a field commander and in mid-September formed part of the great pincer

Walter Model entered the Army in February 1909 with Brandenburg Infantry Regiment 6 as an officer candidate and attended War School from August. At the beginning of the First World War Model served as adjutant of I. Battalion of Infantry Regiment 6 with the rank of *Leutnant*. He was wounded in November 1915, spending time in hospital, and was awarded the Iron Cross 1st and 2nd Classes. From April 1916 he was a Company Leader with his regiment and was promoted to *Hauptmann* in December 1917. He ended the war as chief supply officer of 36th Reserve Division, and he remained in the Army after the war. He served in various artillery and machine gun battalions and was promoted to *Major* in October 1929. Promoted to *Oberstleutnant* in November 1932, he was made Commander of the II. Battalion of Infantry Regiment 2 in October 1933. (*Author's Collection*)

movement that encircled Kiev and took huge numbers of Soviet prisoners of war. The following month he was given command of the motorised XXXXI. Army Corps and took part in the drive towards Moscow, during which time he was promoted to *General der Panzertruppe*.

Knight's Cross with Oakleaves: He became the seventy-fourth recipient on 17 February 1942 as *General der Panzertruppe* and Commanding General of the XXXXI. Army Corps while attached to the 9th Army, awarded for his outstanding leadership and accomplishments during the winter of 1941–42 near Rzhev. The Soviets had tried to force their way out of the encirclement but Model was ready for them and had predicted exactly where they would break out. The final battle did not end until 24 February, when six Soviet divisions

By October 1935 he was Chief of the Technical Office of the Army General Staff and held the rank of *Oberst*, and was promoted to *Generalmajor* in February 1938. That November he was appointed Chief of Staff of the IV. Army Corps. He saw action in Poland, where he was awarded the Bar to the Iron Cross 1st and 2nd Classes, and from October 1939 he was Chief of the General Staff in the 16th Army. In March 1940 was promoted to *Generalleutnant*. (*Author's Collection*)

had been wiped out, another four had virtually been destroyed and dozens more were badly damaged. The Soviet offensive had failed. Here Model would cement his reputation as an energetic and skilful master of defence, and was personally presented with the Oakleaves by Hitler during a special ceremony on 28 February 1942 at *Führer* Headquarters the Wolf's Lair at Rastenburg. The same day he was promoted to *Generaloberst*.

Knight's Cross with Oakleaves and Swords: Awarded on 2 April 1943 to become the twenty-eighth recipient as *Generaloberst* and Commander-in-Chief of the 9th Army part of Army Group Centre for his further achievements during the fighting and his skilful retreat near Rzhev. It was one of the best-planned and executed tactical withdrawals of the war. Model's army suffered very few casualties, unlike the Soviets. All efforts were made by the Red Army to annihilate the 9th Army while it was on the move. He was personally presented with the Swords by Hitler on 27 April 1943 at the Berghof on the Obersalzburg in Austria. Model later commanded the 9th Army during the Battle of Kursk, where his strategy was responsible for the German defeat, but he survived this setback and was given command of the 2nd Panzer Army (while still commanding the 9th Army), and continued to inflict heavy losses on the Soviets. On 31 May 1944 he flew to *Führer* Headquarters, where he was presented with his *Marshals'* Baton having been officially promoted to that rank on 1 March 1944, and at fifty-three he was Germany's youngest *Generalfeldmarschall.* At the end of March he was appointed Commander-in-Chief of Army Group North Ukraine, and at the same time from June he was Deputy Commander of Army Group Centre. He now controlled forty-three divisions, of which five were panzer divisions, however the situation on the Eastern Front was by now critical and Army Group Centre was now defending the 450-mile Belorussian salient.

Knight's Cross with Oakleaves, Swords and Diamonds: He became the seventeenth recipient on 17 August 1944 as *Generalfeldmarschall* and Commander-in-Chief of Army Group Centre, and it was awarded for his management of the Eastern Front following the collapse of his Army Group. It was his leadership and skill that made it possible to ensure that the Soviet advance could be brought to a halt at the area of the Vistula River. The Diamonds were personally presented to Model by Hitler at *Führer* Headquarters the Wolf's Lair sometime in late August. Hitler said to Model during the ceremony, 'Were it not for you, your heroic efforts, and your leadership … the Soviets might have been in East Prussia today or even before the gates of Berlin.' Model transferred to the Western Front, where he took over as Commander-in-Chief West as well as Commander-in-Chief of Army Group B. In September he defeated the British at Arnhem and later during the fighting in the Siegfried Line and during the Battle of the Bulge, and in the fighting in the Ruhr his pleas to be allowed to break out eastwards were rejected. As the war came to an end and with no hope of withstanding the Allied superiority and no intention of being a witness to the final destruction of Germany, Model drove himself to a wood outside Düsseldorf on 21 April 1945 and rather than surrender he shot himself.

Ernst Hermann Walther SCHROTH

General der Infanterie

* 3 June 1882, Alteichenau, Silesia
+ 6 October 1944 near Bad Nauheim, Hesse

Knight's Cross: Awarded on 9 July 1941 as *General der Infanterie* and Commanding General of the XII. Army Corps, part of the 4th Army, for his part in the attack on the Brest-Litovsk Fortress. He carefully prepared the assault on the reinforced fortress and carried out the operation with great skill. As a result, almost the entire Soviet garrison was annihilated. Later in July he led his corps across the Dnieper River to reinforce the 2nd Army in the Gomel area and at the end of August his corps was assigned to the 4th Army. From

Walther Schroth joined the Army in February 1902 as an officer candidate with the Royal Prussian Army and was commissioned as a *Leutnant* in August 1903. He served as an adjutant of a command district in Hirschberg and later with 1st Lower Silesian Infantry Regiment from November 1908 and was promoted to *Oberleutnant* in August 1911. He was a general staff officer at the start of the First World War with the rank of *Hauptmann* and was awarded both classes of the Iron Cross during the war. He stayed in the Army after the war and continued to serve with the General Staff. By October 1931 he had been promoted to *Oberst* and was serving as a leader of a training course at the Infantry School in Dresden. In April 1935, now with the rank of *Generalmajor*, he served as Artillery Leader 1 in Königsberg and by February 1938 he had been promoted to *General der Infanterie*, serving as Commanding General of the XII. Army Corps. He saw action in Poland at the start of the Second World War. (*Deutsches Wehrkundearchiv*)

early October he saw action as part of Operation Typhoon as part of Panzer Group 4 and broke through the Soviet front near Spas-Demensk. Schroth led his corps during the clearing out of the Vyazma Pocket but later, as a result of the Soviet counteroffensive near Moscow, his corps was in full retreat. Schroth was transferred to the Reserves on 19 February 1942 for rest and on 1 May was named Commanding General of the Deputy Commando of IV. Army Corps and Commander of Military District IV, Dresden. In August 1944 he was a member of the Court of Honour that investigated those members of the *Wehrmacht* who had participated in the 20 July 1944 plot to kill Hitler. Schroth was killed in a car accident on the road to Bad Nauheim on 6 October 1944.

Hermann-Heinrich BEHREND

Generalmajor

* 25 August 1898, Perleberg, Brandenburg
+ 19 June 1987 in Soltan, Lower Saxony

Knight's Cross: Behrend was awarded the Knight's Cross on 15 July 1941 as *Major* and Commander of the I. Battalion of Infantry Regiment 489 for his successful breakthrough of the enemy's heavily defended lines south-east and east of Tauroggen in Lithuania on 22 June 1941. He had decided to strike early before the planned attack in order to take advantage of the morning fog and

Hermann-Heinrich Behrend entered the Army as a war volunteer in June 1915, with Fusilier Regiment 90. In November he transferred into Infantry Regiment 43, and was commissioned as a *Leutnant* in April 1917. Four months later he was the Ordnance Officer with the Staff of II. Battalion. He ended the war as a Company Leader and in March 1920 he left the Army, only to return in February 1924. Two years later he was promoted to *Oberleutnant* and after attending a weapons training course he later became a Signals Officer, then from May 1928 was a Company Officer. In October 1930 he transferred into Infantry Regiment 18, and was promoted to *Hauptmann* in September 1933. In 1935 he was a training officer and from February 1939 he was appointed head of the Non-commissioned Officer Course with Infantry Regiment 16. (*Deutsches Wehrkundearchiv*)

dust that had been created by the artillery's preparation. Behrend was seriously wounded in September 1941, transferred into the Reserves the following month to recuperate and promoted to *Oberstleutnant*.

Knight's Cross with Oakleaves: He became the 421st recipient of the Oakleaves on 6 March 1944 as *Oberst* and Commander of Grenadier Regiment 154 for actions west of Luga near Leningrad at the beginning of February 1944. His regiment became separated and was attacked by an entire Soviet division and Behrend acted with iron resolve while being encircled by enemy forces. He led his command during fierce fighting and managed to reach the Pljussa River under the cover of darkness, crossing it and reaching the German lines on 13 February 1944. He was personally presented with the Oakleaves by Hitler on 27 April at the Berghof on the Obersalzburg. In June he was given command of Infantry Regiment 529, and saw action during the massive Soviet summer offensive, which saw more than 2½ million troops taking part. His command was decimated by the Soviets and only remnants, which included Behrend and a few members of his regiment, managed to escape.

Knight's Cross with Oakleaves and Swords: Awarded on 26 April 1945, without a recipient number, (although some sources state it was number 148) as *Generalmajor* and Commander of the 490th Infantry Division for actions during the defence of the Fladder Canal in Lower Saxony, Germany. During the fighting Behrend destroyed an Allied tank with a *Panzerfaust*, a hand-held anti-tank weapon, and led his troops in a successful breakout, destroying fourteen US Sherman tanks. He was captured and taken prisoner by the British on 8 May, remaining in captivity until 15 May 1947.

Adolf Robert Erich BRANDENBERGER

General der Panzertruppe

* 15 July 1892, Augsburg, Bavaria

+ 21 June 1955, Ludwigshafen am Rhein, Rhineland-Palatinate

[insert photo No: 013]

Knight's Cross: Awarded on 15 July 1941 as *Generalmajor* and Commander of the 8th Panzer Division attached to the LVI. Motorised Army Corps for his leadership during the opening stages of Operation Barbarossa. It was stated that he directed the division with great energy and discipline during the breakthrough of the border positions at the crossing over of the Dubysa River and the

Brandenberger was awarded the Bar to the Iron Cross 2nd Class during the Polish campaign and in May 1940 he was awarded the Bar to the Iron Cross 1st Class. (*Author's Collection*)

Brandenberger entered military service in August 1911 and saw action during the First World War with Bavarian Field Artillery Regiment 6, rising to the rank of *Hauptmann* by the war's end, and having been awarded both classes of the Iron Cross. He remained in the Army after the war and was for a time assigned to the Reich Defence Ministry. From July 1921 he was assigned to the infantry. Promoted to *Major* in February 1928, he transferred to the War Ministry in 1933 and from October 1936, now with the rank of *Oberst*, he was Commander of Artillery Regiment 4. (*Deutsches Wehrkundearchiv*)

subsequent battles. His men captured two large bridges over the river that the Soviets had prepared for demolition, and their swift action enabled Army Group North to continue its advance without problems. The division broke through the Soviet defences very successfully and during the early stages his troops covered more than 200 miles in just four days. Brandenberger was promoted to *Generalleutnant* in August 1942 and remained in command of his division until January 1943, when he took temporary command of the LIX. Army Corps. He was promoted to *General der Panzertruppe* in November 1943.

Knight's Cross with Oakleaves: Awarded on 12 November 1943 to become the 324th recipient as *General der Panzertruppe* and Commanding General of the XXIX. Army Corps while attached to the 6th Army for the distinguished leadership of his Corps during the fighting along the Mius River in the summer of 1943 as well as in the subsequent withdrawal battles back to the Dnieper River. The Oakleaves were personally presented to Brandenberger by Hitler at his mountain retreat, the Berghof on the Obersalzburg in the Bavarian Alps, on 24 February 1944. From August 1944 he led the 7th Army on the Western Front and again did a great job – his forces managed to bog down the Americans at Aachen and in the Hürtgen Forest, giving Hitler precious time for his Ardennes Offensive. He knew he would face a counteroffensive from Patton's forces in the Bastogne area and demanded Hitler send him a panzer division. Hitler refused and Brandenberger kept asking until he felt that Hitler's answers became curt and threatening. Hitler did, however, eventually promise fifty assault guns, although Brandenberger only ever received twelve. He had no tanks and faced a well-equipped US Army. In February 1945 he was relieved of his command by *Generalfeldmarschall* Walter Model, who disliked him. Model referred to Brandenberger as 'the professor, a typical product of the general staff system', but Model was known to be a tough taskmaster and fell out with most officers under his command. On 22 February Brandenberger did not wait for the new commander, instead he handed over command to *General der Infanetrie* Hans Felber and left for home. An hour later bombers flattened his headquarters. Felber was wounded and several staff officers were killed. On 25 March he was called out of retirement and given command of the 19th Army, which he led until his capture by US forces on 6 May 1945, and remained in US captivity until 1948.

Walter Kurt Thilo Graf von BROCKDORFF-AHLEFELDT

General der Infanterie

* 13 July 1887. Perleberg, Prignitz in Brandenburg
\+ 9 May 1943, Berlin-Zehlendorf hospital

Knight's Cross: Awarded on 15 July 1941 as *General der Infanterie* and Commanding General of the II. Army Corps, attached to the 16th Army, for actions in the Soviet Union. On 24 June 1941 he planned the attack to capture the Soviet fortress at Kaunas, and its seizure was of vital importance for the continuation of operations in the area. On 27 and 28 June he attacked with great effectiveness several Soviet divisions north-east of Kaunas, his troops fighting in very heavy combat over a difficult terrain.

Knight's Cross with Oakleaves: He became the 103rd recipient while still *General der Infanterie* and Commanding General of the II. Army Corps on 27 June 1942, for his brave steadfastness of his troops and his own leadership. The award also represents clear recognition of his soldiers, who fought with honour in combat during the Battle of Demyansk, and he received the award for

Brockdorff-Ahlefeldt entered Army service with *Jäger* Battalion 3 in April 1907, and was commissioned as a *Leutnant* the following year. He served as a Company Leader from 1915 to 1917 and on the General Staff of the VII. Army Corps for the rest of the war. He was awarded both classes of the Iron Cross and remained in the Army after the war. From March 1934, now with the rank of *Oberst*, he served as Commander of the Infantry Regiment 8, and from March 1938 he was Commander of the 23rd Division with the rank of *Generalmajor*. Promoted to *Generalleutnant* in March 1939, he was appointed Commanding General of the II. Army Corps in June 1940 and two months later was promoted to *General der Infanterie*. (*Author's Collection*)

both the efforts of the six divisions he commanded as well as his own personal disposition. His corps almost surrounded he was able to inspire his troops and push them beyond human endurance and escape encirclement. The Oakleaves were personally presented to him by Hitler at Rastenburg, his headquarters in East Prussia. Brockdorff-Ahlefeldt was known as the 'Fieseler Storch General'* because he travelled around visiting his troops whenever he could, and although he suffered from severe rheumatic pain he never showed it. By November 1942 his health had deteriorated so much that he was transferred to the Military Hospital in Berlin-Zehlendorf, where he died in May 1943.

*The Fieseler Fi 156 Storch was a liaison aircraft flown before and during the war.

Wilhelm CRISOLLI

Generalleutnant

* 20 January 1895, Berlin
+ 12 September 1944, Pistoia, Italy

Knight's Cross: Awarded on 15 July 1941 as *Oberstleutnant* and Commander of Rifle Regiment 8 while attached to the 8th Panzer Division for actions on the Russian Front. On 24 June his command blocked the road from Kaunas to Daugavpils, trapping a Soviet fighting force. The following day he took advantage of the situation, capturing various bridges and occupying the town of Daugavpils, during which he took many Soviet prisoners. In August 1941 Crisolli was promoted to *Oberst* and from December he took temporary command of

Crisolli entered the Army in August 1914 as a war volunteer with Horse Jäger Regiment 4, and was awarded the Iron Cross 2nd Class and commissioned as a *Leutnant* in December 1915. He was awarded the Iron Cross 1st Class in April 1918 and became Company Leader with Reserve *Jäger* Battalion 15. He remained in the Army after the war, joining the mounted troops from April 1920 and was promoted to *Oberleutnant* five years later. At the beginning of the Second World War he was Commander of the III. Battalion of Rifle Regiment 8 with the rank of *Oberstleutnant* and was at this time awarded both classes of the Bar to the Iron Cross. (*Author's Collection*)

the 13th Panzer Division, part of the 1st Panzer Army, and saw action in the Caucasus. From May 1943 he took over leadership of the 16th Panzer Grenadier Division and at the same time was temporary leader of the 333rd Infantry Division. He was named as leader of the 6th Panzer Division while attached to Army Group South from July until 22 August 1943. On 7 December he became commander of the newly created 20th Luftwaffe Field Division in Italy, seeing action in Vetralla, Tuscania and Lake Bolsena. On 1 February 1944 he was promoted to *Generalmajor* but on 12 September he was killed by partisans in Pistoia in the Tuscany region of central Italy.

Hans Emil Richard Freiherr von FUNCK

General der Panzertruppe

* 23 December 1891, Aachen
\+ 14 February 1979, Viersen

Knight's Cross: Awarded on 15 July 1941 as *Generalmajor* and Commander of the 7th Panzer Division, part of the XXXIX. Army Corps, for his outstanding leadership and bravery during the crucial formation of a bridgehead during the fierce fighting during the occupation of Vilnius in Lithuania. Funck and his forces captured both bridges over the Nieman River during heavy enemy counter-attacks and as a result the Soviet forces suffered heavy losses. He also took part in the destruction of Soviet troops trapped in the Smolensk Pocket and from October fought during the battles of Vyazma and Bryansk. Funck and his Panzer Division pushed forwards until winter fell, when he was forced to withdraw and wait for the weather to improve. He saw heavy action during February and March 1942 and from April moved to an area near Vyazma in order

Hans von Funck entered Army service as a *Fahnenjunker* in August 1914, served in the field with Dragoon Regiment 2 and was wounded in December that year. He was commissioned as a *Leutnant* in June 1915 and in October he was taken ill, but returned to combat in March the following year. He later served with Reserve Dragoon Regiment 2 and then with a machine gun company, being awarded both classes of the Iron Cross. He remained in the Army after the war and by August 1934 had been promoted to *Major* and was serving as an adjutant of the Commander-in-Chief of the Army. From August 1936 he served as Chief of Operations in the General Staff of the IV. Army Corps and was promoted to *Oberstleutnant* in September that year. From August until November 1936 he transferred briefly to the *Luftwaffe* and in January 1939 was promoted to *Oberst*. From August he was the Military Attaché at the German Embassy in Lisbon. In October 1939 he served as Commander of Panzer Regiment 5 of the 3rd Panzer Division. (*Deutsches Wehrkundearchiv*)

to link up with other parts of his division. Funk was promoted to *Generalleutnant* on 1 September 1942, and by early 1943 he was leading his division back on the Eastern Front. He saw action south of Kharkov and then after being refreshed his division was made ready for the Kursk offensive.

Knight's Cross with Oakleaves: He became the 278th recipient on 22 August 1943 while *Generalmajor* and while Commander of the 7th Panzer Division, now attached to the III. Panzer Corps, and was recognised for his leadership in the Soviet Union. He was awarded specifically for the capture of Vilnius, the encirclement of the Soviet armies at Bialystok and Minsk and during the Battle of Vyazma. In fact, Funck had been recommended for the Oakleaves twice, once in March 1943 and then again in August. The award was finally presented to him by Hitler at Führer Headquarters in Rastenburg on 29 October 1943, when Funck was appointed Commanding General of the XXIII. Army Corps. After the collapse of the 9th Army during the Soviet summer offensive, Funck and his Army Corps was deployed in the area south of Luninez in support of the 2nd Army. On 1 March Funck was promoted to General *der Panzertruppe*, was appointed Commanding General of the XXXXVII. Panzer Corps and saw action in France, which included the fighting during the Allied invasion. Briefly in August for just twenty-four hours Funck was Leader of the 7th Army and continued to see action in France until he was relieved in September 1944. He ended the war as a reservist and in May 1945 the western Allies deported him to the Soviet Union, where he was sentenced to prison and where he remained until October 1955.

Richard KOLL

Generalleutnant

* 7 April 1897, Koblenz
+ 13 May 1963, Berlin

Knight's Cross: Awarded on 15 July 1941 as *Oberst* and Commander of Panzer Regiment 11 while attached to the 6th Panzer Division for actions on the Russian Front. He saw action during the opening phase of the invasion of the Soviet Union as the German troops broke through the Stalin Line. He later saw action during the early stages of the Siege of Leningrad and his regiment, as well as the whole division, suffered heavy losses in the Soviet winter offensive of 1941–42. In December 1941 the division lost its only tank and Panzer Regiment 11 reorganised as a battalion and fought as a marching infantry unit. By the end of January 1942, the division had fewer than 1,000 troops left and only three operational guns. In April during the spring thaw the division and Koll's regiment were sent to France to rest and refit. In September Koll was appointed Chief of Motor Vehicle Repairs, and from July 1943 he was appointed Chief of Repair Matters under the General of Mechanisation in the *OKW* (High Command of the Armed Forces), being promoted to *Generalmajor* in August 1943. From 16 November he attended the 6th Divisional Leaders Course in Döberitz and from 6 January 1944 he was named Commander of the 1st Panzer Division. It was a brief command and he spent only four weeks in Vinnitsa at the front before returning to Germany as Chief of the *Wehrmacht* Motor Transport Matters and Plenipotentiary for Motor Transport Matters in the Four Year Plan. He was promoted to *Generalleutnant* in January 1945 and surrendered to British troops in May 1945. He was released on 24 February 1946.

Eugen Walter KRÜGER

General der Panzertruppe

* 23 March 1892, Zeitz, Saxony
+ 11 July 1973, Baden-Baden

Knight's Cross: Awarded on 15 July 1941 as *Generalmajor* and Commander of 1st Rifle Brigade, part of the 1st Panzer Division, for his leadership and success during the first weeks of the invasion of the Soviet Union. Between 23 and 25 June he distinguished himself during the tank Battle of Raseiniai with great success and captured various towns on 28 June and 4 July. On 17 July he was

Walter Krüger entered Army service in March 1910 as a *Fahnenjunker* with Infantry Regiment 181 and attended War School in Metz until May 1911, being commissioned as a *Leutnant* three months later. He served as a Platoon Leader at the beginning of the First World War and was promoted to *Oberleutnant* in October 1915. He was awarded the Iron Cross 1st and 2nd Classes and later saw action as a staff officer with the 24th Reserve Division and as a Company Chief with Infantry Regiment 107. He was promoted to *Rittmeister* in August 1918. He remained in the Army after the war and was attached to the cavalry. By October 1936, now with the rank of *Oberstleutnant*, he was head of the Cavalry Department in the War Ministry. In October the following year he was Commander of Cavalry Regiment 10 with the rank of *Oberst* and from November 1939 he was given the leadership of the 1st Rifle Brigade. He was named as Commander of the 1st Rifle Brigade in November 1939 and he saw action during the Western campaign. (*Deutsches Wehrkundearchiv*)

delegated with the leadership of the 1st Panzer Division and fought through the Courland against strong Soviet counter-attacks. In early August his command had reached the railway line to Leningrad. He began the attack on the city in early September and took part in the attack on Moscow and the Rzhev Salient, among other battles. On 1 October 1942 Krüger was promoted to *Generalleutnant* and appointed the official Commander of the 1st Panzer Division. He continued to see action as part of the 9th Army in Rzhev and took part in heavy battles. Then, in December, he took the remnants of his command to France to rebuild. From the end of May 1943 he led his division in the Balkans and then into Greece, and finally to the Ukraine and the southern sector of the Eastern Front.

Knight's Cross with Oakleaves: He became the 373rd recipient on 24 January 1944 as *Generalleutnant* and Commander of the 1st Panzer Division while attached to the XXXXVIII. Panzer Corps for his distinguished service during the fighting near Zhytomyr in the Ukraine and for his role in the clearing of the Western Bank of the River Teteriv. He was personally presented with the Oakleaves by Hitler at the Wolf's Lair in Rastenburg, and on 1 February 1944 Kruger was promoted to *General der Panzertruppe* and appointed Commanding General of the LVIII. Panzer Corps. He led his new command in Normandy and later during the Ardennes Offensive and by March was leading his forces during the retreat across the Rhine. From 10 April 1945 he was appointed Commanding General of the Replacement IV Army Corps and Commander in Military District IV, Dresden. He surrendered to British troops on 10 May 1945. They handed him over the Americans, who held him prisoner until 26 June 1947.

Karl LOHMEYER

Generalmajor

* 25 December 1893, Königsberg, East Prussia
+ 4 January 1942, Volkhov in the Soviet Union

Karl Lohmeyer entered Army service as a war volunteer in August 1914 and served with Infantry Regiment 57 from 1915. He was commissioned as a *Leutnant* in September 1917 and served with Infantry Regiment 299 as a Platoon Leader and later as a Company Leader. He was awarded the Iron Cross 1st and 2nd Classes and transferred into the *Reichswehr* at the war's end. From October 1920 he served with Infantry Regiment 4 and from January 1934, now with the rank of *Hauptmann*, he served as Tactics Instructor at the War School in Munich. He was promoted to *Oberstleutnant* in October 1937 and from November 1938 he was Commander of the II. Battalion of Infantry Regiment 24. In 1940 he served during the French campaign and was promoted to *Oberst* in October 1940. (*Deutsches Wehrkundearchiv*)

Knight's Cross: Awarded on 15 July 1941 as *Oberst* and Commander of Infantry Regiment 505 while attached to the 291st Infantry Division for his leadership and bravery during the initial invasion in which the division penetrated 44 miles in the first thirty-four hours of the invasion. He was later involved in the attack near Riga in which Lohmeyer and his regiment took part in the fight with the Soviet garrison trying to break out of the city. Both sides fought well and casualties were high but the Germans eventually destroyed the Soviet garrison, and later that year they seized the Russian naval base at Liepaja. On 4 January Lohmeyer was killed in action in Volkhov near Tigoda in the Soviet Union, and was posthumously promoted to the rank of *Generalmajor*. He is buried today in the German War Cemetery in Sologubovka, plot 2, row, 82 and grave 8565.

Hartwig von LUDWIGER

General der Infanterie

* 29 June 1895, Beuthen, Silesia
+ 3 or 5 May 1947, Belgrade, Yugoslavia

Hartwig von Ludwiger entered the Army in August 1914 with Grenadier Regiment 11 as a *Fahnenjunker* and attended officer training courses in Döberitz. On 30 July 1915 he was commissioned as a *Leutnant* and was Platoon Leader in the machine gun company of his regiment from October 1915. He was later made adjutant and then training officer, and was awarded the Iron Cross 2nd Class in July 1915 and the Iron Cross 1st Class in May 1917. A few months before the end of the war he transferred back to Grenadier Regiment 11 and remained in the Army after the Armistice. He served as a Signals Officer, a Weapons Officer and a Company Officer and was promoted to *Oberleutnant* in July 1925 and to *Hauptmann* five years later. In October 1935 he was Company Commander with Infantry Regiment 43 and was promoted to *Major* a month later. From October 1936 he served with Infantry Regiment 28. Promoted to *Oberstleutnant* in October 1938, he saw action in Poland. (*Deutsches Wehrkundearchiv*)

Knight's Cross: Awarded on 15 July 1941 as *Oberstleutnant* and Commander of Infantry Regiment 83, part of the 28th Infantry Division, for actions on the Russian Front, where he showed outstanding leadership and bravery. He particularly distinguished himself in the initial opening days of the invasion during the heavy action in the areas around Suwalki and to the northernmost area of the front near Smolensk. His regiment achieved further success during the march through Grodno and thereafter in the formation of a bridgehead over the Nemunas on 28 June 1941. On 1 September 1941 he was promoted to *Oberst* and later saw action in the drive towards Moscow, where the whole division suffered heavy casualties, and from November his regiment was transferred to France and converted into a *Jäger* Division.

Knight's Cross with Oakleaves: He became the 163rd recipient on 23 December 1942 as *Oberst* and while still Commander of *Jäger* Regiment 83 of the 28th *Jäger* Division for his part in the prevention of the Soviet breakthrough near

Sinjawino near Leningrad in September 1942. His regiment repelled the first assault of the enemy and at one point, after the Germans temporarily went over to the offensive, a total of six Soviet battalions as well as tank forces were encircled and destroyed. He was presented with the Oakleaves personally by Hitler at *Führer* Headquarters in Rastenburg, the Wolf's Lair. On 20 February 1943 he was delegated with the leadership of the 704th Infantry Division and saw action in Yugoslavia, then from April he was Commander of the 104th Jäger Division, which had been formed from the 704th Infantry Division. He was promoted to *Generalmajor* in May 1943 and in June his division was stationed in Greece, remaining there until the rapidly advancing Soviet armies threatened to take Army Group F and the Balkans. Promoted to *Generalleutnant* in January 1944, his division became involved in heavy combat towards the end of the year and by early 1945 was involved in fighting with Tito's partisans. He was promoted to *General der Infanterie* in April and was appointed Commander of the XXI. Mountain Army Corps, taking part in fierce fighting with partisans in Serbia and Macedonia. On 13 May he was captured by Allied forces and handed over to the Yugoslavian government to stand trial as a war criminal. He was charged with the torture and murder of Yugoslavian prisoners of war. He stood trial together with other German officers between 27 March and 4 April 1947. They were all found guilty and sentenced to death, and Ludwiger was executed in Belgrade in early May 1947.

Karl Maria Blasius ALLMENDINGER

General der Infanterie

* 3 February 1891, Abtsgemünd in Baden-Württemberg
+ 2 October 1965, Ellwagen in Baden-Württemberg

Knight's Cross: Awarded on 17 July 1941 as *Generalmajor* and Commander of the 5th Infantry Division for the successful attack, as part of the V. Army Corps, on the bridgehead over the Niemen River on the Russian Front. On 22 June 1941 he personally led his division during a difficult attack near Lazdijai and in doing so managed to establish an important bridgehead over the Niemen. The creation of the bridgehead was of great operational importance and Allmendinger was recognised for this achievement by being awarded the Knight's Cross. The award was presented to Allmendinger by *General der Infanterie* Ruoff together with the commander of the 9th Army, *Generaloberst* Adolf Strauss.

Karl Allmendinger entered the Army in October 1910 with Fusilier Regiment 122. Commissioned as a *Leutnant* in January 1913, he served as battalion adjutant until April 1916, when was made regimental adjutant with the rank of *Oberleutnant*. He remained in the Army after the war with Infantry Regiment 13 until October 1923, when he transferred to the Mounted Regiment 13 as a *Hauptmann*. From October 1929 he served as Company Commander with Infantry Regiment 1 and was promoted to *Major* three years later. In July 1934 he was promoted to *Oberstleutnant* and twelve months later was appointed Chief of Operations on the General Staff of the 1st Army under *Generalleutnant* Walter Schroth. (*Author's Collection*)

Knight's Cross with Oakleaves: He became the 153rd recipient of the Oakleaves on 13 December 1942 as *Generalleutnant* and Commander of the 5th Jäger Division attached to the II. Army Corps for his part in the successful offensive between 27 September and 9 October 1942, during the fighting near Demyansk and in the encirclement and destruction of Soviet forces south-east of Lake Ilmen. He was presented with the Oakleaves by Hitler at his Wolf's Lair

Shortly before the outbreak of the Second World War in September 1939 he served as Chief of the General Staff of the V. Army Corps, seeing action in both the Polish and French campaigns. Promoted to *Generalmajor* in August 1940, he took command of the 5th Infantry Division two months later, and from June 1941 led the division during the opening stages of the invasion of the Soviet Union, Operation Barbarossa. He was promoted to *Generalleutnant* in August 1942 and continued to demonstrate great leadership during the heavy fighting in the attacks on the bridgehead near Niemen. During September he led his division during the successful attacks on Soviet forces near Demyansk, where the fighting was tough and Allmendinger's forces received many casualties. (*Author's Collection*)

headquarters in East Prussia in early 1943. From May 1944 he commanded the 17th Army during the retreat from the Crimea across the Black Sea and in July he was granted leave and entered the Reserves. He was captured by US forces on 16 May 1945 and finally released after eighteen months.

Albert Eugen Emil BUCK

Generalmajor

* 23 January 1895, Stuttgart, Württemberg
+ 6 September 1942, near Novrossijsk, Soviet Union

Buck entered Army service as a war volunteer with Grenadier Regiment 119. He was commissioned as a *Leutnant* in March 1915 and was awarded both classes of the Iron Cross. He was captured by US troops in October 1918 and released in January 1920. Upon returning to Germany entered the police, rising to the rank of *Polizei-Major*. He saw action during the Polish campaign with Infantry Replacement Battalion 5 and awarded the Bar to the Iron Cross 2nd Class in April 1940. At the same time he and was promoted to *Oberst* and during the French campaign he was awarded the Bar to the Iron Cross 1st Class. (*Deutsches Wehrkundearchiv*)

Knight's Cross: Awarded on 17 July 1941 as *Oberst* and Commander of Infantry Regiment 305 while attached to the 198th Infantry Division for actions on the Russian front. On 22 June 1941 his men created a bridgehead over the Prut River near Sculeni, defending it successfully against two well-equipped Soviet divisions. At times he personally led his men in counter-attacks during multiple situations, and all attempts by Soviet forces to retake the bridgehead were thwarted. He continued to see action in and around Dnepropetrovsk as part of the 1st Panzer Army until April 1942, when he was transferred and took command of the 198th Infantry Division. Buck was promoted to *Generalmajor* on 5 July and saw action in Mius, now part of Ukraine, while attached to the XXXXIX, Army Corps. Shortly after noon on 6 September Buck was ambushed while driving his command car over a bridge near Novorossiysk in the Soviet Union. A reconnaissance unit from a Soviet Rifle Regiment was hiding under a bridge along this route, and they recognised the division commander's pennant on his vehicle and opened fire, destroying the car with anti-tank hand grenades and he killing Buck.

Walter KEINER

General der Artillerie

* 30 December 1890, Benshausen
+ 23 January 1978, Gelnhausen

Walter Keiner entered Army service in March 1910 as a *Fahnenjunker* with Foot Artillery Regiment 3 and was commissioned as a *Leutnant* in August 1911. From October 1913 he served as adjutant with II. Battalion with the same regiment and then served as battery leader. He was promoted to *Oberleutnant* in August 1915 and before the war ended he was awarded both classes of the Iron Cross. He remained in the Army after the war and served in various artillery commands. By October 1935 he held the rank of *Oberst* and was serving as Commander of Artillery Regiment 60. From October 1936 he served with Artillery Regiment 24. Promoted to *Generalmajor* in August 1938, twelve months later he was appointed Commander of the 62nd Infantry Division. (*Deutsches Wehrkundearchiv*)

Knight's Cross: Awarded on 17 July 1941 as *Generalleutnant* and Commander of 62nd Infantry Division, part of the XVII. Army Corps, for actions on the Russian Front. He saw action on the southern sector of the Russian Front, fighting at Cholm, and in the Dnieper crossings and in Kiev. On 17 September Keiner was seriously wounded and hospitalised, and then placed on the *Führer* Reserve. He was promoted to *General der Artillerie* in January 1943 and from August served as Army Field Equipment Master as he was not fit enough for front-line duty. On 1 August he was appointed Chief of the General Army Office with the Chief of Army Armaments and Commander-in-Chief of the Replacement Army. On 8 May 1945 he surrender to Allied troops, and was released in 1947.

Otto LASCH

General der Infanterie

* 25 June 1893, Pless, Silesia
+ 29 April 1971, Bonn, North Rhine-Westphalia

Knight's Cross: Awarded on 17 July 1941 as *Oberst* and Commander of Infantry Regiment 43, part of the 1st Infantry Division, for his outstanding leadership

Otto Lasch entered Army service in March 1913 as a *Fahnenjunker* with *Jäger* Battalion 2. He was commissioned as a *Leutnant* in August 1914 and served as a Company Leader. He was wounded in November and then served with the Observer and Flying Battalion 52, and later as adjutant of the Commander of Flying with Artillery Regiment 19. He joined the police about a year after the end of the war and was promoted to *Polizei-Major* in November 1933. He served as Chief Intelligence Officer in Breslau until October 1935. He transferred to the Army and served as Commander of the III. Battalion of Infantry Regiment 3 from October 1936, being promoted to *Oberstleutnant* the following year. He served as Commander of Infantry Regiment 43 at the beginning of the Second World War and was awarded the Bar to the Iron Cross 1st and 2nd Class during the Polish campaign. (*Deutsches Wehrkundearchiv*)

during the invasion of the Soviet Union. During the summer of 1941 he led his regiment from Bauske to Riga, Latvia, and was able to bridge the Dvina River while fighting with the enemy without loss of his own forces. Lasch pushed his men hard and he broke into Riga as planned. He led his men and was mentioned in an official *Wehrmacht* Communiqué on 1 July 1941. He continued to lead his regiment during the many battles around Leningrad and was promoted to *Generalmajor* in January 1942, being appointed Commander of the 217th Infantry Division in September. Lasch was now fully committed to fighting a defensive battle south of Leningrad, and he led a skilful retreat to the Dnieper River before his division was completely wiped out, and very few managed to escape, including Lasch. He was promoted to *Generalleutnant* in April 1943 and in October he was sent to Calais in France with the remnants of his division, which were absorbed into the newly created 349th Infantry Division that Lasch took command of in November. He took his new command to the Soviet Union in April 1944, where he saw action during the massive Soviet summer offensive. His division was encircled at Brody in Belorussia in July, but Lasch led it in a successful breakout attempt, but with heavy losses. Lasch was transferred and the division was reformed as the 349th *Volksgrenadier* Division in early September, commanded by *Generalmajor* Karl Kötz.

Knight's Cross with Oakleaves: Awarded on 10 September 1944 to become the 578th recipient as *Generalleutnant* and Commander of 349th Infantry Division while attached to the XXXXVIII. Army Corps for his leadership during the tough fighting in the Lvov area of the Eastern Front. After his division was surrounded by the Soviets, he launched a successful breakout of the night of 21–22 July, although his division took heavy losses in the process. Lasch was presented with the Oakleaves by *Reichsführer-SS* Heinrich Himmler on 7 November 1944 in Posen. After some leave, Lasch took over as the Commanding General of the LXIV. Army Corps in France as part of the 19th Army. It was involved in some defensive battles in Vesoul and from 12 September saw action against a strong Allied force, and three days later his men were fighting in the north-eastern area of *Épinal*. The Allies launched another offensive on the 24th to breakthrough to the east and three days later Rasch decided to retreat while the Allies continued their heavy attacks. Over the next few days the Allied attacks became stronger and by the end of October Lasch was exhausted and returned to Germany. On 9 November he was promoted to *General der Infanterie* and was appointed the Commanding General of the Replacement I Army Corps and Commander in Military District 1. On 28 January 1945 Lasch was appointed Fortress Commandant of Königsberg and was responsible for the defence of the city against the approaching Red Army of thirty-six divisions. Lasch only had three divisions under his command and on 9 April he surrendered to Soviet troops to save further bloodshed. Hitler was furious and ordered the arrest and execution of Lasch and his family. His wife and daughters were arrested in Berlin by the *Gestapo*, but they were not executed and were released at the end of the war. Lasch remained a prisoner of the Soviets until his release on 8 October 1955.

Willibald Erich Franz Josef BOROWIETZ

Generalleutnant

* 17 September 1893, Ratibor, Upper Silesia
\+ 1 July 1945, Clinton, Mississippi, USA

Knight's Cross: Awarded on 24 July 1941 as *Oberstleutnant* and Commander of Rifle Regiment 10 of the 9th Panzer Division when he distinguished himself during the invasion of Yugoslavia and on the Russian Front. He fought in the battles at Uman, Kiev and Bryansk, during the drive on Moscow. In the summer of 1941 his unit destroyed ninety-two enemy tanks, sixteen guns and twelve anti-aircraft guns in a single battle. In July he took part in the Battle of Uman and on 16 August his regiment took part in the conquest of Krivoy-Rog, reaching the Dnieper two days later. After the Battle of Kiev had ended the division, together with the regiment commanded by Borowietz, advanced towards Orel and in November German forces captured the city of Kursk. On

Willibald Borowietz entered military service in March 1914 with Infantry Regiment 156 and was wounded on 22 August. Commissioned as a *Leutnant* in January 1915, he saw action with a machine gun company and then with the infantry until the end of the war. Wounded during the last weeks of the war, he transferred to the police in 1919 rising to the rank of *Polizei-Major* in August 1931. He transferred to the Panzer forces in October 1937 and saw action in Poland with the 4th Light Division, where he was awarded the Bar to the Iron Cross 2nd Class. (*Deutsches Wehrkundearchiv*)

1 February 1942 he was promoted to Oberst. On 5 October 1942 he resigned his command and was transferred to the Reserves. On 10 November 1942 he was appointed commander of the 10th Panzer Grenadier Brigade, and eight days later he was delegated with the leadership of the 15th Panzer Division. He was promoted to *Generalmajor* on 1 January 1943 and appointed actual commander of the 15th Panzer Division in North Africa. He fought with great bravery there and was promoted to *Generalleutnant* in May 1943.

Knight's Cross with Oakleaves: He became the 235th recipient on 10 May 1943 as *Generalmajor* and Commander of the 15th Panzer Division while attached to Army Group *Afrika* in Tunis. It was here that the enemy attacked the German lines with an overwhelming superiority that included strong support from artillery and fighter aircraft. Borowietz fought the Allied onslaught at the head of his soldiers and they inflicted heavy losses on the enemy. The enemy continued to show great resistance and outnumbered the Germans in men and tanks but once again Borowietz and his men fought back. On the very day he was awarded the Oakleaves he was captured by US forces in Tunisia and he remained in Allied captivity until the end of the war. He was killed during an accident in his prison camp at Clinton, Mississippi, almost two months after the end of the war.

Gerhard FRANZ

Generalmajor

* 26 February 1902, Bobeck, Stadtroda
+ 24 December 1975, Bad Wildungen

Gerhard Franz joined the Army as a pupil in the Unteroffiziers Preparatory School in October 1917 and transferred into the *Reichswehr* two years later. He attended many courses, was commissioned as a *Leutnant* in December 1924 and at the time was attached to the 14th Company of Infantry Regiment 17. He served in the same regiment until October 1933, when he was attached to the War Academy, and he was promoted to *Hauptmann* in July 1934. In November 1938 Franz was a Company Commander with Infantry Regiment 5 and in April 1939 he was promoted to *Major*. At the beginning of the Second World War in September 1939 he was Chief of Operations on the General Staff 29th Motorised Infantry Division and saw action in Poland and later France. (*Deutsches Wehrkundearchiv*)

Knight's Cross: Awarded on 24 July 1941 as *Oberstleutnant im Generalstab* as Operations Officer with the 29th Motorised Infantry Division, part of the XXXXVII. Army Corps, for actions during the containment of the Bialystok Pocket at the beginning of the invasion of the Soviet Union. The commander of the division was forward with a Battle Group when a group of Soviet tanks tried to push through to seize control of the Zelwa Bridge. In the absence of the commander, Franz organised a new defensive line on his own initiative and led his troops in the attack. The Soviet attempt to break out from the Bialystok Pocket was defeated. From late December 1941 he was sent to Poland as Chief of Staff of Corps Command XXXV., a special-purpose unit that was part of the 9th Army. From May 1942 he was Chief of the General Staff of XXXX. Army Corps under *General der Panzertruppe* Georg Stumme, and Franz was promoted to *Oberst* on 1 July 1942. On 26 July he was relieved of his command, along with Stumme, after a security violation a month earlier, when an aircraft crashed with the secret plans on board for the German drive on Stalingrad and the Volga. Stumme and Franz had been told not to make copies of the plans but they had and they were being carried by a *Major* Reichel of Stumme's staff. The aircraft was later found and the pilot and Reichel were found dead, but the plans for the attack were missing. When Hitler was informed he was furious and Stumme was sentenced to five years' detention, while Franz received a two-year sentence. However, von Bock appealed to Hitler and both officers were released after just four weeks. From December 1942 Franz was Chief of the General Staff of the Afrika Korps and after a short illness was transferred and appointed Chief of the General Staff of the XXXXII. Army Corps in August 1943. Franz saw action on the Eastern Front and fought in Kharkov, in the retreats to the Dnieper and during the Battle of Cherkassy. In fact, Franz and his men had to swim a freezing river in February 1944 to escape capture by Soviet troops. From September 1944 he took over leadership of the 256th *Volksgrenadier* Division, and his new command suffered heavy losses at Vitebsk as part of the 3rd Panzer Army. On 1 December Franz was promoted to *Generalmajor*, and towards the end of the year he fought in eastern France and in during the battles of the Siegfried Line. By the end of March 1945 his division was defending a sector in the Rhine area against a tough US fighting force and, without getting replacements, his division was soon down to just Battle Group strength. He briefly saw action near Bitburg before being captured by US forces on 8 April 1945.

Erich Adolf Ernst FRONHÖFER

Generalmajor

* 27 December 1895, Ragaischen
+ 12 January 1970, Dortmund-Berghofen

Knight's Cross: Awarded on 24 July 1941 as *Oberstleutnant* and Commander of Panzer Regiment 10 while attached to the 8th Panzer Division for his success and bravery while fighting on the Eastern Front and the Soviet Union. On 25 June 1941 he was ordered to break through strong enemy forces near Utena in Lithuania that were blocking the way for other German divisions advancing on Daugavpils, Latvia. Fronhöfer succeeded in pushing back the enemy forces and on his own initative managed to break through the enemy forces to a depth of over 20 miles. He was promoted to *Oberst* in November 1941 and remained on the Russian Front until he was admitted to hospital in February 1942 due to an illness. From May he was Commander of Fast Troops in Military District XVII, Wiesbaden, and from November he was the commanding officer of the Officer Candidates School for Fast troops in Zossen. From April 1943 he took up a similar position in Gross-Glienicke, Berlin, and at the same time, although very briefly, he was delegated with the leadership of the 20th *Luftwaffe* Field Division in Denmark. From 14 July 1944 he attended the 12th Divisional Leaders Course and was promoted to *Generalmajor* on 1 August. On 8 September he was

Erich Fronhöfer entered Army service as a war volunteer with the 1. Replacement Battalion with Fusilier Regiment 34 and saw action during the beginning of the First World War. He was wounded in November 1914 and was hospitalised. He was transferred to a replacement battalion and from May 1915 he served back with his old regiment. He was commissioned as a *Leutnant* in June 1915 but was taken ill the following month and was in hospital until December that year. He then served as a Company Officer and then an Orderly Officer but in June 1917 he was wounded once again. He was awarded both classes of the Iron Cross during the war, which he ended recovering from a gas attack. He remained in the Army and was promoted to *Oberleutnant* in July 1925, when he was attached to the Weapons School. He was promoted to *Hauptmann* in May 1930 and in October 1935 he was adjutant with the Staff of the Command of Panzer Troops. Two months later he was promoted to *Major*. (*Deutsches Wehrkundearchiv*)

delegated with the temporary leadership of the 114th Jäger Division, and from 28 September he was Commander of the 20th *Luftwaffe* Assault Division after its commander, *Generalleutnant* Wilhelm Crisolli, had been killed by partisans. On 1 April 1945 he took over as Commander of the 547th *Volksgrenadier* Division but there was hardly anything left as most of the division had been crushed in East Prussia a month earlier. Within a few weeks of him taking over most of his division transferred to the 170th Infantry Division. On 4 May he was captured by British forces and kept in Allied captivity until 18 May 1948.

Walther Kurt Josef NEHRING

General der Panzertruppe

* 15 August 1892, Stretzin, West Prussia
+ 20 April 1983, Düsseldorf, North Rhine-Westphalia

Knight's Cross: Awarded on 24 July 1941 as *Generalmajor* and Commander of 18th Panzer Division while attached to Army Group 2 after achieving great success against the Soviet Army on 1 and 2 July. The continuation of the German operations in that area were made possible only by Nehring's skill as a commander. The Soviets tried to prevent his division from crossing the Berezina River by using elite forces and large tank forces, but their efforts were in vain. Nehring's command was able to cross the river, capture the bridge undamaged and

Walther Nehring entered the Army in September 1911 and at the start of the First World War he served as a Company Leader and then a battalion adjutant. Commissioned as a *Leutnant* in February 1913, he was appointed Company Leader with Infantry Regiment 22 in December 1916 with the rank of *Oberleutnant*. He was later awarded both classes of the Iron Cross and ended the war as an adjutant of the Commander of Replacement Troops of the XX. Army Corps. He remained in the Army after the war, was promoted to *Hauptmann* in March 1923 and served in various staff roles. (*Deutsches Wehrkundearchiv*)

created a safe crossing, despite all the Soviet counter-attacks. He was officially presented with the Knight's Cross by the Commander of Panzer Group Guderian, *Generaloberst* Heinz Guderian. Nehring continued to lead his division with great success and in January 1942 he successfully rescued the 216th Infantry Division, which had been surrounded at Ssuchinitshy in the Soviet Union. In February he was promoted to *Generalleutnant* and from early March he was given the leadership of the Afrika Korps, and had his success there, playing a major role in the breaking of Gazala Line and played a part in the capture of Tobruk. On 1 July 1942 he was promoted to *General der Panzertruppe* and at the end of August he was wounded near El Alamein and hospitalised until November, when he was ordered by *Generalfeldmarschall* Kesselring to assist Rommel and prevent Anglo-American forces taking Tunisia. He was appointed Commanding General of the LXXXX. Army Corps but he said his task was a waste of time as he believed that Allied air and naval power would one day cause the collapse of the Axis supply lines in the area. As a result of his outburst, he was branded a coward by Goebbels but in May 1943 Nehring's prediction came true when the Germans were defeated in North Africa.

Knight's Cross with Oakleaves: He became the 383rd recipient on 8 February 1944 as *General der Panzertruppe* and Commanding General of the XXIV. Panzer Corps while attached to the 4th Panzer Army when the Soviets broke through the front near Kiev. Nehring was brought to the area by air with the mission to stabilise the front using whatever forces were present. With these, which included badly battered divisions from his own command, he managed to bring the Soviet advance to a halt. On 26 April 1944 Nehring attended the funeral of *Generaloberst* Hans Hube, who had been killed when the Heinkel He 111 aircraft he was travelling in crashed near the Obersalzburg, shortly after he had attended the presentation of his Knight's Cross with Oakleaves, Swords and Diamonds. The following day Nehring was presented with the Oakleaves by Hitler at the Berghof. On 19 August 1944 Nehring became ill with bronchial catarrh flu and spent a few weeks in the Reserve Hospital at Wünsdorf. On 17 October he was appointed Commanding General of the XXIV. Panzer Corps and saw action in the Soviet Union once again.

From October 1935 Nehring served with Panzer Troops in Berlin with the rank of *Oberstleutnant*, and he was serving as Chief of the General Staff of the XIX. Army Corps with the rank of *Oberst* when the Second World War broke out. He was awarded the Bar to the Iron Cross 1st and 2nd Classes during the Polish campaign, and he was promoted to *Generalmajor* in August 1940 as Chief of the General Staff of Panzer Group Guderian. (*Deutsches Wehrkundearchiv*)

Knight's Cross with Oakleaves and Swords: Awarded on 22 January 1945 to become the 124th recipient while *General der Panzertruppe* and Commanding General of the XXIV. Panzer Corps while still attached to the 4th Panzer Army. However, on 17 January he found his command was miles behind Soviet lines surrounded by a dozen Russian armies. Nehring called upon all of his skill and experience and formed a 'Floating Pocket', maintaining his perimeter as he retreated to the north-west, picking up stragglers from shattered divisions on the way. He later managed to link up with *General der Panzertruppe* Dietrich von Saucken's *Grossdeutschland* Panzer Corps and continued pushing west. Finally, after covering more than 150 miles, he reached the German lines, and Hitler was thrilled by Nehring's accomplishment and personally decorated him with the Swords. Hitler appointed Nehring Commander-in-Chief of the 1st Panzer Army in Upper Silesia in March 1945 but never forgot his outburst regarding Tunisia and refused to promote him to *Generaloberst*. He surrendered to American troops on 9 May 1945 and for a time he was held at the former concentration camp of Dachau with other generals but he was released without charge in September 1947.

Friedrich-August SCHACK
General der Infanterie

* 27 March 1892, Schmiedeberg an der Netze-Schubin, Posen
+ 24 July 1968, Goslar, Lower Saxony

Friedrich-August Schack entered the Army as a war volunteer in August 1914, was promoted to *Leutnant* in 1915 and was later battalion adjutant. He later served as Ordnance Officer on the Staff of Landwehr Infantry Brigade 23 and was awarded the Iron Cross 1st and 2nd Classes. He later served as Company Officer and before the end of the war he served as deputy brigade adjutant. He remained in the Army after the war and by April 1928 he had been promoted to *Hauptmann* and went on to command a machine gun company. From April 1934 he was an instructor at the War School in Dresden. Promoted to *Major* in February 1935 and to *Oberstleutnant* in October 1937, he was Commander of Machine Gun Battalion 15 in Brieg from November 1938. In January 1940 he was appointed Commander of Infantry Regiment 392 and was awarded the Bar to the Iron Cross 1st and 2nd Classes. He was promoted to *Oberst* in October 1940. (*Deutsches Wehrkundearchiv*)

Knight's Cross: Awarded on 24 July 1941 as *Oberst* and Commander of Infantry Regiment 392 while attached to the 169th Infantry Division for his outstanding leadership during the Battle for Salla, Lapland, against the Soviets. His personal conduct in the battle was crucial for the German success here and after eight days of fighting, Schack's regiment had destroyed thirty-two Soviet tanks and Salla was in German hands. He led his division during the initial drive to Murmansk as part of the XXXVI. Army Corps and the division remained in Lapland for more than two years. Schack, however, left the front in mid-September 1942, and from October served as Commander of School III for Officer Candidates of the Infantry. Towards the end of March 1943 he attended the 3rd Divisional leader Course and from May he was delegated with the leadership of the 216th Infantry Division and saw action during the Battle of Kursk, where the unit suffered heavy losses. In July Schack was promoted to *Generalmajor* and confirmed as Commander of the 216th Infantry Division, continuing to see heavy action. On 10 December 1943 he was appointed Commander of the 272nd Infantry Division and was stationed near Antwerp for training. He was promoted to *Generalleutnant* on 1 January 1944.

Knight's Cross with Oakleaves: He became the 597th recipient on 21 September 1944 as *Generalleutnant* and Commander of 272nd Infantry Division of the 5th Panzer Army for his leadership during the battle for Normandy. He and his men distinguished themselves during Operation Goodwood, where they played a vital role in ensuring the Allied breakthrough attempt was unsuccessful. By the time he had received the Oakleaves he had already been transferred as leader of the LXXXI. Army Corps and saw action in Aachen as part of the 7th Army. On 24 November 1944 he was delegated the leadership of the LXIII. Army Corps as part of the 19th Army in Alsace in north-eastern France. From 21 March he was attached to the General Staff of Army Group Vistula, and from April he took over as commander of the XXXII. Army Corps in the Mecklenburg area. Schack was promoted to *General der Infanterie* on 20 April. He surrendered to Allied forces just ten days later and remained in captivity until his released at the end of September 1947.

Otto Qurin LANCELLE

Generalleutnant

* 27 March 1885, Xanten, Rhine Province
+ 3 July 1941 near *Krāslava*, Soviet Union

Otto Lancelle entered service with the Navy in April 1905, but in December he transferred to the Army as a *Fahnenjunker* with Field Artillery Regiment 43. He was commissioned as a *Leutnant* in January 1907 and shortly before the First World War began he was promoted to *Oberleutnant*. He served with Field Artillery Regiment 6 and was wounded twice in 1915. He was promoted to *Hauptmann* that year and became Leader of I. Battalion of Foot Guards Artillery Regiment 5 from December 1915. On 9 October 1918 he was awarded the Pour le Mérite as Leader of II. Battalion of Guard Field Artillery Regiment 2. He remained in the Army after the war and in March 1920 he retired and became one of the founders of the Stahlhelm Organisation, a First World War veterans association. He rejoined the Army in October 1935 with the rank of *Major* and from April 1938 was Commander of the 43rd Artillery Regiment. In January 1939 he was promoted to *Oberst* and from October he was Commander of the 168th Artillery Regiment and saw action during the invasion of Poland. (*Author's Collection*)

Knight's Cross: Awarded on 27 July 1941 posthumously as *Generalmajor* and Commander of the 121st Infantry Division while attached to the II. Army Corps for actions in the northern sector of the Russian Front. He was hit by small arms fire (some reports say a sniper) while leading his division in an attack near *Krāslava* on the Dvina River. Lancelle was posthumously promoted to the rank of *Generalleutnant* on 21 July 1941, and is buried in the German War Cemetery in Daugavpils near Belarus.

Joachim Hermann August LEMELSEN

General der Panzertruppe

* 26 September 1888, Berlin
+ 30 March 1954, Göttingen, Lower Saxony

Joachim von Lemelsen entered the Army in July 1907 as a *Fahnenjunker* with Artillery Regiment 40 in Magdeburg, and was commissioned as a *Leutnant* the following year. He was adjutant of II. Battalion of his regiment when the First World War began and in December 1914 was promoted to *Oberleutnant*. He later served as regimental adjutant of Field Artillery Regiment 104 and was promoted to *Hauptmann* in August 1916. The following month he was serving as 1st Orderly Officer of the 52nd Infantry Division. He later served as Chief Supply Officer for the 21st Infantry Division and later for the VI. Reserve Corps, and was awarded both classes of the Iron Cross during the war. He stayed in the Army after the war and was Commander of III. Battalion of Artillery Regiment 5 in October 1931, being promoted to *Oberstleutnant* the following month. When the Second World War began in September 1939 Lemelsen held the rank of *Generalleutnant* and served as Commander of the 29th Motorised Division in Poland. (*Author's Collection*)

Knight's Cross: Awarded on 27 July 1941 as *General der Panzertruppe* and Commanding General of the XXXXVII. Motorised Army Corps, part of the 4th Panzer Army, for his leadership during the opening weeks of the invasion of the Soviet Union. His men closed in on a particular area around Smolensk and closed off a pocket full of Soviet troops near Słonim (in 1941 it became a ghetto for the SS to house Jews, and where around 25,000 were killed). Lemelsen showed great leadership during his time on the Eastern Front and would often take off in his Fieseler Storch light aircraft looking for enemy troops. Once he located them he would radio their position to his artillery commanders, who would then bombard them with high-explosive shells. His command saw action during the encirclement of Kiev in September and towards the end of the month took part in the attack near Bryansk. He later led his command during the heavy fighting in December with temperatures of minus 30 degrees, and by mid-December his corps had been pushed back to the area north-east of Orel. By the end of April 1942 the fighting had moved further north towards Rzhev, and from May Lemelsen had taken over as temporary commander of the 2nd Panzer Army. From 21 June 1942 the XXXXVII. Motorised Corps was renamed the XXXXVII. Panzer Corps and continued to see action in the area between Orel and Rzhev.

Knight's Cross with Oakleaves: He became the 294th recipient on 7 September 1943 as *General der Panzertruppe* and Commanding General of the XXXXVII.

General der Panzertruppe Lemelsen conducting a military orchestra seen wearing his Knight's Cross and German Cross in Gold, sometime after 1941. (*Author's Collection*)

Panzer Corps while attached to the 8th Army for his achievements during the summer battles of 1943, specifically the retreat to the Dnieper in August of that year. Lemelsen was personally presented with the Oakleaves by Hitler at his Wolf's Lair headquarters at Rastenburg. In October he was given temporary leadership of the 10th Army in Italy before being transferred to France in May 1944, where he was appointed temporary commander of the 1st Army. From 7 June he replaced *Generaloberst* Eberhard von Mackensen as Commander-in-Chief of the 14th Army and made responsible for the slowing of the advance of the Allies in France. From mid-October he left the front and reported sick with a sinus infection. He returned in October as commander of the 10th Army, replacing *Generaloberst* Heinrich von Vietinghoff, who had taken over from *Generalfeldmarschall* Albert Kesselring after he had been involved in a car accident. In February 1945 Lemelsen returned to the 14th Army in Italy, where he was taken prisoner by British forces on 6 May 1945. He later testified in Venice at the trial of Kesselring and he was eventually released from Allied captivity on 10 April 1948.

Friedrich August Eberhard von MACKENSEN
Generaloberst

* 24 September 1889, Bromberg, Posen
+ 19 May 1969, Alt-Mühlendorf, Schleswig-Holstein

Eberhard von Mackensen entered the Army as a *Fahnenjunker* with the Lifeguards Hussar Regiment No.1 in Danzig on 1st October 1908. He was commissioned as a *Leutnant* in March 1910 and served as adjutant of his regiment from January 1914. He was promoted to *Oberleutnant* in February 1915 and was wounded a few months later. Awarded the Iron Cross 1st and 2nd Class, he was promoted to *Hauptmann* in May 1917 and was then assigned to the General Staff, where he remained until the end of the war. He remained in the Army after the war and from April 1935, now with the rank of *Oberst*, he was Chief of the General Staff of the X. Army Corps. He was promoted to *Generalmajor* in January 1938 and at the start of the war he was Chief of the General Staff of the 14th Army in Poland. (*Author's Collection*)

Knight's Cross: Awarded on 27 July 1941 as *General der Kavallerie* and Commanding General of the III. Motorised Army Corps, part of Panzer Group 1, for his success during the first weeks of the invasion of the Soviet

Eberhard was the second son of *Generalfeldmarschall* August von Mackensen and brother of Hans-Georg von Mackensen (26 January 1883–28 September 1947). He was Adjutant to Prince August Wilhelm in the First World War and married Winifried Christine Helene, daughter of Hitler's First Foreign Minister Konstantin von Neurath, former State Secretary in the Reich Foreign Ministry and later Ambassador in Rome. Mackensen is seen here with General Ewald von Kleist, both wearing their Knight's Cross with Oakleaves. (*Author's Collection*)

Union. He and his corps distinguished themselves during the breaking of Soviet resistance near Włodzimierz, and in crossing the Horyn River, the penetration of the Stalin Line and the capture of Zhitomir. By the end of July his command had reached the Dnieper and Dnepropetrovsk, and in November moved into the Rostov area. Later his corps was forced to retreat from Rostov by a Soviet counter-attack and was pushed back to the Mius in the winter of 1941. Mackensen was forced to divert some of his armour to deal with the Red Army threat, and then on 25 November 1941 the main Soviet forces fell upon his weakened corps, and just three days later he was ordered to withdraw his troops from Rostov.

Knight's Cross with Oakleaves: He became the ninety-fifth recipient on 26 May 1942 as *General der Kavallerie* and Commanding General of III. Panzer Corps while attached to the 1st Army and was awarded for his leadership during the Second Battle of Kharkov. His corps formed the southern pincer of the German encirclement during the battle linking up with the 6th Army south of Balakliya in the Ukraine on 22 May 1942, and with this successful manoeuvre the Soviet

6th and 57th Armies were cut off. He was presented with the Oakleaves by Hitler at the Wolf's Lair, Rastenburg. His command had captured 128,607 Soviet troops, 417 tanks, 827 assault guns and 1,300 heavy weapons. On 21 June his command became known as the III. Panzer Corps and he took part in the summer offensive as part of the 1st Panzer Army. He then saw fighting in late 1942 and his corps withdrew from the Caucasus after the beginning of the Soviet counteroffensive. From 21 November he was appointed Commander-in-Chief of the 1st Panzer Army and took part in defensive battles on the Don and Mius Rivers, followed by defensive battles near Isyum and in the Dnepropetrovsk area once again. Mackensen was promoted to *Generaloberst* on 6 July 1943 and in mid-November was transferred and took over command of the 14th Army, where he saw action in Italy and where he was ordered to liquidate the Anzio bridgehead, but was unsuccessful. He saw further action in the Allied breakthrough and from May 1944 took part in the fighting retreat to the Gothic Line. In June he was replaced by *General der Panzertruppe* Joachim Lemelsen and went into the Reserves. He then entered the Reserves, where the war ended for him. In May 1945 he went into British captivity and was tried with war crimes by a British Military Court. Together with *Generalfeldmarschall* Kesselring, he was charged with complicity in the Ardeatine Cave massacre of March 1944. A column of Italian soldiers from a police regiment were ambushed by partisans and twenty-eight were killed and others seriously wounded. The German Commandant of Rome, *Luftwaffe Generalmajor* Kurt Mälzer, demanded reprisals and so did Hitler, and Mackensen endorsed the recommendation but was not involved in any reprisals. Funck was found guilty on 6 May 1947 for his part in the reprisals and was initially sentenced to death. This was later commuted to a life sentence and then to twenty-one years' imprisonment, but he was subsequently released on 2 October 1952.

Hans von OBSTFELDER

General der Infanterie

* 6 September 1886, Steinbach-Hallenberg, Hesse-Nassau
+ 20 December 1976, Kassel, Hesse

Knight's Cross: Awarded on 27 July 1941 as *General der Infanterie* and Commanding General of the XXIX. Army Corps while attached to the 6th Army for his leadership during the fighting in the southern sector of the Soviet Front, especially around Kiev. At the beginning of October his corps advanced towards Kursk and Belgorod, where it remained until the first half of 1942, and

Hans von Obstfelder entered the Army with Thuringia Infantry Regiment 32 in March 1905 and was commissioned as a *Leutnant* he following year. He attended the War Academy from late 1913 and in February 1914 he was promoted to *Oberleutnant* and appointed adjutant of the Reserve Infantry Regiment 71. He was awarded the Iron Cross 2nd Class in September 1914 and the Iron Cross 1st Class in June 1915, being promoted to *Hauptmann* at the same time. He then served in the General Staff and was Operations Officer with the 4th and 7th Cavalry Divisions before the end of the war. He stayed with the Army after the war and served in various regiments and divisions. By January 1936 had been promoted to *Generalmajor*. From October that year he was appointed Commander of the 28th Infantry Division in Breslau and saw action during the invasion of Poland, where he was awarded the Bar to the Iron Cross 1st and 2nd Classes. On 20 May 1940 Obstfelder was appointed Commanding General of the XXIX. Army Corps and was promoted to *General der Infanterie* on 17 June 1940. (*Deutsches Wehrkundearchiv*)

later moved to a more defensive position near the Don River. Obstfelder led his command during the summer offensive of 1942, and by the end of December the XXIX. Army Corps had been savaged by Soviet attacks and had begun to retreat. They then moved south to the area of Army Group Hollidt. By the end of February 1943, during the Soviet winter General Obstfelder and his corps were pushed back to the Mius River near Taganrog.

Knight's Cross with Oakleaves: He became the 251st recipient on 7 June 1943 as *General der Infanterie* while still the Commanding General of the XXIX. Army Corps and still part of the 6th Army, receiving the award for his outstanding command. He was particularly recognised for his command during the advance to the Don in the summer of 1942, the retreat in early 1943 and the subsequent defensive battles that took place. Obstfelder took over command of the LXXXVI. Army Corps in northern France on 25 August 1943, and three days later was presented with the Oakleaves by Hitler at *Führer* Headquarters at Rastenburg, together with *General der Infanterie* Paul Laux, *Majors* Bruno Kahl, Karl Langesee and Friedrich Höhne.

Knight's Cross with Oakleaves and Swords: Awarded on 5 November 1944 as *General der Infanterie* and Commanding General of the LXXXVI. Army Corps, part of the 5th Panzer Army, for his leadership during the Allied invasion of

France. After the success of the Allied landings in Normandy in June 1944, the LXXXVI. Army Corps formed the defensive front in southern Holland, where it held back the Allied forces for a time. Obstfelder proved a capable corps commander and the success of the defence was down to his skill as a leader. In December 1944 Hitler decorated Obstfelder with the Swords at his Adlerhorst headquarters in Bad Nauheim. He had now become the temporary leader of the 1st Army on the Western Front and from early March 1945 he was given temporary leadership of the 19th Army. He later served as Commander-in-Chief of the 7th Army during the final weeks of the war as part of Army Group G on the Western Front. On 8 May 1945 Germany surrendered and Obstfelder turned himself in to American troops and remained in captivity until August 1947. He later served as the German Liaison Officer to the 123rd US Army Group.

Hans Wilhelm Karl ZORN

General der Infanterie

* 27 October 1891, Munich, Bavaria
+ 2nd August 1943, Krassnaya-Roschtocha, Oryol Oblast, Soviet Union

Knight's Cross: Awarded on 27 July 1941 as *Generalmajor* and Commander of the 20th Motorised Infantry Division for actions in the Soviet Union, where

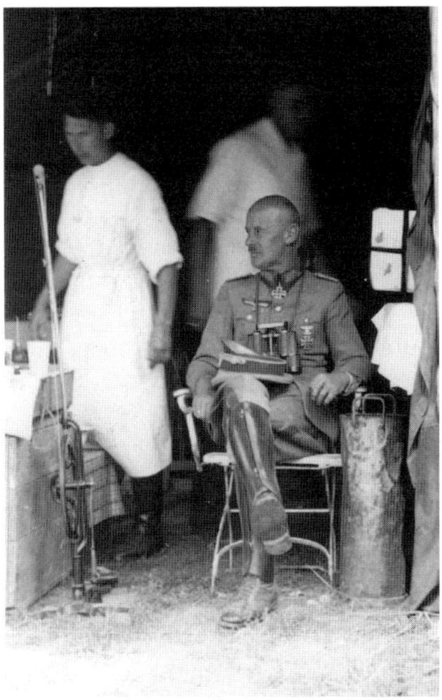

Hans Zorn was a member of the Bavarian Cadets from 1905 before he joined the Army in July 1911 as an officer cadet. He was commissioned as a *Leutnant* in October 1913 and from August 1914 was assigned as an adjutant with Bavarian Infantry Regiment Crown Prince 2. He was promoted to *Oberleutnant* in January 1917 and was awarded the Iron Cross 1st and 2nd Classes. He remained in the Army after the war. He served with various regiments and with the *Reichswehr* Ministry, and from 1926 he served on the Staff of the 7th Division. In October 1935, now with the rank of *Oberstleutnant*, he was Office Head in the Army Transport Department of the General Staff. Promoted to *Oberst* in August 1936, he was named as Commander of Infantry Regiment 19 in May 1938 and at the beginning of the Second World War he served as Chief of the General Staff of the XXII. Army Corps. He was awarded the Bar to the Iron Cross 1st and 2nd Classes in France in May 1940. (*Deutsches Wehrkundearchiv*)

he established a bridgehead at Vitebsk following heavy combat. He held this during heavy Soviet counter-attacks, which was of great importance for further Panzer Group operations, and a report stated that the success was primarily due to the courageous spirit and aggressive leadership of *Generalmajor* Zorn. On 15 January 1942 he was promoted to *Generalleutnant* and delegated with the leadership of the XXXX. Panzer Corps, being responsible for the defence of a sector of the 4th Army's front near Yukhnov. From February 1942 he served in Demyansk as an advisor to the commander of the II. Army Corps, *General der Infanterie* Walter Graf von Brockdorff-Ahlefeldt. On 1 June Zorn was promoted to *General der Infanterie* and appointed Commanding General of the XXXXVI. Panzer Corps, seeing action in north-western France. In September he was sent back to the Russian Front, and two months later he became ill but he returned to active service in June 1943, two weeks before the Battle of Kursk.

Knight's Cross with Oakleaves: He became the 291st recipient on 3 September 1943, awarded posthumously as *General der Infanterie* and Commanding General of XXXXVI. Panzer Corps while attached to the 2nd Army for actions near Rzhev in the Soviet Union. Awarded for his successful leadership where his troops participated in the elimination of a Soviet pocket south of the Smolensk–Vyazma railway line, which secured the rear of the 9th Army. During this process his corps took 50,131 prisoners as well as twenty-six tanks, and 763 guns were either destroyed or captured. On 2 August 1943 Zorn's staff car was attacked by a Soviet fighter plane near Krassnaya-Roschtocha and he was killed.

Walther DÜVERT

Generalleutnant

* 2 October 1893, Görlitz
+ 4 February 1972, Düsseldorf

Knight's Cross: Awarded on 30 July 1941 as *Generalmajor* and Commander of the 13th Panzer Division while attached to the III. Army Corps for actions on the Russian Front. During the fighting around Słucz in north-eastern Poland, Düvert showed great energy and leadership, which he passed on to his men with great results. They broke through the Stalin Line near Hul's'k and pushed ahead towards the Zviahel–Zhytomyr road and pursued the Soviet forces, and managed to hold them back for a time. His division advanced further and by 22 August he had reached Dnepropetrovsk and took part in heavy fighting until the end of

Düvert entered Army service as a *Fahnenjunker* in September 1911, and saw action at the beginning of the First World War as a *Leutnant* with Foot Artillery Regiment 8. He was awarded the Iron Cross 1st and 2nd Classes and promoted to *Oberleutnant* in June 1916, remaining in the Army after the war. From 1933 he served as an Operations Officer with various commands and by August 1934 had been promoted to *Oberstleutnant*. From May 1940 he served in France as Chief of the General Staff of the VI. Army Corps. (*Author's Collection*)

August, when his division was relieved. From the end of September until 10 October his division advanced towards the Azov Sea and then towards Rostov, and after attempting to capture Rostov the division withdrew in early December 1941. He then entered the Reserves and from the end of June 1942 he was commander of the 20th Panzer Division, seeing action on the Russian Front, and from August transferred to the area near Smolensk. From October until April 1943 Düvert was once again on the reserve list. From January until May 1943 he was attached to the office of the Chief of Army Armaments & Commander of the Replacement Army. From June he was commander of the 265th Infantry Division, now with the rank of *Generalleutnant*, and took part in coastal protection while part of the 7th Army in Brittany. He later saw action during the Allied landings in Normandy and on 30 November 1944 he retired from active service.

Konstanz Johann Georg Maximilian Reichsfreiherr von EDELSHEIM

General der Panzertruppe

* 6 July 1897, Berlin
+ 26 April 1994, Konstanz, Baden-Württemberg

Knight's Cross: Awarded on 30 July 1941 as *Oberstleutnant* and Commander of Bicycle Battalion 1 of the 1st Cavalry Division in recognition of his gallantry and leadership during an attack on enemy positions on the Russian Front. During the advance his battalion played a vital role in the capture of important strategic bridges despite strong Soviet resistance, and as a result his battalion cleared the way for the rest of the division. The Knight's Cross was personally presented to him by the Commander of 1st Cavalry Division *Generalmajor* Kurt Feldt. In September Edelsheim was appointed Commander of Mounted Regiment 22 and on 17 December he was promoted to *Oberst*.

Maximilian von Edelsheim entered Army service as an officer candidate on 11 August 1914 and was commissioned as a *Leutnant* in December 1915. He served with Infantry Regiment 59 from January 1917 and was awarded both classes of the Iron Cross. After the war he served briefly with the Freikorps and re-entered the Army in May 1919. He was assigned to Mounted Regiment 4 in April 1920. (*Deutsches Wehrkundearchiv*)

Knight's Cross with Oakleaves: He became the 162nd recipient on 23 December 1942 as *Oberst* and Commander of Panzer Grenadier Regiment 26 while attached to the 24th Panzer Division for continued actions on the Russian Front. It was awarded for his leadership during the breakthrough to Voronezh between 28 June and 8 July 1942, and for the battle in the Don Bend between 9 July and 21 August 1942. The Oakleaves were personally presented to him by Hitler at the Wolf's Lair in Rastenburg on 12 January 1943. Shortly after, Edelsheim attended a Divisional Leader's course and after the destruction of the 24th Panzer Division in the Stalingrad Pocket he was flown out of Stalingrad to raise the new 24th Panzer Division in France. On 1 June he was promoted to *Generalmajor* and while still in France he was promoted to Generalleutnant on 20 May 1944. In August he was transferred to the Reserves and from 21 September he was given the leadership of the XXXXVIII. Panzer Corps.

Knight's Cross with Oakleaves & Swords: Awarded on 23 October

By October 1935 he was serving in the cavalry with the rank of *Rittmeister*, and at the beginning of the Second World War in September 1939 he served as an *Oberstleutnant* with the 1st Cavalry Brigade during the invasion of Poland, where he won the Bar to the Iron Cross 1st and 2nd Classes. Edelsheim is seen here in a relaxed mood, wearing his Knight's Cross. (*Author's Collection*)

1944 as the 105th recipient while *Generalleutnant* and Commander of the 24th Panzer Division attached to the LIX. Army Corps for his outstanding leadership. This was primarily during the defensive battles in the Dnieper Bend, the Nikopol Bridgehead, in Cherkassy, between the Dnieper and Bug Rivers, and during the defence in the Dukla Pass during September 1944. On 1 December he was promoted to *General der Panzertruppe* and confirmed as Commanding General of the XXXXVIII. Panzer Corps. He saw action near the Vistula River in Poland and by February 1945 had begun the retreat to Silesia. He then moved his troops to the Elbe River section to defend against the Americans, and then to the west in defence of Halle and Leipzig. On 19 April Halle fell to the Americans after five days of heavy fighting and from the 25th his command took up defensive positions between Wittenberg and Dessau. On 3 May the Germans sent their wounded, including civilians, across the river near Stendal and Fishbeck in Saxony-Anhalt in order to reach the Americans. Two days later his command crossed the Elbe to escape the Soviet advance and Edelsheim surrendered to the Americans on 7 May near Tangermünde after he had negotiated the surrender.

Walter HOERNLEIN

General der Infanterie

* 2 January 1893, Blüthen near Karstädt
+ 14 September 1961, Cologne-Merheim, North Rhine-Westpahlia

Walter Hoernlein entered Army service in November 1912 and saw action in France from October 1914 with Infantry Regiment 140. He was commissioned as a *Leutnant* in June 1913 and was captured by French troops in October 1914 and remained a prisoner of war for the remainder of the war. He was interned in Switzerland until August 1919 and then returned to Germany. He was soon promoted to *Oberleutnant* and was appointed Company Officer with Infantry Regiment 4. In October 1934 he was appointed Commander of a training battalion and was promoted to *Major* and named as Commander of the I. Battalion of Infantry Regiment 69 the following year. Promoted to *Oberstleutnant* in April 1937, he remained with this command until the Polish campaign during the Second World War, during which he was awarded the Bar to the Iron Cross 2nd Class. He saw action during the French Camping from June 1940, was awarded the Iron Cross 1st Class and soon after was promoted to *Oberst*. (*Deutsches Wehrkundearchiv*)

Knight's Cross: Awarded on 30 July 1941 as *Oberst* and Commander of Infantry Regiment 80, part of the 34th Infantry Division, for his part in the rapid advance of his forces on Fortress Brest-Litovsk during the early stages of the invasion of the Soviet Union. His regiment then launched a swift thrust to the bridge over the Mukhavets River in western Belarus, capturing it undamaged. This was crucial for the German advance as it enabled the 3rd Panzer Division to cross the river and drive towards the Soviet Union. In August he took over command of Infantry Regiment *Großdeutschland*, and on 1 April 1942 Hoernlein was promoted to *Generalmajor*, and just over a week before he took command of the newly formed Infantry Division *Großdeutschland.* He led his new command at Kursk, Rzhev and later at Smolensk, and from 1 January 1943 he was promoted to *Generalleutnant*.

Knight's Cross with Oakleaves: He became the 213th recipient on 15 March 1943 as *Generalleutnant* and Commander of Infantry Division *Grossdeutschland* for continued actions on the Russian Front. From 10 to 13 March 1943 he had led his division during the bitter defensive fighting west of Belgorod, against a large Soviet force consisting of three infantry divisions and two anti-tank brigades. His forces pushed back the large Soviet formations and captured more than 400 Soviet soldiers, while a total of twenty-nine tanks, 146 artillery pieces and 107 mortars and anti-tank guns were either captured or destroyed. The Oakleaves were personally presented by Hitler at *Führer* Headquarters in Rastenburg. During the summer of 1943 his division took part in the Battle of Kursk, and with the failure of the offensive the division was deployed in the Kharkov area. In August 1944 Hoernlein took temporary command of the LXIV. Army Corps and from September he took temporary command of the LXXXII. Army Corps in the Metz area. On 9 November he was promoted to *General der Infanterie* and his command was confirmed and took part in a large-scale attack against American troops in the area north of Metz. From December he was assigned to Military District X and in February 1945 he transferred as the Commanding General of the Replacement II. Army Corps and Commander in Military District II, in Stettin. He was recalled to front-line duty on 28 April as the Commanding General of the XXVII. Army Corps, part of the 2nd Army, seeing action in West Prussia against US forces. He surrendered on 3 May and was held in captivity until his release in 1947.

Hans Valentin Robert Friedrich HUBE
Generaloberst

* 29 October 1890, Naumburg, Saxony-Anhalt
+ 21 April 1944, air crash near Thundorf, Bavaria

Knight's Cross: Awarded on 1 August 1941 as *Generalmajor* and Commander of the 16th Panzer Division, part of the XIV. Motorised Army Corps, for actions on the Russian Front. On 7 July 1941 Hube led his division through Soviet defences towards Starokostiantyniv and during the fighting that followed his forces prevented the advance of Soviet tank and artillery formations. Hube had already proven to be a gifted commander during the invasion of France, where he accepted the surrender of the XXI. French Army Corps. His Panzer Division proved itself during the early stages of the invasion of the Soviet Union and Hube proved to be a very capable commander when his division spearheaded Kleist's 2nd Panzer Group.

Hans Hube entered the Army as a *Fahnenjunker* in February 1909 with Infantry Regiment 26 and was commissioned as a *Leutnant* in August 1910. He served during the First World War as adjutant of II. Battalion of his regiment and was severely wounded in September 1914, losing his left arm in the Battle of Verdun. He was promoted to *Oberleutnant* in February 1915 and became Company Leader of his regiment from January 1916. By November he was regimental adjutant. (*Deutsches Wehrkundearchiv*)

Knight's Cross with Oakleaves: He became the sixty-second recipient on 16 January 1942 as *Generalmajor* and Commander of the 16th Panzer Division while attached to the XIV. Motorised Army Corps for his decisive contributions to the capture of Nikolayev and during the encirclement of Kiev. He was presented the Oakleaves personally by Hitler in March 1942 during a ceremony at *Führer* Headquarters in Rastenburg. On 8 April Hube was promoted to *Generalleutnant* and in May led his command near the Volga area. His men captured 31,500 Russian soldiers and sixty-nine tanks and other vehicles. His command was, however, seriously depleted by casualties during street fighting in Stalingrad in September. On 1 October he was promoted to *General der Panzertruppe* and made Commanding General of the XIV. Panzer Corps.

Hube was awarded both classes of the Iron Cross and was promoted to *Hauptmann* in January 1918, ending the war in hospital suffering from a gas attack. He remained in the Army after the war and was a Tactics Instructor from October 1928. He was promoted to *Major* in February 1931, and in June 1934 he was promoted to *Oberstleutnant*. He served as a Battalion Commander and was promoted to *Oberst* in August 1936. He saw action in the Polish campaign as Commander of Infantry Regiment 3 and from May 1940 he served as Commander of the 16th Infantry Division. He was awarded both classes of the Bar to the Iron Cross and was promoted to *Generalmajor* in June 1940. (*Author's Collection*)

Knight's Cross with Oakleaves and Swords: Awarded on 21 December 1942, the twenty-second recipient, as *General der Panzertruppe* and Commanding General of the XIV. Panzer Corps while attached to the 9th Army for his bold thrust to the Volga River north of Stalingrad and his defence there against repeated and fierce Soviet counter-attacks. The Swords were presented personally by Hitler on 28 December 1942 at *Führer* Headquarters in Rastenburg. After the ceremony Hube spoke to Hitler and tried to persuade him to let the 6th Army breakout of Stalingrad, but Hitler refused. However, on 18 January 1943 during the Stalingrad encirclement Hitler ordered Hube to be flown out of the Pocket. Despite Hube's protests, he was flown out from Gumrak Airfield on 19 January by *Leutnant* Hans Gilbert. In July 1943 Hube was sent to the Mediterranean Front, where he created Group *Hube* in Sicily, a four-division force whose task was to defend the island. With the advent of Operation Husky, the Allied invasion of Sicily, he was also made Commander-in-Chief of all Army and *Luftwaffe* anti-aircraft troops on the island. He was also made responsible for the evacuation to the Italian Peninsula and prepared a strong defensive line that would enable the Germans to retreat from the area. On 20 September 1943 he was delegated with the leadership of the 10th Army in Italy but only very briefly and was granted leave a week later. He prepared a strong defensive line around Messina that enabled the Germans to make a successful retreat to the mainland. He later became involved in the battles defending Salerno from Patton's forces. From October he

Hans Hube seen here in an official portrait photograph wearing his Knight's Cross with Oakleaves and Swords. (*Deutsches Wehrkundearchiv*)

was delegated with the leadership of the 1st Panzer Army as part of Army Group South on the Eastern Front, and in early 1944 one of his units was required to assist German forces breaking out of the Cherkassy Pocket. Soon after this Hube's entire force was trapped and with the help of Manstein's Army Group he managed to extricate his unit and avoid disaster. On 1 April he was promoted to *Generaloberst* and officially took over as Commander-in-Chief of the 1st Panzer Army.

Knight's Cross with Oakleaves, Swords and Diamonds: He became the thirteenth recipient on 20 April 1944 as *General der Panzertruppe* and Commanding General of the 1st Panzer Army, part of Army Group North Ukraine, for his outstanding leadership in Kamenets-Podolsky, known as the '*Hube Pocket*'. Despite being encircled by several Soviet Armies and armoured corps, Hube managed to prevent the annihilation of his army by breaking out towards the west. He was also recognised for his masterful command achievements during the fighting for Sicily and around Salerno in 1943, and he organised the evacuation. The Diamonds were personally presented to Hube by Hitler at his mountain retreat, the Berghof on the Obersalzburg, on 20 April 1944. The following day, on the return journey, Hube was killed when his aircraft, a Heinkel He 111, crashed shortly after take-off near Thundorf in Bavaria. Only his false metal hand was recovered from the wreckage and he was given a state funeral in Berlin on 26 April 1944, which Hitler attended. Hube's coffin was laid out in the Reich Chancellery and the eulogy was delivered by the Inspector of Panzer Troops, *Generaloberst* Heinz Guderian. The honour guard consisted of generals Walther Nehring, Hermann Breith, Heinrich Eberbach and Hans Gollnick.

Christian HANSEN

General der Artillerie

* 10 April 1885, Schleswig
+ 7 August 1972, Garmisch-Partenkirchen

Knight's Cross: Awarded on 3 August 1941 as *General der Artillerie* and Commanding General of the X. Army Corps, part of the 16th Army, in recognition of his leadership and bravery during an attack towards the end of July 1941. His troops crossed the River Velikaja towards the Staraya area, where his corps advanced eastwards towards Pskov against the Soviet 34th Army. By 15 August the Soviet advance threatened to cut off the X. Army Corps east of Lowyat, and the LVI. Army Corps had to be redeployed from

Christian Hansen entered Army service in March 1903 with Foot Artillery Regiment 9, being commissioned as a *Leutnant* eighteen months later. He attended Military Technical Academy from October 1906 and attended various training courses. He was promoted to *Oberleutnant* in August 1912, and two years later he was attached to the General Staff. He remained in the Army after the war and by December 1930 had risen to the rank of *Oberstleutnant* and was Army Liaison Officer in Hamburg. He attended various courses and from October 1936, now with the rank of *Generalmajor*, he was appointed Commander of the 25th Division in Ludwigsburg. He was promoted to *Generalleutnant* in March 1938 and saw action during the invasion of Poland from September 1939 as Commander of the 25th Infantry Division. He was appointed Commanding General of the X. Army Corps in October 1939, and saw action in the Netherlands from May 1940. (*Deutsches Wehrkundearchiv*)

Luga, a town near Leningrad, to push back the Soviet Army. By the 20th the Soviet resistance south of Lake Ilmen was broken and the Germans advanced further east. By the end of August the X. Army Corps was able to expand a bridgehead over the River Pola. In early January 1942 the Soviets pushed through the German defences to the south of Staraya Russa in Novgorod and cut the railway line to Shimsk. By the beginning of February Hansen's Corps together with the II. Army Corps was trapped in the Demyansk Pocket, but by the end of March the Pocket was relieved by German forces as part of Operation Bridge Building and Demyansk was held for the next twelve months. At the beginning of September 1943 Hansen was at the same time made temporary commander the 16th Army, and then in early November was named officially as Commander-in-Chief. He took part in the defensive battles in the Staraya Russa area and from 18 February 1944 had to withdraw from the area around Leningrad, during months of trench warfare. At the end of June and early July the 16th Army retreated along the Daugava River to Riga, and it was during this time that Hansen was taken ill and relieved of command. He entered the Reserves in late December 1944 and retired from Army Service.

Walther Ludwig Otto Karl Bernhard FISCHER VON WEIKERSTHAL

General der Infanterie

* 15 September 1890, Stuttgart
+ 11 February 1953, Stuttgart

Walther Fischer von Weikersthal entered army service with Grenadier Regiment 119 in June 1909. He was commissioned as a *Leutnant* in November 1910 and saw action during the First World War, being wounded in September 1914. He was awarded both classes of the Iron Cross during the war and remained in the Army after war, later serving with both the 5th and 6th Division. Promoted to *Oberstleutnant* in December 1932, he was appointed Battalion Commander with Infantry Regiment 13 in July 1933 and was promoted to *Oberst* in November 1934. In October 1935 he took command of Infantry Regiment 9 and at the start of the Second World War he saw action as a *Generalmajor.* He was Chief of the General Staff of the 7th Army during the invasion of Poland and later in France, and was awarded both classes of the Bar to the Iron Cross. (*Deutsches Wehrkundearchiv*)

Knight's Cross: Awarded on 6 August 1941 as *Generalleutnant* and Commander of the 35th Infantry Division, part of the V. Army Corps, for actions on the Russian Front. He sent an advance battalion into the Bialystok Pocket that contributed to the success of the V. Army Corps, securing a major victory. As a result, Fischer von Weikersthal was personally thanked and had the Knight's Cross presented by the Commanding General of the V. Army Corps, *General der Infanterie* Richard Ruoff. He later led his command during the opening stages of Operation Typhoon, the advance on Moscow, with his division crossing the Dnieper River south of Yartsevo and taking part in the Battle of Vyazma. On 1 December he was appointed Commanding General of the LIII. Army Corps and the following month he was promoted to *General der Infanterie,* later taking part in the battle for Tula and the advance on Ryazan and Kashira. From February 1942 he served six months in the Reserves before returning to active duty in September 1942 as Commanding General of the LXVII. Reserve Corps, with its initial purpose to lead reserve divisions of Commander-in-Chief West. In mid-1942 it was renamed the LXVII. Army Corps and served in Belgium as part of the 15th Army. From the end of January 1944 it served in the Amiens area for coastal protection on the Pas-de-Calais. He entered the Reserves once again from July 1944 and on 27 March 1945 was appointed Commanding General of Higher Command Upper Rhine and saw action while defending the fortifications in Baden-Baden. Von Weikersthal was captured by Allied troops in May 1945 and imprisoned until his release in 1947.

Friedrich 'Fritz' Wilhelm HOLZHÄUSER

Generalmajor

* 8 July 1902, Schwäbisch-Gmünd, Württemberg
+ 14 December 1982, Freiburg im Breisgau, Baden-Württemberg

Knight's Cross: Awarded on 6 August 1941 as *Major* and Commander of III. Battalion of Panzer Regiment 29, part of the 12th Panzer Division, for the crucial area his command held during the fighting in the Smolensk Pocket, which prevented the Soviets from outflanking the XXXIX. Army Corps. On 4 August he had been wounded and was hospitalised until the beginning of October, and while recovering he was presented with the Knight's Cross. In January 1942 he became Commander of Special Staff Panzer Repair East and was promoted to *Oberstleutnant* in March. From June he worked with Professor Porsche, Director of the Work Companionship on Air-Cooled Engines in the Reich Ministry for Armaments and Munitions. From July 1942 until September 1944 he was Department Head of the Weapons Testing Office 6 of the High Command of the Army, and at the same time he was Director of Motor Vehicle Commission and Office Head with the Ministry for Armaments and Munitions. He had been promoted to *Oberst* in July 1943, and from October 1944 he was Head of the Office Group for Panzer and Mechanisation in the Army Weapons Office. He was promoted to *Generalmajor* on 20 April 1945. He surrendered to the British on 8 May 1945 and remained in captivity until 17 May 1947.

Theodor Otto Friedrich BOHLMANN-COMBRINCK

Generalmajor

* 18 November 1891, Delmenhorst, Oldenburg
+ 18 November 1956, Bad Honnef, North Rhine-Westphalia

Knight's Cross: Awarded on 8 August 1941as *Oberst* and Commander of Rifle Regiment 111 while attached to the 11th Panzer Division for his excellent leadership during the battles around Ostrog in the Ukraine. It was his command that bore the brunt of combat at this time and the victories achieved were solely down to his leadership, according to press releases of the time. From 23 August his regiment was deployed in the operational area for the Battle of Kiev and was later moved to the area of Army Group South and Centre. As part of 11th Panzer Division, his command took part in the twin battles at Vyazma and Bryansk, and by mid-October was part of the advance on Moscow. From December his

Bohlmann-Combrink entered Army service as a volunteer in October 1913 with Infantry Regiment 94. He saw action at the beginning of the First World War and was awarded the Iron Cross 2nd Class in December 1914. He was wounded and hospitalised in July 1915. He returned to the front in October and was wounded again in August 1916, returning to his regiment in December. He was awarded the Iron Cross 1st Class in May 1917. He was taken ill three more times before the end of the war and was promoted to *Leutnant* in 1918. He joined the police after the war, rising to the rank of *Major*. He re-entered the Army in October 1935 and he was awarded both the Bar to the Iron Cross 1st and 2nd Classes during combat in Poland between September and October 1939. (*Deutsches Wehrkundearchiv*)

regiment was on the defensive near Moscow, and from 22 March until 18 April 1942 his command was involved in the terrible battles at Vyazma, followed by action near Vyazma from mid-May. From May 1942 Bohlmann-Combrinck was appointed commander of Fast Troops in the Military District IV, Dresden. He was promoted to *Generalmajor* on 10 November 1943 and attended a Divisional Leaders Course shortly afterwards before being appointed Commander of Panzer Troops in Dresden from February 1944. He later moved to Military District VI in Münster and his last appointment was that of Commander of Panzer Training Unit *Westfalen* in north-west Germany. He surrendered to the Allies in May 1945 and remained in captivity until May 1947.

Fritz HERTZSCH

Generalmajor

* 15 June 1892, Zittau, Saxony
+ 15 July 1941 near Kutnjany, Belarus, Soviet Union

Knight's Cross: Awarded on 8 August 1941, posthumously, as *Oberst* and Commander of Infantry Regiment 77 while attached to the 26th Infantry Division for actions in Belarus on the Soviet Front. On 15 July his regiment crossed the river near Kutnjak and came under enemy fire, when Hertzsch was told that some of his regiment were lagging behind due to strong enemy forces. He immediately went across the battlefield towards his men to take personal command but on the way he was seriously wounded by gunfire. Within a very short time he succumbed to his injuries and died. Herztsch was posthumously promoted to the rank of *Generalmajor*. At the beginning of the war his regiment was used for border security and on 10 May 1940 he crossed the Luxembourg border and travelled through the Ardennes into France. After the defeat of France and Belgium he remained there as part of the occupation force and was transferred to eastern Poland in May 1941, ready for the invasion of the Soviet Union. On 22 June the division crossed the German and Russian border and Hertzsch took part in the tough and challenging opening battles.

Karl-Friedrich von der MEDEN

Generalleutnant

* 3 December 1896, Samplau, West Prussia
+ 25 December 1961, Hannover, Lower Saxony

Karl-Friedrich von der Meden (third from the left pointing at the map) was a war volunteer from August 1914 as part of Jäger Regiment 12 and saw action on both fronts. He was commissioned as a *Leutnant* in August 1917 and was awarded the Iron Cross 2nd Class. He left the Army at the end of the war but rejoined in November 1922 and attended the Cavalry School at Hannover. Promoted to *Oberleutnant* in April 1925, he was appointed Squadron Chief with Mounted Regiment 1 from February 1932 and was promoted to *Hauptmann* in April 1933. From October 1934 he was Training Officer of the Riding School for the Army in Hannover and from April 1939, now with the rank of *Major*, he was Commander of the I. Battalion of the 5th Cavalry Regiment and saw action in Poland. (*Author's Collection*)

Knight's Cross: Awarded on 8 August 1941 as *Oberstleutnant* and Commander of Bicycle Troop Battalion 12 while attached to the 12th Infantry Division for actions on the Russian Front. From the beginning of the invasion in June 1941 his unit played an important part in the capture of Dvinsk and the sweep across northern Russia. It saw action in Demyansk and Meden was promoted to *Oberst* in October. In February 1942 he was made Commander of Rifle Regiment 1, part of the 1st Panzer Division, and took part in the fighting in the area south-west of Rzhev in March and April. The following month his unit became Panzer Grenadier Regiment 1 and he continued to see action near Rzhev. He took part in the counter-attacks against strong Soviet forces and at the end of July his unit was withdrawn from the front to rest. Meden returned to combat in early August, when he was delegated with the leadership of the 1st Panzer Grenadier Brigade and continued to see heavy fighting on the Russian Front. He saw action at the beginning of the Soviet winter offensive and shortly after Christmas 1942 his unit's deployment in the East ended when the whole division was sent to France for refreshment. From 22 July 1943 he took command of the 17th Panzer Division and joined in the Battle of Kursk, and in the subsequent retreats from the Donets, the Dnieper bend and from northern Ukraine as part of the 1st Panzer Army. Meden was promoted to *Generalmajor* and in October he briefly commanded Panzer Division Nr. 178, and then entered the Reserves. Promoted to *Generalleutnant* on 1 July 1944, he was appointed Head of Field Training for Panzer Division No. 178 from January 1945. From February he was Commander of the Special Staff *von der Meden* of the 4th Panzer Army and saw action on the Eastern Front. Just before the surrender most of his staff crossed the Elbe and surrendered to the Western Allies.

Franz Otto SPONHEIMER

Generalleutnant

* 19 December 1886, Nuremberg, Bavaria
\+ 13 July 1982, Theuern, Bavaria

Knight's Cross: Awarded on 8 August 1941 as *Generalleutnant* and Commander of 21st Infantry Division while attached to I. Army Corps for actions on the Russian Front. He took his division through the Baltic States, fought in the battles of Tilsit, Volkhov and Grusino and broke through the Soviet defensive positions on the Msta River, later taking part in the Siege of Leningrad. From May 1943 he was delegated with deputy leadership of the XXVIII. Army Corps as part of the 18th Army on the Russian Front. From 1 July he took

Otto Sponheimer joined the Army in October 1907 as a volunteer and was commissioned as a *Leutnant* in May 1909. He later served as a Company Leader and Ordnance Officer in the Staff of Bavarian Replacement Brigade 9 in 1916 with the rank of *Oberleutnant*. He ended the war as a *Hauptmann* and regimental adjutant and transferred into the police in September 1920. He transferred into the *Landespolizei* in 1935 and was later promoted to *Oberst*. The following year he transferred back to the Army and served with the 102nd Infantry Regiment until October 1937. He then transferred into the 21st Infantry Division and was promoted to *Generalmajor* in June 1939. He took over as Commander of the division in October 1939. (*Deutsches Wehrkundearchiv*)

over the leadership of the X. Army Corps and a month later was promoted to *General der Infanterie*. From 15 August 1943 he was Commanding General of the LIV. Army Corps, part of the 11th Army, and was preparing for the offensive to capture Leningrad. From late January 1944 the corps was known as *Group Sponheimer* and continued to see action on the Russian Front. It was later renamed once again as Army Detachment *Narva*. On 25 July 1944 he was appointed Commanding General of the LXVII. Army Corps and served in Boulogne, France, against the Allied invasion. By October his corps had established a front line north of Antwerp and heavy fighting broke out against Allied – mainly Canadian – troops. Sponheimer and his men were pushed back by the Allies and at the end of November the staff of the LXVII. Army Corps were withdrawn from the front line and transferred to the 1st Parachute Army in the Krefeld Area. Sponheimer, however, was transferred into the Reserves, where he remained until the surrender in May 1945.

Walter HARTMANN

General der Artillerie

* 23 July 1891, Mülheim an der Ruhr, Rhine Province
+ 11 March 1977, Hameln, Lower Saxony

Knight's Cross: Awarded on 10 August 1941 as Artillery Commander 140 with the rank of *Oberst* while part of the 17th Army for his decisive role in the successful breakthrough of the 100th Light Infantry Division through the Stalin line at Koserow in July 1941. He led his unit with great skill and

Walter Hartmann entered the Army in October 1910 as a *Fahnenjunker* attached to Field Artillery Regiment 12 and he was commissioned as a *Leutnant* in May 1912. He saw action during the First World War with the same regiment and was promoted to *Oberleutnant* in March 1916, being awarded the Iron Cross 1st and 2nd Classes. During the last months of the war Hartmann served as a staff officer and remained in the Army after the defeat of Germany. In March 1934 he was appointed Commander of IV. Battalion of Artillery Regiment 60 and was promoted to *Oberstleutnant* in April 1936. In October 1937 Hartmann was appointed Commander of 24th Artillery Regiment and promoted to *Oberst* in June 1938. He was awarded both classes of the Bar to the Iron Cross during the invasion of Poland in 1939. (*Deutsches Wehrkundearchiv*)

gallantry, always leading from the front while under constant enemy fire, and in October was promoted to *Generalmajor*. During this time Hartmann was seriously wounded in an explosion and lost both his left arm and left leg, and he remained in hospital until the spring of 1942. Despite his wounds he formally requested to be returned to full duty as soon as he was fit enough. In May he was appointed Commander of Special Purpose Division 407. In September he was appointed Commander of the 390th Field Training Division, part of Army Group Centre, seeing action once again in the Soviet Union.

Knight's Cross with Oakleaves: Awarded on 30 November 1943 to become the 340th recipient as *Generalleutnant* and Commander of the 87th Infantry Division, now part of the 3rd Panzer Army, for actions on the Soviet Front. He led two platoons of *Jäger* Battalion 1 to Beljanskaja to seal off a Soviet penetration, and later led the divisional Reserves with twenty of his staff against Soviet forces that had pushed more than 10 miles beyond the German front lines. The Oakleaves were personally presented by Hitler at *Führer* Headquarters the Wolf's Lair, Rastenburg. He attended a course for Commanding Generals in January 1944 and in February took command of the I. Army Corps, part of the 16th Army, in Nevel, Soviet Union. In May 1944 he was promoted to *General der Artillerie* and from the 10th he was appointed Commanding General of the XXXXIX. Mountain Corps, succeeding *General der Gebirgstruppe* Rudolf Konrad and seeing action in the Crimea and later in Romania. From 28 May until 13 June he was given leadership of the 17th Army and from September was appointed Commanding General of the VIII. Army Corps, part of the 9th Army in Warsaw.

Knight's Cross with Oakleaves and Swords: He became the 139th recipient on 18 March 1945 as *General der Artillerie* and Commanding General of the VIII. Army Corps, part of Army Group Centre, for holding the Oder front against strong enemy attacks. Hartmann repeatedly dealt with dangerous Soviet advances and his forces achieved many defensive successes north-east of Racibórz in Poland and east of the Sobotka. The Swords were personally presented by Hitler at the Reich Chancellery *Führer* Bunker in Berlin, and then he was granted leave. On 18 April he was appointed Commander of the XXIV. Panzer Corps part of the 1st Panzer Army in Moravia, Czechoslovakia, and saw action against Soviet forces. He managed to retreat as far as the American lines, where he surrendered together with his panzer corps on 8 May 1945. He was released from captivity on 20 June 1947.

Walter Hugo Thurow von BOLTENSTERN

Generalleutnant

* 26 November 1889, Breslau, Silesia
+ 19 January 1952, Prisoner-of-War Camp 5110/48 Woikovo, Soviet Union

Boltenstern joined the Army in March 1910 as an officer candidate and was commissioned as a *Leutnant* in August 1911. He served as a Company Leader with Reserve Infantry Regiment 262 at the beginning of the First World War. He was awarded both classes of the Iron Cross and was promoted to *Oberleutnant* in August 1915. He transferred to the 79th Reserve Division from February 1917. He ended the war with the rank of *Hauptmann* and remained in the Army in various regiments. In October 1934 he was promoted to *Oberstleutnant* and served as adjutant of Military District Command III. From October 1937, now an *Oberst*, he served as Commander of Infantry Regiment 71. (*Author's Collection*)

Knight's Cross: Awarded on 13 August 1941 as *Generalmajor* and Commander of the 29th Motorised Infantry Division while attached to the XXXXVII. Army Corps for personally leading his division during a fresh drive over the Dnieper River near Kopek. There, on the following day, he led his men during the push that took them to the gates of Smolensk, breaking all Soviet resistance along the way and achieving a great victory. The Knight's Cross was presented personally to him by *General der Panzertruppe* Joachim Lemelsen, Commanding General of the XXXXVII. Army Corps. Boltenstern was promoted to Generalleutnant on 15 July 1942 and continued to command his infantry division until February 1943, when he was transferred to the Reich War Court. In May 1944 he transferred to the Reserves and in January 1945 he retired from the Army. He was abducted by Soviet forces in May 1945 and imprisoned in Woikovo, where he died.

Helmut Martin Karl Otto FRIEBE

Generalleutnant

* 4 November 1894, Droschkau, Silesia
+ 14 January 1970, Friedrichshafen, Baden-Württemberg

Helmut Friebe entered Army service as a war volunteer in September 1914 and was attached to the Replacement Battalion of Fusilier Regiment 38. He was commissioned as a *Leutnant* in March 1916. He was Leader of the Signals Battalion of his Regiment from March 1917 and was awarded the Iron Cross 1st and 2nd Classes, ending the war as a Regimental Signals Officer. He returned to the Army in 1924 and was attached to Engineer Battalion 3 from 1925. That same year he was promoted to *Oberleutnant*. Promoted to *Major* in March 1937, he became Chief of Operations of the 20th Division from June 1938 and was promoted to *Oberstleutnant* in April 1939. He was awarded both classes of the Bar to the Iron Cross in 1939 and in January 1941 he was appointed Chief of the General Staff of XXXXVIII. Motorized Army Corps with the rank of *Oberst*. (*Deutsches Wehrkundearchiv*)

Knight's Cross: Awarded on 13 August 1941 as *Oberst* and Commander of Infantry Regiment 164 while attached to the 67th Infantry Division in recognition of his outstanding bravery and leadership, which resulted in the enemy being pushed back towards Kocury in Poland. On 24 June 1941 he had been seriously wounded and it would be several months before he was ready to return to front-line duty. On 4 April 1942 he was appointed Commander of Infantry Regiment 419 and saw action in the southern sector of the Eastern Front. On Christmas Eve Friebe was given leadership of the 125th Infantry

Division and his command was confirmed in March 1943 with his promotion to the rank of *Generalmajor*. On 17 April he led his division together with the 4th Mountain Division under *Generalleutnant* Hermann Kress to crush the Malaya Zemlya Bridgehead with a counteroffensive designated Operation Neptun. They attacked the Soviet beachhead with five battalions, without much combat support and with no air cover. The terrain was very hilly and heavily wooded, and his forces soon found that Soviet resistance was extremely fierce and did not advance more than 4½ miles. By May the planned operation was cancelled and Friebe continued to serve with the 17th Army in the Soviet Union, being promoted to *Generalleutnant* in October 1943. By March 1944 he was back in the Reserves and in May was named Commander of the 22nd Infantry Division, assigned to Crete until September when the island was evacuated and his division was deployed in Macedonia to fight partisans. In January 1945 he led his division against Titos partisans and from 26 March the division was renamed the 22nd *Volksgrenadier* Division, seeing action in Croatia. In April he was transferred and was delegated with the leadership of the LXIV. Army Corps, part of the 19th Army in the Upper Rhine area. He was taken prisoner by the Allies on 8 May and released in 1947.

Otto-Ernst OTTENBACHER

Generalleutnant

* 18 November 1888, Esslingen, Württemberg
+ 7 January 1975, Stuttgart, Baden-Württemberg

Knight's Cross: Awarded on 13 August 1941 as *Generalleutnant* and Commander of the 26th Motorised Infantry Division while attached to the XXXXI. Army Corps for actions in the northern part of the Soviet Union. He saw action during the fighting through the Baltic States, which was especially heavy near Kalinin where his forces established a bridgehead on the upper Volga. From 6 October he took over the leadership of the XXXXI. Army Corps until he was wounded during the opening stages of the Battle of Kalinin on 15 October when his observation aircraft was shot down by Soviet fighters. He was burned severely and was invalided back to Germany to recuperate. He returned to the front line in mid-January 1942, when he was delegated with the leadership of the XIII. Army Corps and saw action on the Russian Front once again. In April he entered the Reserves once again and from 20 July he was named as Commissioner General under the Military Commander of France. He became responsible for all training of the *Wehrmacht* security forces in northern France. Ottenbacher later

Otto Ottenbacher entered the Army with Infantry Regiment 121 in June 1907 and was commissioned as a *Leutnant* the following year. He remained with his regiment until 1916 and was promoted to *Hauptmann* in August of that year, also being awarded the Iron Cross 1st and 2nd Classes. He stayed in the Army after the war and served as a Platoon Leader and Company Commander. By October 1933 had been promoted to the rank of *Oberstleutnant*. In October 1935, now with the rank of *Oberst*, he was appointed Commander of the 54th Infantry Regiment in Glogau. He was promoted to *Generalmajor* in April 1939 and saw action during the invasion of Poland. (*Deutsches Wehrkundearchiv*)

led a small group that became responsible for the withdrawal of the *Wehrmacht* from Clermont-Ferrand and he did everything he could to prevent further destruction of munitions factories and he made sure that the population were kept fed. He entered the Reserves again in October 1944 and from December was attached to the Reich Court Martial Service. From February 1945 he was once again put into the Reserves, suffering from exhaustion.

Josef HARPE

Generaloberst

* 21 September 1887, Gelsenkirchen-Buer, Westphalia
+ 14 March 1968, Nuremberg, Bavaria

Knight's Cross: Awarded on 13 August 1941 as *Generalmajor* and Commander of the 12th Panzer Division while attached to the XXXIX. Army Corps for actions during the defensive battles on the Russian Front, where Harpe and his division had to cover a 25-mile sector. On 24 and 25 July 1941 his troops were attacked by a large Siberian corps and through a combination of good leadership and excellent *Luftwaffe* support not only was the enemy repelled, the 91st Siberian Division was completely destroyed. Later that year Harpe led his division during the Minsk encirclement, the crossing of the Dnieper and the Battle of Smolensk.

Knight's Cross with Oakleaves: Awarded on 31 December 1941 as the fifty-fifth recipient while still *Generalmajor* and Commander of the 12th Panzer

Josef Harpe entered the Army in September 1909 with Infantry Regiment 56, was commissioned as a *Leutnant* in March 1911 and appointed adjutant of the III. Battalion in October 1913. He served with the same regiment, the 56th, throughout the First World War, was awarded both classes of the Iron Cross and was promoted to *Hauptmann* in April 1918. He stayed in the Army after the war and was promoted to *Major* in April 1931, shortly before he retired. (*Deutsches Wehrkundearchiv*)

Division, part of Army Group North, for his command and for the seizure of the town of Tikhvin, Leningrad. Harpe was further praised as he had been wounded in the head but had stayed with his troops, and even though the area was almost completely surrounded, his division did an outstanding job as a rearguard unit that enabled three German divisions to retreat. In January 1942 Harpe was presented with his Oakleaves by Hitler at the Wolf's Lair his headquarters in Rastenburg, and shortly after was promoted to *Generalleutnant*. From July, now with the rank of *General der Panzertruppe*, he took command of the XXXXI. Panzer Corps and saw action against the Soviet 41st Army. The fighting continued into February 1943 and from May he saw action near Orel.

Harpe returned to the Army in November 1933, was promoted to *Oberstleutnant* in August 1934 and named as Commander of the I. Battalion of Motor Transport Instruction Command Zossen in October that year. From October 1935 he commanded the 3rd Panzer Regiment and was promoted to *Oberst* in January 1937. He was Commander of the 1st Panzer Brigade during the invasion of Poland, where he won the Bar to the Iron Cross 1st and 2nd Classes. He is seen here collecting his Oakleaves from Hitler at the Wolf's Lair, Rastenburg, in early 1942. (*Deutsches Wehrkundearchiv*)

Knight's Cross with Oakleaves and Swords: He became the thirty-sixth recipient on 15 September 1943 as *General der Panzertruppe* and Commanding General of the XXXXI. Panzer Army Corps and achieved considerable success on the Eastern Front. Harpe saw action during the defensive battles of Rzhev during Operation Citadel in July 1943 and during the fighting north-west of Orel. He was presented with the Swords by Hitler at Führer headquarters in Rastenburg on 29 October 1943. In March 1944 Harpe established a makeshift prison camp at Ozarichi in Belarus, where there were no buildings or sanitary facilities. Soldiers of the 35th Infantry Division marched 40,000 civilians into the camp, of which 400 were shot during the journey. The camp was liberated by Soviet soldiers on 19 March 1944, after at least 9,000 people, including women and children, had died in the camp. Shortly after he was appointed Commander-in-Chief of the 9th Army and took part in the beginning of the Russian summer offensive. On 20 May 1944 he was promoted to *Generaloberst*. In September he was appointed Commander-in-Chief of Army Group A, but after the Soviet breakthrough near Baranov he was blamed for the defeat and replaced by *Generaloberst* Ferdinand Schörner in January 1945. He was dismissed by Hitler and placed on the *Führer* Reserve until he was recalled in March as Commander-in-Chief of the 5th Panzer Army. The unit crossed the Rhine but was trapped in the Ruhr basin by US forces. On 17 April Harpe surrendered and remained in US captivity until 14 April 1948. He was never prosecuted with regard to the prison camp in Belarus.

Alfred Karl Martin HEMMANN

Generalleutnant

* 13 October 1895, Gleiwitz, Silesia
+ 26 September 1957, Friedberg, Hesse

Knight's Cross: Awarded on 21 August 1941 as *Oberstleutnant* and Commander of Infantry Regiment 426 while attached to the 126th Infantry Division for actions in the Soviet Union. He saw action on the northern sector of the Russian Front from June 1941, remaining at the front until he was taken ill in December of that year. He was away from the front for almost twelve months because of his illness and had been promoted to *Oberst* in February 1942. The Knight's Cross was personally presented by *General der Artillerie* Christian Hansen, Commanding General of X. Army Corps. In November he was assigned as Tactics Instructor with the Regimental Leaders Course of Instruction Staff II of the Infantry School, and from 6 November 1943 he

Alfred Hemmann entered Army service with Infantry Regiment 22 in October 1914 and attended officer training school in Döberitz from December. He was commissioned as a *Leutnant* in May 1915 and served as a Platoon Leader and then adjutant of III. Battalion of Infantry Regiment 22, where he served until the end of the war. In August 1920 he joined the ranks of the police, rising to the rank of *Polizei-Major* in January 1934. From October 1935 he served once again in the Army and was assigned to Infantry Regiment 28. Promoted to *Major* in March 1936, he served as Commander of I. Battalion of Infantry Regiment 51 from October 1937. (*Deutsches Wehrkundearchiv*)

served as a Commander of Staff at the Infantry School. On 15 August he was delegated with the leadership of the 263rd Infantry Division and took part in the retreat through the Baltic States. Promoted to *Generalmajor* in October he was confirmed as divisional commander, and his command became isolated in the Courland Pocket, holding the sector during six unsuccessful Soviet attempts to crush the pocket. He was promoted to *Generalleutnant* in April 1945 and his command still had not been defeated when the war finished. Taken prisoner on 9 May 1945, he was held in Soviet captivity until his release on 6 October 1955, together with most of his staff.

Erhard Walther MELZER

General der Infanterie

* 7 October 1894, Leipzig
\+ 23 June 1961, Bremen

Knight's Cross: Awarded on 21 August 1941 as *Oberst* and Commander of Infantry Regiment 151, part of the 61st Infantry Division, for his outstanding leadership during the heavy fighting on the Eastern Front. On 22 July 1941 his regiment took part in the attack on Põltsamaa in Estonia and, despite his forces suffering heavy losses, his men stormed the city with great courage. In addition his regiment captured many important bridges across the major rivers and by midday the city was in German hands. From 25 February 1942 Melzer

Walther Melzer entered the Army in April 1914 and was commissioned as a *Leutnant* in September 1916. He was awarded both closes of the Iron Cross and from January 1918 he served as an Intelligence Office in Regimental Headquarters. He stayed in the Army after the war and served as a legal officer and later with the 10th Mounted Regiment with the rank of *Oberleutnant*. From October 1924 he served as an adjutant and three years later he was Welfare Officer with the 11th Infantry Regiment in Freiburg. Promoted to *Major* in November 1934, he served on the Staff of the Commander of a military training area, and from October 1935 he was a Battalion Commander with Infantry Regiment 43 with the rank of *Major*. On 26 August 1939 *Oberstleutnant* Melzer was Commander of the 151st Infantry Regiment and saw action during the opening days of the Second World War in Poland, where he was awarded both classes of the Bar to the Iron Cross. (*Author's Collection*)

was Commander of Infantry Regiment 694 in France. From early December 1942 until 9 January 1943 he took temporary command of the 332nd Infantry Division and was promoted to *Generalmajor* in February of that year. He took permanent command, seeing action during the defence of Yelnya. On 1 August 1943 Melzer was promoted to *Generalleutnant* and his division fought against eight rifle divisions and two tank bridges from the Soviet 43rd and 6th Guards Armies. In fact, the Soviet forces fired 50,000 artillery shells into the division – more than five shells for each soldier of his division! Losses were high on both sides, the Soviets lost 100 tanks and the Germans lost many men and equipment.

Knight's Cross with Oakleaves: He became the 558th recipient on 23 August 1944 as *Generalleutnant* and Commander of 252nd Infantry Division, part of the IX. Army Corps, for his outstanding leadership in the fighting during Operation Bagration, the Soviet attack on the German Army Group Centre. In fact, from April 1944 the division underwent a massive reorganisation and from July his command took part in the retreat across Lithuania and into Poland. During the summer offensive he saw action north-west of Vitebsk and during the fighting around Narew his command managed to hold back the Red Army until reinforcements arrived to prevent a severe crisis. On 12 October he took command of the XXIII. Army Corps. He led his troops into East Prussia in January 1945, shortly after he had been promoted to *General der Infanterie*, and fought his final battle near Gdansk, where he was captured by the Allies.

Carl-Heinrich Rudolf Wilhelm von STÜLPNAGEL

General der Infanterie

* 2 January 1886, Berlin, Brandenburg
+ 30 August 1944, Berlin-Plötzensee, Brandenburg

Carl-Heinrich von Stülpnagel entered the Army in October 1904 as a *Fahnenjunker* with the Royal Prussian Army and was commissioned as a *Leutnant* in 1906. He was at the War Academy from 1911 until 1913 and was then assigned as Company Leader with Infantry Regiment 115. He was promoted to *Oberleutnant* and saw action on the Western Front at the beginning of the First World War, being promoted to *Hauptmann* in January 1915. From January 1916 he was Operations Officer with the 18th Division and was wounded towards the end of the war. He remained in the Army and by October 1935 had been promoted to *Generalmajor.* The following year he took command of the 30th Infantry Division. He was promoted to *General der Infanterie* and served as Senior Quartermaster on the General Staff of the Army. (*Deutsches Wehrkundearchiv*)

Knight's Cross: Awarded on 21 August 1941 as *General der Infanterie* and Commander-in-Chief of the 17th Army for actions in the Soviet Union as part of Army Group South. He led his command through the Galician border fortifications, advanced towards the Stalin Line and was successful during the heavy fighting near Lviv. Between 2 and 25 July 1941 his division broke though the Stalin Line and advanced towards the Dnieper until October, when he was relieved of his command – at his own request. On 13 February 1942 he was appointed Military Commander of France and would take severe measures against resistance fighters. From the summer of 1944 he became one of the leaders of the military resistance against Hitler and when the bomb plot failed he was advised by *Generalfeldmarschall* Günther von Kluge to go into hiding. Stülpnagel refused but was removed from office and ordered to report to Berlin, which he did but on the way he tried to commit suicide near Verdun and in the process he went blind. He was then arrested by the Gestapo and taken to Berlin. He was tried by the People's Court on 30 August 1944 and that same day he was hanged in Plötzensee Prison.

Kurt Friedrich Konrad FELDT

General der Kavallerie

* 22nd November 1887, Schmentau, Prussia
+ 11 March 1970, Berlin, Brandenburg

Kurt Feldt entered the Army in September 1908 and served with the cavalry during the First World War, rising to the rank of *Rittmeister* in June 1917. He remained in the Army after the war, serving in various mounted regiments, and was named as Commander of Cavalry Brigade 1 In November 1938, now with the rank of *Oberst*. He saw action in East Prussia and then in Poland at the beginning of the Second World War, where he was awarded the Bar to the Iron Cross 1st and 2nd Classes. On 25 October 1939 he was named as Commander of the 1st Cavalry Division and was promoted to *Generalmajor* in February 1940. (*Deutsches Wehrkundearchiv*)

Knight's Cross: Awarded on 23 August 1941 as *Generalmajor* and Commander of the 1st Cavalry Division while attached to the XXXXVII. Army Corps in recognition of his leadership while covering and protecting the southern flank of *Generaloberst* Heinz Guderian's Panzer Group during the attack through the Pripyat Marshes in the Soviet Union. It soon became apparent that a cavalry force could not fully function in the area it was fighting in and so it was refitted in December 1941 and renamed the 24th Panzer Division, with Feldt continuing as its commander. From February 1942 the division was relocated to France for refitting, training and reorganisation, during which Feldt was promoted to *Generalleutnant*, and in April he was transferred into the Reserves. On 15 July he was appointed Chief of the Military Administration in District B, south-west France. He remained there until January 1943, when he was appointed District Commander in south-west France. He was promoted to *General der Kavallerie* in February 1944 and was appointed Commander of Section III in Marne, a district of Paris. On 12 September he was appointed Commanding General of Corps *Feldt* and was stationed on the Lower Rhine while attached to the 1st Parachute Army under *Generaloberst* Kurt Student. He saw action against the US 82nd Airborne Division on 17 September when they tried to take Nijmegen Bridge as part of the Allies' Operation Market Garden. At the end of November 1944 most of his command had transferred to the Saar-Palatinate and on 10 December the Medical Corps *Feldt* transferred to the 1st Army. Feldt entered the Reserves and from 5 February 1945 he was made *General* with special duties on the Staff of the *Wehrmacht* Commander in Denmark, *Generaloberst* Georg Lindemann, where he remained until the end of the war. He surrendered to British forces on 8 May 1945 and was in Allied captivity until his release on 23 December 1947.

Otto-Wilhelm FÖRSTER

General der Pioniere

* 16 March 1885, Ilmenau, Weimar
+ 24 June 1966, Walsrode

Otto-Wilhelm Förster entered the Army as a *Fahnenjunker* in March 1903 and by the time of the First World War he held the rank of *Oberleutnant* and was a company commander. From March 1915 until the end of the war he served as a general staff officer with various infantry divisions and had been promoted to *Hauptmann*. He remained in the Army after the war and served in various staff positions until February 1933 when, as an *Oberst*, he was appointed Inspector of Engineers and Fortresses. Promoted to *Generalmajor* in October 1934, he was promoted to *Generalleutnant* in January 1938. He was appointed Commanding General of the VI. Army Corps in November 1938, when he held the rank of *General der Pioniere*. (*Deutsches Wehrkundearchiv*)

Knight's Cross: Awarded on 23 August 1941 as *General der Pioniere* and Commanding General of the VI. Army Corps while attached to the 9th Army for actions on the Russian Front. On 15 July 1941, during an attack against the Stalin Line, his troops had achieved a 7-mile breakthrough and captured the city of Polotsk in Belarus that same day. The capture of Polotsk was of defensive importance for the 9th Army's operations east of the Daugava River, which flowed through Belarus and Latvia. His corps pushed east and took part in two battles near Vyazma and Bryansk during October as part of the Moscow campaign. At the beginning of the Russian winter offensive his corps began to withdraw towards Rzhev and just before the first decisive battles around Rzhev took part Förster was transferred to the Reserves at the end of December 1941 for some rest. He never returned to the front line and remained in the Reserves until his retirement on 31 January 1944. In August 1945 he was handed over to the Soviets and was deported to a prison camp, where he remained until October 1955.

Richard Walter Horst GROSSMANN

General der Infanterie

* 19 November 1891, Sybba-Lyck, Eastern Prussia
\+ 4 May 1972, Rüsselsheim, Hesse in Germany

Horst Grossmann entered the Army in September 1911 with Infantry Regiment 175, and was commissioned as a *Leutnant* two years later. He saw action during the opening phase of the First World War and was awarded the Iron Cross in October 1914. The following month he was appointed adjutant of the II. Battalion of his Regiment. He was promoted to *Oberleutnant* in August 1916 and was awarded the Iron Cross 1st Class in October, spending the rest of the war as a staff officer. He stayed in the Army after the war and continued to serve as an adjutant, and after attending various courses from October 1931 he was an Instructor at the Infantry School in Döberitz. Promoted to *Major* in August 1933, he was appointed Commander of the II. Battalion of Infantry Regiment 22 in 1935 and was promoted to *Oberstleutnant* the following year. During the opening phase of the Second World War in September 1939 he served on the military staff of Hitler and from October he served with Infantry Regiment 84, seeing action in the invasion of France. (*Deutsches Wehrkundearchiv*)

Knight's Cross: Awarded on 23 August 1941 as *Oberst* and Commander of Infantry Regiment 84, part of the 8th Infantry Division, for the storming of the Grodno Bridgehead, which his troops held successfully against all Soviet counter-attacks. On 1 August his regiment had made a 5-mile penetration into the Soviet front line and two days later took the Dnieper Bridge and all opposing attempts by Soviet forces to retake the bridgehead failed. The Knight's Cross was personally presented to Grossmann by the Commanding General of the VIII. Army Corps *General der Artillerie* Walter Heitz. In mid-December Grossmann was promoted to *Generalmajor* and appointed Commander of the 6th Infantry Division. He led his troops across the Volga, where his division met a Soviet counteroffensive. From early 1942 he took part in trench battles and heavy fighting against partisans north-west of Bryansk, and was promoted to *Generalleutnant* in January 1943. In early summer Grossmann led his division in the Dorogobuzh area and from July took part in the opening phase of Operation Citadel.

Knight's Cross with Oakleaves: He became the 292nd recipient on 4 September 1943 as *Generalleutnant* and Commander of the 6th Infantry Division, part of the XXXXVII. Panzer Corps, in recognition of his success during the opening phase of Operation Citadel, the Battle of Kursk. The Oakleaves were presented to Grossmann by Hitler on 25 October 1943 at *Führer* Headquarters in Rastenburg, the Wolf's Lair. From January 1944, while still in command of the 6th Infantry Division, he was appointed Acting Commander of the LV. Army Corps and saw action in Rogachev and later in Bobruisk, Belarus. At the same time he was also named as Acting Commander of the XXXV. Army Corps for almost four weeks while its commander *General der Infanterie* Friedrich Wiese was on leave. He was appointed leader of the VI. Army Corps in August 1944 and on 9 November was promoted to *General der Infanterie.* His command was pushed back to the Baltic area and from March 1945 it was trapped in the Heiligenbeil Pocket and smashed. Grossmann had at this time managed to get away from the area with a small number of staff and headed towards the western borders. They were captured by the British on 9 May 1945 and Grossmann remained in British captivity until 8 July 1947.

Bruno Ritter von HAUENSCHILD

Generalleutnant

* 9 June 1896, Würzburg, Bavaria
+ 10 March 1953, Munich, Bavaria

Knight's Cross: Awarded on 25 August 1941 as *Oberst* and Commander of 4th Panzer Brigade while attached to the 10th Panzer Division for his successful leadership during the swift thrust from the Berezina River to the Dnieper River. His command seized several bridges that were of great importance to the advance of his Panzer Brigade and the 2nd Panzer Group. His command eliminated thirty-six tanks, 115 anti-tank guns, sixty-two artillery guns, eighty machine guns and 182 military trucks. In mid-October 1941 his brigade broke through two defensive positions about 40 miles west of Moscow, but had to retreat soon afterwards. Towards the end of December Hauenschild was attached to the Staff of the 24th Panzer Division, and saw action on the Russian Front, fighting near Smolensk and protecting the southern flank of Heinz Guderian's 2nd Panzer Army. From April 1942 Hauenschild, now newly promoted to *Generalmajor*, took command of the 24th Panzer Division, seeing action from June as part of the 6th Army during the summer offensive.

Bruno Ritter von Hauenschild entered the Army in August 1914 with Bavarian Field Artillery Regiment 11 and was commissioned as a *Leutnant* in April 1915. He served with the same regiment throughout the war and was awarded the Iron Cross 1st and 2nd Classes. He remained in the Army after the war and was promoted to *Hauptmann* in February 1929. Later that year he transferred into Artillery Regiment 7. From October 1935, now with the rank of *Major*, Hauenschild was appointed Commander of Reconnaissance Battalion 7, and was promoted to *Oberstleutnant* in January 1938. From August he took over as Commander or Reconnaissance Regiment 9. (*Deutsches Wehrkundearchiv*)

Knight's Cross with Oakleaves: He became the 129th recipient on 27 September 1942 as *Generalmajor* and Commander of the 24th Panzer Division with the XXXXVIII. Panzer Corps in recognition of his successful leadership. His division played a major role in the German offensive victories near Voronezh, during the battle in the Don area and in the drive towards Stalingrad. He was seriously wounded during the fierce fighting and evacuated to hospital. He was awarded the Wound Badge in Gold and while in hospital was presented with his Oakleaves personally by Hitler on 16 November 1942. Almost a year later he was finally fit for battle and he was promoted to *Generalleutnant* in January 1944. He was appointed Commander of Panzer Troops Schools and from 30 October he co-ordinated the merger of Panzer Troop School Krampnitz with Panzer School Bergen. From 26 January 1945 he was appointed Commanding General of the Replacement III. Army Corps and Commander of Military District III in Berlin, and at the same time he was also Battle Commandant in Berlin. On 20 March he was once again seriously wounded and surrendered to Allied troops in hospital in Feldafing in the Starnberg district of Bavaria in April 1945, where he remained until the end of June that year.

Georg Ritter von HENGL

General der Gebirgstruppe

* 21 October 1897, Lailling, Landau
+ 19 March 1952, Sonthofen

Knight's Cross: Awarded on 25 August 1941 as *Oberstleutnant* and Commander of Mountain Jäger Regiment 137, part of the 2nd Mountain Division, for actions

Georg Ritter von Hengl entered Army service as a war volunteer in August 1914, serving with Bavarian Infantry Regiment 11. He served as an NCO during the war and was finally commissioned as a *Leutnant* in March 1918 while serving with a Flying Battalion. He was awarded the Iron Cross 1st and 2nd Classes during the war as well as the Wound Badge in Gold in 1916. In March 1921, with the war over, he transferred into the State Police in Augsburg, rising to the rank of *Polizei-Hauptmann* in June 1931. (*Author's Collection*)

against positions just east of Petsamo, Finland, on the Soviet border in June 1941. The Knight's Cross was personally presented to Hengl by the Commanding General of Mountain Corps Norway, *General der Gebirgstruppe* Eduard Dietl. In December Hengl was promoted to *Oberst* and from March 1942 he served as Leader of the 2nd Mountain Division, seeing action in Lapland, in April he was promoted to *Generalmajor* and continued to fight in Lapland as part of the XIX. Mountain Corps.

Hengl was promoted to *Generalleutnant* on 21 January 1943, and continued to see action in Lapland against the Finnish Army until October 1943, when he took over as Commanding General of the XIX. Mountain Corps. He was promoted to *General der Gebirgstruppe* in January 1944 and from 15 May was appointed chief of the Personnel Office of the High Command of the Army. On 25 January 1945 he was delegated with the leadership of the LIX. Army Corps but his command never became effective because he was taken ill suddenly and never returned to front-line duty. He was taken prisoner by the Western Allies in May 1945 and remained in captivity until 1947.

In August 1939 Hengl was appointed Commander of the III. Battalion of Mountain Infantry Regiment 99, now with the rank of *Oberstleutnant*. He saw action during the Polish campaign, when he was awarded the Bar to the Iron Cross 1st and 2nd Classes in September 1939. (*Author's Collection*)

Hyazinth Graf STRACHWITZ VON GROSS-ZAUCHE UND CAMMINETZ

Generalleutnant der Reserve

* 30 July 1893, Gross-Stein, Upper Silesia
+ 25 April 1968, Prien am Chiemsee, Bavaria

Hyazinth Graf von Stachwitz joined the Army in 1912 and saw action during the First World War. He was commissioned as a *Leutnant* in 1914 and awarded both classes of the Iron Cross. He joined the *Freikorps* after the war and from 1931 served with Mounted Regiment 7 in Breslau with the rank of *Oberleutnant*. (*Author's Collection*)

Knight's Cross: Awarded on 25 August 1941 as *Major der Reserve* and Commander of I. Battalion of Panzer Regiment 2 while attached to 16th Panzer Division for his role in the successful seizure of the city of Pervomais'k. The award was presented to Strachwitz by *Generalmajor* Hans-Valentin Hube, the Commander of the 16th Panzer Division. In September he saw action at Kremenchug in the encirclement around Kiev, before plunging on towards the Don and eventually being driven back from the Rostov salient in December. He was promoted to *Oberstleutnant der Reserve* in January 1942.

Knight's Cross with Oakleaves: He became the 144th recipient on 13 November 1942 as *Oberstleutnant der Reserve* and while still Commander of I. Battalion of Panzer Regiment 2 for the role he played in the battles near Stalingrad in August 1942. During the armoured battles his division destroyed 275 Soviet tanks and advanced on the city from the Volga River. Towards the middle of November, because of his age and effect of his latest wound, he was evacuated to hospital in Breslau before the Soviet ring closed around the city of Stalingrad, thus escaping the annihilation of the 16th Panzer Division. The Oakleaves were eventually presented to him by Hitler at the Wolf's Lair, Rastenburg, in early January 1943 and shortly after he was promoted to *Oberst der Reserve* and appointed commander of Panzer regiment *Großdeutschland*, part of the Panzer Grenadier Division *Großdeutschland*.

Knight's Cross with Oakleaves and Swords: Awarded on 28 March 1943 to become the twenty-seventh recipient as *Oberst der Reserve* and Commander of Panzer Regiment '*Grossdeutschland*' for his success at Kharkov, especially during the fighting to recapture Belgorod in the north. In addition, his regiment managed to capture or destroy 150 Soviet tanks during a five-day struggle, of which ninety were destroyed in just two days. The Swords were personally presented to Strachwitz by Hitler in a special ceremony at the Berghof on the Obersalzburg on 31 March 1943. In November Strachwitz left his regiment due to ill health and after a month's sick leave he was recalled to active duty. He was promoted to *Generalmajor der Reserve* on 1 April 1944.

In 1933 von Stachwitz joined the SS and from 1935 he also served as an officer in the Army. In 1937 he served as Supply Officer with Panzer Regiment 2 and saw action in Poland and later in France with the 1st Panzer Division. He was awarded both classes of the Bar to the Iron Cross. (*Deutsches Wehrkundearchiv*)

Knight's Cross with Oakleaves, Swords and Diamonds: He became the eleventh recipient on 15 April 1944 as *Generalmajor der Reserve* and Commander of Panzer Battle Group while attached to Army Group North for his actions on the Narva Front. On 22 February 1944 he led a panzer and assault gun formation through a hostile area. By doing they were able to break through Soviet positions located behind woods and contributed significantly to the defence of the Narva Front. His efforts and those of his men thwarted all attempts by the Soviets to penetrate the German lines and this significantly contributed to the holding of the entire defensive front. Strachwitz was decorated with the Diamonds by Hitler at the Reich Chancellery in Berlin during a special ceremony in May 1944. In October he was seriously injured while travelling in a car and suffered a fractured skull, broken ribs, legs and hands. In January 1945 he was appointed Commander of Panzer *Jäger* Brigade in Upper Silesia; this was an ad hoc brigade made up of various units, and was, for the most part poorly trained and equipped. On 30 January he was promoted to *Generalleutnant der Reserve* and later his unit managed to destroy many enemy tanks and vehicles. In April he led his men in a successful breakout from a Soviet encirclement and surrendered to US troops in May 1945. While in Allied captivity he learned of the death of his son, and in 1946 his wife was run over by a US tank and Strachwitz was not permitted to attend her funeral.

Werner KIENITZ

General der Infanterie

* 3 June 1885, Kallies, Dramburg
+ 31 December 1958, Hamburg

Werner Kienitz entered the Army in March 1904 as a *Fahnenjunker* with Infantry Regiment 64 and he was commissioned as a *Leutnant* in August 1905. He was promoted to *Oberleutnant* in February 1913 while serving as a regimental adjutant at the beginning of the First World War. Promoted to *Hauptmann* in December 1914, he was serving as Company Chief and a year later he was serving with the General Staff. He was promoted to *Major* in February 1925 and served with the 4th Division from 1926. He was promoted to Oberstleutnant in October 1929 and appointed Commander of Infantry Regiment 15 in April 1932. He was made Commander of the 24th Division in October 1935 and was promoted to *Generalleutnant* in April 1937. The following year he served as Commanding General of the XVII. Army Corps and was promoted to General der Infanterie in April 1938. (*Deutsches Wehrkundearchiv*)

Knight's Cross: Awarded on 31 August 1941 as *General der Infanterie* and Commanding General of the XVII. Army Corps while attached to the 6th Army for his outstanding bravery during the attack on Kiev. In January 1942 he returned to Germany and from May was Commanding General of the Replacement II. Army Corps and Commander in Military District II, Stettin. From February 1945 until the end of the war he served in the Reserve and he was taken prisoner by the Allies in May 1945. He was sent to the Island Farm Special Camp 11 on 9 January 1946 and he remained there until his release on 12 May 1948.

Wilhelm von LENGERKE

Generalmajor

* 17 June 1894, Salchow
+ 26 August 1942, Hill 118, near Krasnoarmeysk, Stalingrad

Knight's Cross: Awarded on 31 August 1941 as *Oberstleutnant* and Commander of I. Battalion of Mounted Regiment 1 of the 1st Cavalry Division for his leadership and bravery during the fighting in Kiev on the Russian Front. He was presented with the Knight's Cross by the Commander of Mounted Brigade 2, *Oberst* Heinz von Randow. By the time he had been notified of his Knight's Cross award he had already left his battalion and was on the Staff of the German Army Mission in Romania. In December 1941 he was named as Commander of Mounted Regiment 21 and within days the unit was transferred to France and converted to panzers. Lengerke returned to Russia with his new command, Panzer Grenadier Regiment 21, in July 1942, now with the rank of *Oberst*, and attached to the 6th Army. However, on 26 August Lengerke was shot and killed on Hill 118, near Krasnoarmeysk, Stalingrad, and was posthumously promoted to *Generalmajor* on 2 January 1943.

Otto STAPF

General der Infanterie

* 13 November 1890, Hellmitzheim, Middle Franconia
+ 30 March 1963, Munich, Bavaria

Otto Stapf entered the Army in August 1910 with Royal Bavarian Infantry Regiment 22 and was commissioned as a *Leutnant* in October 1912. He served as a Company Officer during the First World War and was awarded both classes of the Iron Cross. He was promoted to *Oberleutnant* in January 1916. He remained in the Army after the war, serving in various Bavarian regiments until 1925, when he entered the General Staff. From 1931 he was attached to the Defence Ministry in Berlin and was promoted to *Oberstleutnant* in October 1933. He then served with Bavarian Motor Battalion 7. Promoted to *Oberst* in August 1935, he was appointed a department head with the General Staff of the Army from October 1938, now with the rank of *Oberst*. From November 1938 he served as Senior Quartermaster III and liaison officer to the Commander-in-Chief of the *Luftwaffe* and was promoted to *Generalmajor* in April 1939. He is seen here with *Generalfeldmarschall* Walter von Reichenau. (*Author's Collection*)

Knight's Cross: Awarded on 31 August 1941 as *Generalleutnant* and Commander of 111th Infantry Division while attached to LV. Army Corps, part of the 6th Army, for actions in the Soviet Union during the early campaigns of Army

Group South. He saw action at Zhitomir and at Kiev, and from December 1941 was delegated with the leadership of the XXXXIV. Army Corps. From January 1942 he saw action against the Red Army across the Donets and in the Soviet advance towards Kramatorsk in the Ukraine. In October he was promoted to *General der Infanterie* and during February 1942 the Germans carried out counter-attacks on the Soviet Army that slowed down their success. From 17 May his corps took part in the German counteroffensive to encircle the Soviets that had broken through the German defences, which lasted until 27 May and ended with the annihilation of the encircled Soviet troops. From July 1942 Stapf was Chief of Economic Defence Staff East, and was awarded the Knight's Cross of the War Merit Cross on 10 September 1944. At that time he was the only army officer to have been awarded this Order, ending the war as Head of the Army Field Economic Office.

Hans-Jürgen Bernhard Theodor 'Dieter' von ARNIM

Generaloberst

* 4 April 1889, Ernsdorf near Reichenbach, Silesia
+ 1 September 1962, in Bad Wildungen, Waldeck-Frankenberg.

Hans-Jürgen von Arnim entered the Army as a *Fahnenjunker* in April 1908, attended the War School in Danzig and was commissioned as a *Leutnant* in August 1909. When the First World War started in 1914 von Arnim was serving as a battalion adjutant with Reserve Infantry Regiment 93 in Belgium. He was severely wounded on 17 September 1914 and on his return to duty in January 1915 he was promoted to *Oberleutnant*. Wounded again in June that same year, he returned to field duty in November and commanded a company in France. He was wounded yet again in July 1916 and was promoted to *Hauptmann* in January 1917. He later served with the 4th Guards Infantry Division as an adjutant, a post he held until the end of the war. (*Author's Collection*)

Knight's Cross: Awarded on 4 September 1941 as *Generalleutnant* as Commander of the 17th Panzer Division while attached to the XXXXVII. Panzer Corps for his leadership during the first week of Operation Barbarossa. During that time his division blazed a trail of destruction that included the capture of Brest-Litovsk on 22 June, and the prevention of a breakout by Soviet forces from

Hans-Jürgen von Arnim, seen here with the Chief of Air Fleet 1, Luftwaffe Generaloberst Alfred Keller. On 15 October 1935 von Arnim was appointed Commander of Infantry Regiment 68, part of the 23rd Infantry Division. In January 1938 he was promoted to *Generalmajor* and on 4 February was named as Commander of the 4th Service Depot at Schweidnitz, Silesia. The position was deemed a demotion. It had been assumed that von Arnim would take over as Commander of the 23rd Infantry Division but the anti-Nazi general, Erwin von Witzleben, the Commander in Berlin, arranged for 'one of his own' to take command. Arnim was politically neutral, he was not a Nazi, but he was not an anti-Nazi either. At the beginning of the Second World War he received the command he deserved; on 12 September he assumed command of the 52nd Infantry Division. (*Author's Collection*)

the Bialystok Pocket. On 17 December Arnim was promoted to *General der Panzertruppe* and was by the beginning of 1942 facing a tough enemy, with his command vastly outnumbered as the winter approached, but they managed to hold ground until relieved by elements of the 9th Army and they were finally evacuated in March 1943. They achieved this without their commander, Arnim, who was quite unexpectedly ordered to *Führer* Headquarters, where he was promoted to *Generaloberst*, named as Commander-in-Chief of the newly formed 5th Panzer Army and flown to Tunis.

Arnim led his new command against British, American, and French forces, once again proving himself a great tactician and displaying excellent leadership, winning several victories. He did not get on well with the Commander in North Africa, *Generalfeldmarschall* Erwin Rommel. The two men had different ideas on strategy and Arnim would more often than not make his own decisions without consulting Rommel. Arnim viewed Rommel as a 'commoner' and it seems very likely that Arnim considered himself better than the field marshal. It was Arnim who succeeded Rommel as Commander-in-Chief of Army Group

Afrika in March 1943. However, on 12 May, Arnim together with 275,000 German and Italian soldiers was forced to surrender to British forces at Tunis. Arnim was transferred to a prison camp in Clinton, Mississippi, in the United States, where he spent the rest of the war and was released in July 1947.

Erik Oskar HANSEN

General der Kavallerie

* 27 May 1889, Hamburg
+ 20 March 1967, Hamburg

Erik Hansen entered Army service in October 1907 with Dragoon Regiment 9 and he was commissioned as a *Leutnant* in January 1909. He served as regimental adjutant until August 1914 and then served in the field at the beginning of the war. He was promoted to *Oberleutnant* in December 1914. He was transferred to a staff position in September 1916 and promoted to *Hauptmann*, ending the war as a Quartermaster assigned to the Guards Reserve Corps. He remained in the Army after the war and by May 1934 had been promoted to *Oberst.* From October 1935 was Commander of Infantry Regiment 39. He was promoted to *Generalmajor* in August 1937 and from November of the following year he was Commander of the 4th Infantry Division. He saw action during the invasion of Poland in 1939, where he won both the Bar to the Iron Cross 1st and 2nd Classes. Now with the rank of *Generalleutnant*, he was appointed Commander of the 14th Panzer Division in August 1940 and on 31 October was promoted to *General der Kavallerie*. (*Deutsches Wehrkundearchiv*)

Knight's Cross: Awarded on 4 September 1941 as *General der Kavallerie* and Commanding General of the LIV. Army Corps while attached to the 11th Army, seeing action in the area from the Dnieper River and towards the Black Sea. From the end of September his corps tried to advance towards the Crimean Peninsula and saw action while supporting both the XXX. and XXXXII. Army Corps during the breakthrough towards the Crimea. In late December the Soviets landed on the Kerch Peninsula and there was heavy fighting near Sevastopol. By the end of May 1942 the Germans had recaptured the peninsula. After June Hansen and his corps moved to the Leningrad area together with the 11th Army and took part in the Siege of Leningrad, which lasted until January 1944. Hansen was transferred in early 1943 to become the Chief of the German Army Mission in

Ludwig Crüwell entered the Army as a *Fahnenjunker* in March 1911 and after attending War School he was assigned to Dragoon Regiment 9 and commissioned as a *Leutnant*. He was awarded both classes of the Iron Cross and remained with the Army after the war, serving with the Defence Ministry until 1925. He transferred to the 6th Division with the rank of *Major* in May 1933. From October 1934 he was Chief of Operations with VI. Army Corps, and was promoted to *Oberst* in 1936. From February 1938 he took over as Commander of Panzer Regiment 9. Promoted to *Generalmajor* in December 1939, he served as Senior Quartermaster of the 16th Army in France, where he was awarded the Bar to the Iron Cross 1st and 2nd Classes. (*Author's Collection*)

Romania, and later he also became Military Attaché to Bucharest. However, after the failure at Stalingrad the Soviets began to advance at speed towards Romania. By the mid-1944 the Red Army were fighting on the Romania border and on 23 August King Michael, supported by all major parties, led a coup d'état and the pro-Nazi government of Ion Antonescu was overthrown. On 26 August Hansen was captured by Soviet forces and just five days later Bucharest fell to the Red Army and Romania joined the Allies. Hansen remained a prisoner until his release on 10 October 1955.

Fritz LINDEMANN

General der Artillerie

* 11 April 1894, Charlottenburg, Prussia
\+ 22 September 1944, Berlin, Brandenburg

Knight's Cross: Awarded on 4 September 1941 as *Oberst* and Artillery Commander 138 while attached to the LIV. Army Corps for actions while serving in the Soviet Union. His command clashed with Romanian units in July and August and then the corps moved into a position on the Dnieper. At the beginning of September the corps reached the isthmus of the Crimean Peninsula and remained there in the weeks that followed. In January 1942 he was promoted to Generalmajor and from 11 February he took command of the 132nd Infantry Division. During the drive to the Dnieper he saw action during the Battle of Kiev, the push to the Crimea and the Siege of Sevastopol. He later took part in the assault that caused the fall of the large Soviet naval fortress in the summer of 1942 and occupied Kertsch Peninsula in August. He then moved to the northern sector of

Fritz Lindemann, together with his sons and grand-daughter, joined the Army on 12 March 1912 as a cadet with Guards Field Artillery Regiment 4. He was commissioned as a *Leutnant* in August 1913. He served throughout the First World War and was awarded the Iron Cross 1st and 2nd Classes, being promoted to *Oberleutnant* in October 1916. He transferred into the *Reichswehr* at the end of the war and was promoted to *Hauptmann* in November 1923, serving as a Battery Officer of Artillery Regiment 3 in Frankfurt. He was promoted to *Major* in March 1932 and served as a staff officer from October 1932 until September 1935. In July 1936 he was appointed Chief of Operations in the General Staff of the X. Army Corps and was promoted to *Oberst* in April 1937. On 27 August 1939 he was appointed Artillery Commander 138 and was awarded the Bar to the Iron Cross 1st and 2nd Classes during the Polish campaign. (*Deutsches Wehrkundearchiv*)

the Eastern Front in October and his division remained in this area for the next two and a half years. Lindemann was promoted to *Generalleutnant* in January 1943 and after sometime in the Reserves he was appointed General of Artillery assigned to the Chief of the Army General Staff. He was officially promoted to *General der Artillerie* in December 1943. Lindemann had made contact with various members of the conspiracy against Hitler, and it was proposed that he would read the conspirators' proclamation to the German people over the radio after the bomb attack on 20 July 1944 but he did not appear at the Bendlerblock in Berlin. Lindemann had gone into hiding. On 3 September 1944 he was hunted down by the Gestapo and shot and severely wounded while being arrested. He died from his injuries on 22 September in Berlin.

Helmuth von PANNWITZ

Generalleutnant

* 14 October 1898, Botzanowitz, Silesia
+ 16 January 1947, Moscow, Soviet

Knight's Cross: Awarded on 4 September 1941 as *Oberstleutnant* and Commander of Reconnaissance Battalion 45 while attached to the 45th Infantry Division for actions in the Pripet Marshes during the first month of the invasion of the Soviet Union. In July he fought with great distinction and skill when he led his

Helmuth von Pannwitz entered the Army as a cadet in April 1914 and by March 1915 he was serving as a Platoon Leader with the rank of *Leutnant*. He was wounded and hospitalised from September 1916 and later was awarded both classes of the Iron Cross. He was promoted in July 1918 to Company Leader of the 10th Company of the 3rd Jäger regiment. Shortly after the end of the war he joined the *Freikorps* movement and the Stormtroopers, and in December 1933 he served as Leader of the SA-Standarte 119 in Breslau. From October 1935 he served back with the Army with the rank of *Rittmeister* and was attached to the Staff Squadron of the 2nd Mounted Regiment. In March 1938 he was promoted to *Major* and was appointed Commander of the II. Bicycle Battalion of the 11th Cavalry Regiment. From August 1939 he served as Commander of Reconnaissance Battalion 45, serving with the 45th Infantry Division. (*Author's Collection*)

battalion near Pinsk in the Marshes against Soviet forces and was later involved in the capture of Brest-Litovsk. In late November he had to give up his command due to a bad back. He was almost unable to move and was sent home to recover. From December he was put in charge of the cavalry while attached to the staff of General of Mobile Troops in the Office of the Army General Staff. He was promoted to *Oberst* in April 1942, and from September was responsible for the forming and training of German Cossack units. In November he was named as Commander of all Cossack formations and charged with the establishment and training of the first Army Cossack Division.

Knight's Cross with Oakleaves: He became the 167th recipient on 23 December 1942 as *Oberst* and Leader of Battle Group *von Pannwitz* while part of the 4th Panzer Army near Stalingrad. On 15 November Pannwitz led his new command comprising of Soviet volunteers who were willing to fight for the Third Reich. His unit later took part in the fighting against the Red Army during the breakthrough on the Don and then smashed three Soviet divisions just west of Stalingrad. On 15 January 1943 he was decorated with the Oakleaves by a grateful Hitler at *Führer* Headquarters at Rastenburg. Pannwitz was promoted to *Generalmajor* on 1 June 1943, and from July was named as Leader of the 1st Cossack Division, taking permanent command from 24 August. Promoted to *Generalleutnant* in April 1944, he continued to command the Cossack division even when it transferred into the Waffen-SS from December. He then took command of the XV. Cossack Cavalry Corps in the Balkans from February 1945, and at the same time he transferred into the Waffen-SS with the rank of *SS-Gruppenführer*. On 9 May 1945 he surrendered together with his Soviet volunteers to the British but less than three weeks later all of his Soviet volunteers were transported to Russia to face trial. Many were badly treated and some were executed for treason. Pannwitz had been told by the British that as a German citizen he would not be handed over to the Soviets. However, he insisted on sharing the fate of his men and voluntarily surrendered to the Soviets, who tried and executed him in Moscow on 16 January 1947.

Karl-Albrecht Theodor von GRODDECK

Generalleutnant

* 18 February 1894, Berlin, Brandenburg
+ 10 January 1944, Breslau Field Hospital, Silesia

Knight's Cross: Awarded on 8 September 1941 as *Oberst* and Commander of Motorised Infantry Regiment 120, part of the 60th Motorised Infantry Division, for his part in the capture of Dnepropetrovsk in the Ukraine and for the fighting in the Dnieper region. From October he led the advance on the Rostov region. When the Soviet winter began his regiment had to retreat to the Mius and from March he took part in the Battle of Kharkov, until on 11 May he was severely wounded at Kerch. He remained in hospital for some time and entered the Reserves. He was promoted to *Generalmajor* on 1 August 1942, and from 10 to 30 July 1943 he commanded the 11th Infantry Division, seeing action once again in the Soviet Union as part of the XXVI. Panzer Corps. On 22 August he was appointed Commander of the 161st Infantry Division and saw action in Kharkov while attached to the XXXXII. Army Corps. Only six days later he was severely wounded once again and hospitalised in Breslau, where on 10 January 1944 he died from meningitis and was posthumously promoted to the rank of *Generalleutnant*.

Karl-Adolf HOLLIDT

Generaloberst

* 25 April 1891, Speyer, Bavaria
+ 22 May 1985, Siegen, North Rhine-Westphalia

Knight's Cross: Awarded on 8 September 1941 as *Generalleutnant* and Commander of the 50th Infantry Division, part of the LIV. Army Corps, for

Karl-Adolf Hollidt entered Army service in July 1909 with Infantry Regiment 117 and was commissioned as a *Leutnant* in November 1910. He saw action from August 1914 as adjutant of the II. Battalion of Infantry Regiment 118, and shortly after being taken ill in January 1915 he was transferred to a replacement battalion and promoted to *Oberleutnant*. He returned to the front in August 1915 and served with Infantry Regiment 117 until May 1916, when he was attached to a Field Recruitment Depot. He was promoted to *Hauptmann* in March 1918 and remained in the Army after the war, during which he won both classes of the Iron Cross. He was promoted to *Major* in February 1930, two years later he was promoted to *Oberstleutnant* and from December 1933 served as Commander of I. Battalion of Infantry Regiment 12. Promoted to *Oberst*, in January 1935 he was appointed Chief of Staff of Military District Command I two months later, and from October he was named as Chief of the General Staff of the I. Army Corps. He was made a *Generalmajor* in April 1938 and appointed Infantry Commander 9 in Siegen from November of that year. He served as Commander of the 52nd Infantry Division from the beginning of the Polish campaign and was promoted to *Generalleutnant* in April 1940. (*Author's Collection*)

actions on the Russian Front. On 25 July 1941 his division crossed over the Dnieper River and became involved in attacks by Soviet troops near the Stalin Line fortifications. For several days his men fought against strong Soviet forces that were defending from their modern bunkers and the fighting lasted several days. Hollidt remained in command of his division until 23 January 1942, when he was appointed Commanding General of the XVII. Army Corps and continued to see action in the Soviet Union. On 1 February he was promoted to *General der Infanterie*. He saw action during the summer offensive and led his corps during the march to the Don area as part of the 6th Army. In November that year his command crossed the Don River and escaped the encirclement at Stalingrad. During this time his corps had been renamed Army Detachment *Hollidt* and consisted of two Romanian and two German corps. It saw fighting in the area near the Donets. On 5 March 1943 the 6th Army, which had fallen at Stalingrad and where 91,000 men were captured, which included twenty-four generals and 2,500 officers, was reformed and placed under the command of Hollidt.

Knight's Cross with Oakleaves: Awarded on 17 May 1943 to become the 239th recipient as *General der Infanterie* and Commander-in-Chief of the

6th Army, part of Army Group South, and despite Soviet superiority Hollidt and his men put up remarkable resistance. The Soviet force proved unable to achieve a breakthrough against Hollidt's forces and as a result he was awarded the Oakleaves. They were presented personally by Hitler at his headquarters in Rastenburg. Hollidt continued to see action in the Donets area of the front and was promoted to *Generaloberst* in September 1943. By November his forces had been withdrawn and he took part in several defensive battles in the Nikopol–Krivoi Rog offensive in November and December. However, Hollidt was away from the front on sick leave for just over three weeks and finally returned on 20 December. However, he became ill again and left the front during April 1944. He entered the Reserves until February 1945, when he was appointed representative of the *Gauleiter* Albert Hoffmann in the Rhine and Westphalia area. He became responsible for all industrial aspects of the area and its defence. In April 1945 he was captured by US forces in the Ruhr Pocket and tried as a war criminal at Nuremberg in 1947. He was sentenced to five years' imprisonment in Landsberg Prison, however, he was released on 22 December 1949.

Meinrad von LAUCHERT

Generalmajor

* 29 August 1905, Potsdam, Brandenburg
\+ 4 December 1987, Stuttgart, Baden-Württemberg

Meinrad von Lauchert joined the Army in April 1924 as a *Fahnenjunker* with Mounted Regiment 5 and was commissioned as a *Leutnant* in February 1931. He was appointed Company Commander of anti-tank Battalion 5 from October 1935 and was *Oberleutnant* and Commander of I. Battalion of Panzer Regiment 35 at the beginning of the Second World War. He was promoted to *Rittmeister* in March 1937 and saw action during the Polish campaign. (*Deutsches Wehrkundearchiv*)

Knight's Cross: Awarded on 8 September 1941 as *Major* and Commander of Panzer Regiment 35 while attached to the 4th Panzer Division for his leadership and bravery during heavy fighting on 19 and 20 July when his regiment prevented breakthrough attempts by a strong Soviet force near Proposk. From December 1942 until June 1943 he was appointed Commander of Panzer Training Battalion 59 in Neuruppin and was then given command of Panzer Regiment *von Lauchert*. This regiment was deployed to the Eastern Front and saw action during Operation Citadel, the German offensive against Soviet forces at Kursk, and in August Lauchert was promoted to *Oberstleutnant*.

Knight's Cross with Oakleaves: He became the 396th recipient on 12 February 1944 as *Oberst* and Commander of Panzer Regiment 15, part of the 11th Panzer Division, for his courage and leadership at the time of Operation Citadel. He and his unit distinguished themselves during the defensive battles at Dnepropetrovsk and Kirovograd in the Ukraine, and on 22 November 1943 his regiment destroyed forty-one Soviet tanks. Lauchert was presented with his Oakleaves personally by Hitler on 27 April 1944 at the Berghof, Obersalzburg. In early August 1944 he attended the 13th Divisional Leaders Course in Hirschberg and was from the 24th appointed Leader of the Panzer Special Unit *Strachwitz* after its original commander had been wounded on the Eastern Front. On 15 December he took over as leader of the 2nd Panzer Division and saw action during the Ardennes Offensive in Belgium, where the unit suffered heavy losses. On 1 March 1945 Lauchert was promoted to *Generalmajor* and confirmed as divisional commander. He saw action against the Americans and was down to the strength of only four tanks, three assault guns, and just 200 troops. Lauchert surrendered with his division to American troops near Plauen in Germany on 19 March 1945.

Karl-Wilhelm SPECHT

General der Infanterie

* 22 May 1894, Herdecke, Hagen
+ 3 December 1953, Soviet Prison Camp in Voikovo, Moscow

Knight's Cross: Awarded on 8 September 1941 as *Oberst* and Commander of Infantry Regiment 55 while attached to the 17th Infantry Division for actions in the Soviet Union. In August Specht and his regiment seized a particularly strong Soviet strongpoint at Veliky Novgorod and held it against fierce counter-attacks. Later they were able to break through the fortified positions at Rekta and pushed into a depth of 12 miles into Soviet territory. By these actions Specht was able to contribute to the German breakthrough north of Gomel, which resulted in the encirclement and destruction of a considerable number

Karl-Wilhelm Specht is seen here with Generalarzt Maximilian Riemer during the latter stages of the Second World War. Specht entered the Army with the 6th Lorraine Royal Infantry Regiment Nr. 145 in January 1914 as a *Leutnant* and was awarded the Iron Cross in January 1915. He served as a Platoon Leader and then Company Leader, and from September 1916 he served as a battalion adjutant and was awarded the Iron Cross 1st Class in April 1917. He stayed in the Army after the war and was promoted to *Major* in May 1934. In October 1936 he was promoted to *Oberstleutnant* while serving as a battalion leader with Infantry Regiment 110. Promoted to *Oberst* in June 1939, he served as Commander of Infantry Regiment 55. (*Deutsches Wehrkundearchiv*)

of Soviet troops. On 15 November Specht was shot in the head by a Soviet sniper and rushed to hospital. He was away from the front line for ten months.

Knight's Cross with Oakleaves: He became the sixtieth recipient on 16 January 1942 as *Oberst* and while still Commander of Infantry Regiment 55 in recognition of his leadership and bravery during the battles of Gomel, Kiev and Bryansk-Vyazma. He proved to be a determined leader and despite shrapnel wounds to his hand and knee suffered during the crossing of the Ugra River he continued to lead his troops. His regimental command post was struck by shellfire three times and Specht lost consciousness. After being revived with oxygen he immediately hurried back to the front. He was promoted to *Generalmajor* in August 1942 and on 10 September he was assigned as Commander of the Infantry School at Döberitz. Promoted to *Generalleutnant* in August 1943, he served as Inspector of the Army Education System from December until March 1944. From August he was a member of the Court of Honour where officers who were thought to have been involved in the 20 July 1944 plot to kill Hitler were tried and dismissed from the Army so they could be tried by the civilian People's Court. On 1 December 1944 he was promoted to *General der Infanterie* and named Commanding General of the Deputy General Commando XX. Army Corps and Commander of Military District XX in Hamburg. He was captured by Soviet troops on 8 May 1945 and as sentenced to twenty-five years imprisonment in Moscow, where he died on 3 December 1953.

Dr Franz Waldemar BEYER

General der Infanterie

* 27 May 1892, Bautzen, Saxony
+ 15 October 1968, Bad Wiesse, Bavaria

Knight's Cross: Awarded on 12 September 1941 as *Oberst* and Commander of Infantry Regiment 131 as part of the 44th Infantry Division in recognition of his extraordinary achievements on 22 and 23 June 1941 on the Eastern Front. After successfully forcing a crossing over the Bug River his regiment became the first to penetrate the enemy bunker positions near Janów, and in doing so played a major role in supporting the division's breakthrough of the Soviet border fortifications. At the end of December he was appointed Commander of the newly formed 331st Infantry Division, and from January 1942 was part of the XXXX. Army Corps and saw action in the Yukhnov area. Here Beyer's division suffered heavy casualties almost immediately upon combat with the Red Army during the Soviet winter offensive. Beyer was promoted to *Generalleutnant* in January and from early February was rested before. He took over as Commander of the 44th *Reichs* Grenadier Division *Hoch-und Deutschmeister* on 1 March, when it had been given an honorary title after it had been reformed when it had been destroyed at Stalingrad. After some training in Belgium, Beyer took his division to northern Italy from August as part of Rommel's Army Group. From April 1944 he was delegated with the leadership of the XII. Army Corps and in July he was promoted to *General der Infanterie.* From early August he took over as Commanding General of the LXXX. Army Corps, his last command of the war. Stationed in France as part of the 1st Army, he was then ordered to move to Trier with the 7th Army. He finished the war in the Upper Rhine region of Germany, where he surrendered to the Allies.

Friedrich Paul GURRAN

Generalleutnant

* 11 January 1893, Alt Zauche, Brandenburg
+ 22 April 1944, Majevo north-west Nevel, Soviet Union

Paul Gurran entered Army service in 1908 and volunteered for service with Grenadier Regiment 12 from 1911, seeing action as a NCO during the First World War with this regiment. He remained in the Army after the war, being commissioned in 1919, and served for nine years with Infantry Regiment 2. In February 1929 he served as a *Hauptmann* with the staff of the training department of his regiment, and from 1932 he served as a Company Leader. In October 1937 he served as a *Major* and Commander of the II. Battalion of Infantry Regiment 45, and was promoted to *Oberstleutnant* in March 1938. Gurran was serving with this unit when the Second World War started. (*Deutsches Wehrkundearchiv*)

Knight's Cross: Awarded on 12 September 1941 as *Oberst* and Commander of Infantry Regiment 506, part of the 291st Infantry Division, and saw action during the opening phase of the invasion of the Soviet Union. During the first two days of the campaign his regiment together with the division managed to advance 44 miles in just two days, an astonishing achievement for a non-motorised combat division. He led his regiment during action near Riga, repulsing several attempts by the Soviet garrison to break out of the city, and for his personal bravery and leadership he was awarded the Knight's Cross. Between

January and March 1942 Gurran saw action during the Battle of Volkhov, later seeing action during the opening phase of the attack on Leningrad. From mid-November 1942 he entered the Reserves as Commander of a company at the Battery Leaders School in Reval. In June 1943 he returned to front-line duty with the temporary leadership of the 12th Infantry Division, seeing action in Demyansk. From September he took over as commander of the 23rd Infantry Division as part of the XXXVIII. Army Corps, seeing action in the area around Novgorod. He was promoted to *Generalmajor* in October 1943 and in early 1944 he took part in the defensive battles near Nevel before being seriously wounded on 20 February. He died in a field hospital in Majevo in north-west Nevel on 22 April 1944 and was posthumously promoted to *Generalleutnant*.

Harry [Arthur] HOPPE*

Generalleutnant

* 11 February 1894, Braunschweig, Lower Saxony
+ 23 August 1969, Wetzlar, Hesse

Harry Hoppe entered Army service in August 1914 as a volunteer with Infantry Regiment 92 and was wounded just two months later. He was attached to a *Fahnenjunker* training course in Döberitz from February 1915 and the following month he was promoted to *Unteroffizier*. he was commissioned as a *Leutnant* in April 1916 and appointed Leader of the 2nd Company of Reserve Infantry Regiment 261 a few months later. He was awarded both classes of the Iron Cross during the war and in April 1917 he was once again wounded. He remained in the Army after the war and served with various regiments between 1919 and 1927, attending many courses. By October 1929 he had been promoted to *Hauptmann* and from October 1935 he served as Commander of Machine Gun Battalion 2 with the rank of *Major*, being promoted to *Oberstleutnant* in June 1938. He saw action during the invasion of Poland, where he was awarded the Bar to the Iron Cross 2nd Class, and from December he served as Chief of Operations with Commander-in-Chief East. (*Author's Collection*)

Knight's Cross: Awarded on 12 September 1941 as *Oberst* and Commander of Infantry Regiment 424, part of the 126th Infantry Division, for the seizure of the city and harbour at Schlüsselburg near Leningrad on 8 September 1941. His regiment had the honour of being the first German unit to attack Leningrad and the Knight's Cross was presented to him by *Generalmajor* Hans Zorn, the Commander of the 20th Infantry Division. On 14 October 1942 Hoppe was delegated with the leadership of the 126th Infantry Division and with his promotion to *Generalmajor* in December he became full Commander of the division. He saw action during the first and second battle south-east of Lake Ilmen in Novgorod Oblast in the Soviet Union during the winter of 1942–43. After Hitler approved the evacuation of the Demyansk Pocket in February 1943, Hoppe led his troops to new positions east of the River Lovat, and later moved to the area south of Staraya Russa. On 1 June 1943 Hoppe was promoted to *Generalleutnant* and by the end of July his division had moved to the area south of Lake Ladoga, where heavy fighting broke out during August. Hoppe then moved his troops towards Leningrad. On 10 December he took over command of the newly formed 278th Infantry Division in the Bologna area of Italy, where he prepared it for battle. From February it was sent to the Castel San Pietro area and deployed for coastal protection, and in June it took part in heavy fighting against Polish troops, where it suffered heavy losses.

Knight's Cross with Oakleaves: Awarded on 18 December 1944 to become the 682nd recipient as *Generalleutnant* and Commander of the 278th Infantry Division while attached to the LXXVI. Panzer Corps for his outstanding leadership during the fighting in Italy. It was for actions Hoppe led during heavy fighting north-west of Urbino in Italy, and from mid-September 1944 he took part in heavy defensive fighting around San Marino. The battle was the result of the Allies trying to capture the city in order to gain possession of a seaport close to the fighting to shorten the lines of communication. Although they achieved their objective, Hoppe and his division held them back for almost thirty days. In April 1945 his division was almost destroyed, suffering heavy losses, and was renamed the 278th *Volksgrenadier* Division. It suffered further losses while breaking through to the American lines between 24 and 29 April. Hoppe surrendered his division to US troops in Belluno in northern Italy on 8 May 1945 and he was imprisoned until 17 May 1948.

* Born with the first name of Arthur, he changed it officially to Harry on 18 February 1943. His nickname was 'Stan Laurel' as his troops thought he resembled the much-loved Hollywood actor.

Ernst SIELER
Generalleutnant

* 22 August 1893, Altenburg, Thüringia
\+ 6 October 1983, Bernau am Chiemsee, Bavaria

Ernst Sieler joined the Army as a *Fahnenjunker* in March 1913 and was commissioned as a *Leutnant* the following year. He served as a Company Officer with the 4th Grand Ducal Hessian Infantry Regiment from the start of the Great War and was awarded the Iron Cross 2nd Class in September 1914 and the Iron Cross 1st Class in July 1916. Promoted to *Oberleutnant* in October 1917, he stayed in the Army after the war and served with the 15th Infantry Regiment until October 1936, when as an *Oberstleutnant* he was transferred to the 17th Infantry Regiment. He was promoted to *Oberst* in August 1939 and saw action during the French campaign from May 1940. (*Deutsches Wehrkundearchiv*)

Knight's Cross: Awarded on 12 September 1941 as *Oberst* and Commander of Infantry Regiment 46 while part of the 30th Infantry Division in recognition of his outstanding combat performance during the defence of the fiercely contested railway line east of Opochka near Pskov Oblast. He later saw action at the Battle of Dvinsk and from November 1942 was delegated with the leadership of the 304th Infantry Division while stationed in Belgium. In December his command was rushed to the Eastern Front, where the southern sector was on the verge of collapse in the Donets area. In January 1943 Sieler was promoted to *Generalmajor* and took official command of the division during Army Group Don's retreat from Stalingrad. He continued to serve as commander on the southern sector of the Mius, and was promoted to *Generalleutnant* in July 1943. His division suffered heavy losses at Taganrog and during the withdrawal to the lower Dnieper Bend in March 1944.

Knight's Cross with Oakleaves: He became the 502nd recipient on 24 June 1944 as *Generalleutnant* and Commander of 304th Infantry Division while attached to the XXIX. Army Corps for his leadership on the southern sector of the Eastern Front from the beginning of 1943 until the spring of 1944. The Oakleaves were presented to Sieler personally by Hitler, together with eight other recipients, including *General der Infanterie* Erich Buschenhagen in July 1944 at the Wolf's Lair in Rastenburg. He later saw action at Tiraspol between May and June 1944, then in the Ukraine and in southern Poland. His division was crushed when the Red Army broke out of the Baranov Bridgehead west of the Vistula River in January 1945. In early February Sieler was delegated with the leadership of the LIX. Army Corps and because of the Soviet winter his corps was pushed back towards Slovakia, where on 8 May Sieler was taken prisoner, not being released until October 1955.

Karl Anton Theodor Graf von SPONECK

Generalleutnant

* 24 January 1888, Offenburg, Baden-Württemberg
+ 13 July 1982, Bächingen an der Brenz

Knight's Cross: Awarded on 12 September 1941 as *Oberst* and Commander of Rifle Regiment 11 while attached to the 9th Panzer Division for his part in the encirclement of Kiev, where 667,000 Soviet soldiers were captured. His rifle regiment remained on the southern sector, facing the Soviet winter offensive of 1941 until he was seriously wounded and hospitalised. Sponeck was away from the front line until September 1942, when he was delegated with the leadership of the 90th *Afrika* Division and involved in the Second Battle of El Alamein between 23 October and 4 November 1942. He was promoted to *Generalmajor* on 1 November and was confirmed as Commander of the 90th *Afrika* Division. He formed part of Rommel's rearguard and retreated through Egypt, Libya and Tunisia, where he surrendered his division on 12 May 1943, shortly after being promoted to *Generalleutnant*. Together with other captured senior commanders, he was sent to a prison camp in Arkansas, USA, where he remained until 1947.

Richard Walter WEISS

Generaloberst

* 5 September 1890, Tilsit
21 December 1967, Aschaffenburg

Knight's Cross: Awarded on 12 September 1941 as *Generalmajor* and Commander of 26th Infantry Division for his mastery of the situation during the tough fighting in the Soviet Union between 30 and 31 July 1941. The Russians were attacking from the north-east and broke through the German lines, which forced Weiss's division to fight a front line more than 15 miles

Walter Weiss entered the Army with Infantry Regiment Nr. 59 in March 1908 and was commissioned as a *Leutnant* that same year. He attended the War School in Potsdam and later served as adjutant during the beginning of the First World War, being promoted to *Oberleutnant* in July 1915. He served mainly as a staff officer during the war and was awarded both classes of the Iron Cross, being promoted to *Hauptmann* just before the end of the war. He stayed in the Army after the war and served in numerous regiments. By the start of the Second World War he had risen to the rank of *Oberst* and was on the Staff of Infantry Regiment 1. He served in Poland as Commander of Infantry Regiment 1 and was awarded the Bar to the Iron Cross 1st and 2nd Class. He was promoted to *Generalmajor* in August 1940. (*Deutsches Wehrkundearchiv*)

wide. His calmness and decisiveness remained unbroken as he led his division to victory and by the evening of 31 July his troops were back in control. His division distinguished itself well when it crossed the Volga between Moscow and Leningrad. It stormed Rzhev but then became bogged down in the winter of 1941–42. On 1 July 1942 Weiss took over command of the XXVII. Army Corps and on 20 July was promoted to *Generalleutnant*, seeing action in Demyansk as part of the 4th Army. On 28 August he was promoted to *General der Infanterie* and continued to see action on the Russian Front as part of Army Group Centre. He led his corps during the difficult defensive actions near Rzhev and from February 1943, serving as Commander-in-Chief of the 2nd Army and holding the front at Kursk throughout the winter of 1943–44. From May to June 1943 he was additionally delegated with the leadership of the 9th Army while *Generaloberst* Walter Model was on leave.

Knight's Cross with Oakleaves: He became the 646th recipient on 5 November 1944 as *Generaloberst* and Commander-in-Chief of 2nd Army while attached to Army Group Centre for his leadership of the 2nd Army following the collapse of Army Group Centre in the summer of 1944. It was reported that his command had fought successfully in the hard, defensive battles in cooperation with the *Luftwaffe* and had thwarted all breakout attempts by the Soviets, destroying 609 tanks. From 12 March until 5 April 1945 Weiss was Commander-in-Chief of the Army Group North in East Prussia. He was taken into US captivity from June 1945 and imprisoned for a time at the former Dachau concentration camp until his release in 1948.

Konrad-Oskar HEINRICHS

Generalleutnant

* 5 May 1890, Wallstawe, Salzwedel
+ 8 September 1944 near Liége, Belgium

Knight's Cross: Awarded on 13 September 1941 as *Oberst* and Commander of Infantry Regiment 24, part of the 21st Infantry Division, for actions during the opening battles of the invasion of the Soviet Union. He saw action during the battles of Tilsit, Volkhov and Grusino, and took part during the opening phase of the Siege of Leningrad from September 1941. He was wounded on 1 May 1942 and five days later he transferred to the 290th Infantry Division, where he took over leadership until his promotion to *Generalmajor* on 1 July 1942, when he was officially named as the new commander. On 1 February 1943 Heinrichs was promoted to *Generalleutnant* and took up new defensive positions in the Staraya Russa area. His unit took part in defensive battles until December, when his division was moved to the Newel area as part of Army Group Centre. On 10 February 1944 he was appointed the first Commander of the 89th Infantry Division, which had been formed from infantry regiments of the Replacement Army. Heinrichs led his division during training until June 1944 and a few weeks after D-Day it was ordered to Normandy, where it suffered heavy losses. The division was encircled at Falaise in August and suffered more losses. Both of its grenadier regiments were destroyed and on 8 September Heinrichs was killed near Liége.

Dr rer.pol. Johannes MAYER

General der Infanterie

* 6 September 1893, Stepenitz-Ostpriegnitz, Brandenburg
+ 7 August 1963, Hamburg, Lower Saxony

Knight's Cross: Awarded on 13 September 1941 as *Oberst* and Commander of Infantry Regiment 501, part of the 290th Infantry Division, in recognition for his infantries and his actions in the northern sector of the Eastern Front. He distinguished himself in battle when his regiment took part in taking an important bridge over the Porussja River. After leading his regiment through a thick forest and arriving to find the bridge on fire they managed to put it out and secure it and maintain it so other elements of the division could cross. He continued to command Infantry Regiment 501 in East Prussia until January

Johannes Mayer volunteered for war in August 1914 with the 5th Pomeranian Infantry Regiment and was awarded the Iron Cross in August 1915. Just two months later was commissioned as a *Leutnant*. From May 1916 he served as an Ordnance Officer with Infantry Regiment 42, and in December he was awarded the Iron Cross 1st Class. He served as battalion adjutant from November 1916 and was Company Leader when the war ended. He then served in the *Reichswehr*. By February 1935 he was serving with Infantry Regiment 25 in Stargard with the rank of *Major* and from October that year he was Tactics Instructor and Training Commander at the Potsdam War School. He served as Commander of the I. Battalion of Infantry Regiment 65 from October 1938 and was awarded the Bar to the Iron Cross 1st and 2nd Class in June 1940. (*Author's Collection*)

1942 and shortly after being promoted to *Generalmajor* in April he was appointed Commander of the 329th Infantry Division. He saw action during the defensive battles on the northern sector of the Eastern Front near Lake Peipus and Mayer was promoted to *Generalleutnant* in February 1943.

Knight's Cross with Oakleaves: He became the 453rd recipient on 13 April 1944 as *Generalleutnant* and Commander of 329th Infantry Division, part of the VIII. Army Corps, for his bravery and leadership on the Eastern Front during an attack by the enemy north-west of Newel. On 10 March his division came under attack by five Soviet rifle divisions and two tank brigades. Following the arrival of reinforcements the following day Mayer launched a counter-attack on his own initiative, which was successful at first but his troops became bogged down. In response, Mayer moved to lead his men from the front, and under heavy fire he directed his troops during an assault on the enemy.

Knight's Cross with Oakleaves and Swords: Awarded on 23 August 1944 as the eighty-ninth recipient as *Generalleutnant* and while still Commander of 329th Infantry Division as part of the XXXVIII. Army Corps for his continuous leadership of his division. On 13 July his division saw action near Małkowo, Lenovo and Borki in Poland, and over the next four days his command fended off thirty-seven Soviet attacks. Throughout all of this time Mayer was at the front with his troops. He was seriously wounded on 16 July and recognised for his devotion to duty. He spent time recovering and did not return to front-line duty until February 1945, when he was appointed Commanding General of the II. Army Corps, against the wishes of his doctor. As part of the 18th Army, he continued to see action in the Courland area until early April. Shortly after being promoted to *General der Infanterie* he fell ill and was taken off the front line to recover. While lying in hospital he was taken prisoner by British troops on 8 May 1945. He was released from both hospital and captivity in December 1946.

Hans-Gustav FELBER

General der Infanterie

* 8 July 1889, Wiesbaden, Hessen
+ 7 March 1962, Frankfurt am Main

Hans-Gustav Felber entered Army service in March 1908 as a *Fahnenjunker* and was for a time attached to the War School in Potsdam, where he trained as an officer. He was commissioned as a *Leutnant* in August 1909 and served as a adjutant with Infantry Regiment 117 during the first three years of the First World War, rising to the rank of *Hauptmann*. By the end of the war he had joined the General Staff and remained in the Army after the war. By 1928 had been promoted to *Major* and was serving with the 7th Division. After a number of training courses, he was transferred to the Staff of the 4th Division and from February 1933 he was an *Oberstleutnant* and Battalion Commander with Infantry Regiment 1. From May until July 1935 he commanded the War Academy, and at the beginning of the Second World War he was Chief of the General Staff of the 2nd Army with the rank of *Generalleutnant*. The photo shows Felber with Baptist Kniess on the right. (*Author's Collection*)

Knight's Cross: Awarded on 17 September 1941 as *General der Infanterie* and Commanding General of the XIII. Army Corps, part of the 2nd Army, for his part in the important victory near Gomel in Belarus over the Soviet 21st Army. Towards the end of the year he led his corps during a strong Soviet counteroffensive and on 14 January 1942 Felber was rested and attached to the *Führer* Reserve. In April he took over command of Special Purpose Higher Command XXXXV., part of the 1st Army in Germany, and at the same time he took temporary leadership of the 1st Army. From 25 May he was appointed Commanding General of the LXXXII. Army Corps, and at the same time he was appointed Commander-in-Chief of Army Group Felber in south-eastern France. Here his command took part in Case Anton, the military occupation of southern France by Germany and Italy, marking the end of the Vichy Regime. Later his corps was used as a coastal protection force on the Mediterranean coastline. On 15 August 1943 Felber was appointed Military Commander South-East and Military Commander of Serbia, commanding all German troops in Serbia, Croatia and Greece. For the first six months of his command he was involved in heavy fighting in the western and southern areas of Serbia against Yugoslavian Partisans. From 26 September 1944 he commanded Army Group Serbia, and from 6 October he was Commanding General of Higher Command Vogesen in Eastern France, which later was reformed as the XIII. Army Corps, part of the 7th Army under *General der Panzertruppe* Erich Brandenberger. On 22 February 1945 he was given temporary leadership of the 7th Army and he surrendered to American troops on 26 March 1945, remaining in captivity until 8 May 1948.

Siegfried Waldemar HAENICKE

General der Infanterie z. V.

* 8 September 1878, Konstanz, Baden
+ 19 February 1946, NKVD Special Camp 1, Mühlberg, Brandenburg

Knight's Cross: Awarded on 17 September 1941 as *Generalleutnant z. V.* and Commander of the 61st Infantry Division while attached to the XXXXII. Infantry Corps for his leadership during the tough defensive breakthrough near Tallinn, Estonia, in August 1941. He had led his division with great success during the invasion of the Soviet Union and similarly during the Polish campaign and during combat on the Eastern Front in Lithuania, Latvia and Estonia. Haenicke also saw action during the Soviet winter offensive and was later involved in the opening phase of the Siege of Leningrad. In early April

Siegfried Haenicke entered Army service in March 1897 as an officer and was a battalion adjutant from September 1900, attending the War Academy from October 1904. At the beginning of the First World War he was a *Hauptmann* with Infantry Regiment 150 and was awarded both classes of the Iron Cross during the first year of the war. On 14 June 1918 Haenicke was awarded the Pour le Mérite, one of the highest awards of the war, given as *Hauptmann* and Commander of the II. Battalion of Infantry Regiment 150 for his leadership and bravery. He remained in the Army until September 1932, and was finally recalled to duty in August 1938 as Commander of the 61st Infantry Division, seeing action during the Polish campaign. (*Deutsches Wehrkundearchiv*)

1942 he served as temporary commander of the XXXVIII. Army Corps and was promoted to *General der Infanterie z. V.* At the beginning of June his troops pushed back the Soviet 2nd Army and together with the I. Army Corps repelled the Soviet advance. As a result the 2nd Shock Army was almost wiped out. In October 1942 he was appointed Commander of the Military District of the General Government in occupied Poland, and from July 1944 he was made Commander of Army Area in General Government. At the end of the war he was discharged from the Army and arrested by Soviet forces in July. He was sent to a NKVD (People's Commissariat for Internal Affairs) Special Camp in Brandenburg, Germany, where he died in February 1946.

Heinrich Otto Ernst von KNOBELSDORFF

General der Panzertruppe

* 31 March 1886, Berlin
+ 21 October 1966, Hannover, Lower Saxony

Knight's Cross: Awarded on 17 September 1941 as *Generalleutnant* and Commander of the 19th Panzer Division while attached to LVII. Panzer Corps for his success against the Soviet Union at Velikiye Luki at the end of July 1941. The counter-attacks made by the Soviets lasted several days and Knobelsdorff's command held its ground and pushed back the Red Army, taking part in fierce hand-to-hand fighting until the Soviets finally retreated.

Otto von Knobelsdorff entered the Army as a cadet in 1905 and a few months later he entered Infantry Regiment 94. He was commissioned as a *Leutnant* in 1906 and served as a regimental adjutant with his regiment, being promoted to *Oberleutnant* in November 1914. He was wounded in August 1915, later served as Company Leader and was promoted to *Hauptmann* in March 1916. He later served as a machine gun officer and adjutant with Infantry Brigade 83, and then served as a general staff officer and was seriously wounded near the end of the war. He was awarded the Iron Cross 1st and 2nd Classes in 1914 and 1915, and remained in the Army, serving with different regiments and later again as a staff officer. He was promoted to *Major* in February 1929. On 15 October 1935, now with the rank of *Oberst*, he was appointed Commander of the 19th Infantry Division and saw action during the Polish campaign, with the rank of *Generalmajor*. He was awarded the Bar to the Iron Cross 2nd Class and during the French campaign he was awarded the Bar to the Iron Cross 1st Class. (*Deutsches Wehrkundearchiv*)

He was also credited with his part in the crushing of the Bialystok–Minsk Pocket during the opening stages of the Soviet campaign as part of Army Group Centre. On 4 January 1942 he was taken off the front line due to ill health and was admitted to hospital in Bad Gastein, Austria, returning to duty in May with the leadership of the X. Army Corps on the northern sector of the Eastern Front. In June he was delegated with the leadership of the II. Army Corps at Demyansk and from early July he took command of Corps *Knobelsdorff*, an ad hoc unit on the Russian Front. On 1 August he was promoted to *General der Panzertruppe* and from October was Commanding General of the XXIV. Panzer Corps. He was heavily engaged in the Don Sector of the front while supporting the Hungarian Second Army as part of Army Group B. Knobelsdorff was taken ill in October 1943 and suffered a nervous breakdown, entering the Reserves.

Otto von Knobelsdorff, seen here together with Major Rudolf Köhler, who was awarded the Knight's Cross in July 1941. (*Author's Collection*)

Knight's Cross with Oakleaves: Awarded on 12 November 1943 as *General der Panzertruppe*, to become the 322nd recipient as Commanding General of the XXXXVIII. Panzer Corps, part of the 4th Panzer Army, and also for for his achievements during the abortive German assault against the Kursk salient in July 1943. Knobelsdorff returned to front-line duty as Commanding General of the XXXX. Panzer Corps in February 1944 and saw action on the southern sector of the Eastern Front. Here he took part in the retreat from the Dnieper region and saw fighting around Jassy in Romania before he and his staff were sent to Lithuania.

Knight's Cross with Oakleaves and Swords: He became the 100th recipient on 21 September 1944 as *General der Panzertruppe* and Commanding General of the XXXX. Panzer Corps in recognition of his bravery and leadership during the fighting near the Nikopol Bridgehead in Ukraine. During the battles that followed all the way to the Romanian border Knobelsdorff demonstrated great skill and was able to prevent his division from being destroyed. He was presented with the Swords by Hitler at the Wolf's Lair, Rastenburg, in September 1944 and took over the leadership of the 1st Army in France. However, he was out of his depth and was still recovering from his mental illness. Hitler took an interest in his career after Knobelsdorff was reported to have stated that he thought Germany should make peace with the Soviet Union or lose the war. On 1 December he was removed as Commander of the 1st Army and spent the remainder of the war in the Reserves. In January 1945 he helped with the evacuation of Dresden and was taken prisoner by US forces on 6 April 1945. He remained in captivity until 21 December 1947.

Albrecht Ernst Eduard Max Otto Hermann SCHUBERT

General der Infanterie

* 23 June 1886, Marienwerder, West Prussia
+ 26 November 1966, Bielefeld, North Rhine-Westphalia

Knight's Cross: Awarded on 17 September 1941 as *General der Infanterie* and Commanding General of the XXIII. Army Corps, part of the 9th Army, for action in the Soviet Union. He led his corps during the advance towards Velikiye Luki from August 1941 together with the XXXX. Army Corps and successfully occupied the area. He later saw action during the Soviet counteroffensive, which began in December around Ostashkov and Torzhok, and managed to hold back the Soviets from the strategically important town of Rzhev. However,

Albrecht Schubert entered the Army in February 1904, was commissioned as a *Leutnant* the following year and served with Infantry Regiment 27. He was promoted to *Oberleutnant* in June 1912 and was serving as adjutant of the 21st Replacement Brigade when the war began. In November 1914 he was promoted to *Hauptmann.* He served as a battalion leader at the front and later on the General Staff of the V. Army Corps, and was awarded both classes of the Iron Cross. After the war he stayed in the Army and was attached to the Naval Station in the Baltic Sea, later serving with the infantry. By 1934 he was serving as an *Oberst* and Commander of the 12th Infantry Regiment, and shortly after his promotion to *Generalleutnant* in March 1938 he was named Commander of the 44th Infantry Division in Vienna. He later saw action during the opening phase of the war in Poland, where he was awarded the Bar to the Iron Cross 1st and 2nd Classes. In October he was appointed Commanding General of the XXIII. Army Corps and was promoted to *General der Infanterie* in June 1940. (*Author's Collection*)

on 31 December the front line collapsed and the 256th and 206th Infantry Divisions were pushed back. From 9 January 1942 the left flank of the XXIII. Army Corps was struck by a Soviet counter-attack and pushed back south. The following month Schubert managed to secure a key position to defend and from 23 May until 2 June was named temporary leader of the 9th Army. In July he was taken off front-line duty because of illness and from March 1943 he was made Commanding General of the Deputy of General Commando XI. Army Corps and Commander of Military District XI in Hannover. From August 1943 he took over a similar command in Vienna. On 8 May 1945 he surrendered to Allied troops and while in an Allied prison, as senior general he was delegated with the leadership of the 6th Army. He was released in 1947.

Rudolf Alexander Karl Wilhelm SIECKENIUS
Generalmajor

* 18 August 1896, Ludwigsthal, Silesia
+ 28 April 1945, Berlin

Rudolf Sieckenius joined the Army as a volunteer in August 1914 and was promoted to *Leutnant* in December 1916, later serving as a battalion adjutant. He joined the police after the war, rising to the rank of *Polizei-Hauptmann* in May 1928. From October 1935 he was a Company Commander with the 2nd Panzer regiment in Eisenach with the rank of *Hauptmann*, and by October 1937 he was Commander of the I. Battalion of the 15th Panzer Regiment. When the Second World War began he was an *Oberstleutnant* and Commander of Panzer Battalion 66. He saw action in Poland, where he was awarded both classes of the Iron Cross. (*Author's Collection*)

Knight's Cross: Awarded on 17 September 1941 as *Oberstleutnant* and Commander of Panzer Regiment 2 while attached to the 16th Panzer Division for actions in the southern sector of the Soviet Union. He saw action almost continuously during the Ukraine campaign, the Battle of Kiev and the drive across the Don and to the Volga. On 17 December Sieckenius was promoted to *Oberst* and between 17 to 22 May 1942 during the Bacaklesa encirclement his regiment played a major role in the capture of 31,500 Soviet soldiers and sixty-nine tanks and 224 other vehicles. However, during September and October the division took many casualties during the street fighting in Stalingrad and from mid-November he had only 4,000 men. When the massive offensive struck his division had been split and at least four regiments were trapped in the Stalingrad Pocket but a few units including Panzer Regiment 2 escaped capture. In the spring of 1943 a second 16th Panzer Division was formed and Sieckenius took command. On 1 June he was promoted to *Generalmajor* and saw action in Italy against the US 5th Army. From March 1944 he was briefly given the leadership of the 13th *Luftwaffe* Field Division, and from May was delegated with the leadership of the 290th Infantry Division in the Courland area. From 23 May he was Commander of the 263rd Infantry Division and saw action on the Russian Front until August, when he took over the leadership of the 221st Security Division. On 5 September he took over command of the 391st Security Division, his last command before he was killed in Berlin during fighting with the Soviets on 28 April 1945 as part of the 9th Army.

Feodor August Gotthard HEINRICI

Generaloberst

* 25 December 1886, Gumbinnen, East Prussia
+ 13 December 1971, Endersbach-Waiblingen, Baden-Württemberg

Gotthard Heinrici entered the Army in March 1905 as a *Fahnenjunker*, was attached to the War School in Hannover and was commissioned as a *Leutnant* in August 1906. He was appointed adjutant of the II. Battalion with Infantry Regiment 95 at the beginning of the First World War, now with the rank of *Oberleutnant*. He was promoted to *Hauptmann* in June 1915 and from August 1916 served on the General Staff, having been awarded both classes of the Iron Cross. He remained in the Army after the war and by February 1926 had been promoted to *Major*. From October 1927 he was attached to the Troop Office in Berlin. By March 1933 he was department head with the Ministry of Defence with the rank of *Oberst*, and he was Commander of the 16th Infantry Division at the beginning of the Second World War. He saw action during the invasion of France in May and June 1940, now with the rank of *Generalmajor* and with leadership of the XII. Army Corps. (*Deutsches Wehrkundearchiv*)

Knight's Cross: Awarded on 18 September 1941 as *General der Infanterie* and Commanding General of the XXXXIII. Army Corps while attached to the 2nd Army for his success during the battles at Mogilev, Smolensk and the advance towards the Berezina River in August 1941. The fast and victorious advance of his Army Corps and the success during the attack on Gomel-Shlobin were crucial, with the success due in particular to the fighting spirit and leadership of Heinrici. In January 1942 he took over as Commander-in-Chief of the 4th Army and saw heavy fighting against a strong Red Army near Yukhnov that lasted until May 1942. He continued to see action in the Soviet Union and was promoted to *Generaloberst* on 30 January 1943.

Knight's Cross with Oakleaves: Awarded on 24 November 1943, the 333rd recipient, as *Generaloberst* and Commander-in-Chief of the 4th Army, part of Army Group South, during the success east of Orsha on the Russian Front, and for the prevention of a strong Soviet breakout. On 9 December 1943 Heinrici was presented with the Oakleaves personally by Hitler at his headquarters in

Rastenburg. He continued to command the 4th Army until he was taken ill with hepatitis in May 1944, being hospitalised for four weeks. He remained resting until August 1944, when he was recalled and named as the Commander-in-Chief of the 1st Panzer Army. He saw action at Vinnitsa, Yampil and Chernovtsy in the Ukraine before taking part in battles near Kamianets-Podilskyi.

Knight's Cross with Oakleaves and Swords: Awarded on 3 March 1945 to become the 136th recipient as *Generaloberst* and Commander-in-Chief of the 1st Panzer Army, part of Army Group Centre, for his success in halting the Soviet offensive in February 1945. On 20 March he took command of Army Group Vistula, and now commanded two armies, the 3rd Panzer Army and the 9th Army, which were tasked with preventing the Soviet attack across the Oder River. However, he faced great shortages of not only manpower but vehicles and ammunition, and Hitler was convinced the Red Army would not attack Berlin. However, on 16 April the Battle of Berlin began and within just three days the Soviet armies had broken through and were entering the city. On 21 April Hitler was told that Heinrici was retreating and was furious after he was told that Heinrici's command post was further from the Soviets than Hitler's Bunker! On 29 April 1945 Heinrici was dismissed from his command by *Generalfeldmarschall* Keitel for ordering an unauthorised withdrawal on the Eastern Front. Keitel named *Generaloberst* Kurt Student as his replacement, but he did not arrive from Holland to assume command until 1 May 1945. With the loss of his command, Heinrici retired to Plön, where he surrendered to the British on 28 May 1945. He was released on 19 May 1948.

Ernst Ulrich Hans von LEYSER

General der Infanterie

* 18 November 1889, Steglitz
+ 23 September 1962, Garstedt

Knight's Cross: Awarded on 18 September 1941 as *Generalmajor* and Commander of 269th Infantry Division while attached to the LVI. Army Corps for his leadership during the fighting and eventual defeat of the Soviet III. Armoured Corps. He later saw action during the Battle of the Volkhov, south-east of Leningrad, and continued to see action until he was transferred and took over command of the XXVI. Army Corps shortly after he had been promoted to *Generalleutnant* in October 1942. He saw action in the area around Leningrad, was promoted to *General der Infanterie* in December and

Ernst von Leyser entered Army service in March 1909 as a *Leutnant* with Foot Guard Regiment 5 and served as a platoon leader, battalion adjutant, Company Leader and regimental adjutant during the First World War. He was awarded the Iron Cross 1st and 2nd Classes during the war and held the rank of *Hauptmann* when it was over. He entered the police in December 1920 with the rank of *Polziei-Hauptmann* and rose to *Polizei-Major* in April 1922. He transferred into the Army in October 1935 as Commander of an anti-tank battalion and was promoted to *Oberstleutnant* in March 1936 and to *Oberst* the following year. In late August 1939 he was named Commander of Infantry Replacement Regiment 6 and from October 1939 he was Commander of Infantry Regiment 169. He was awarded the Bar to the Iron Cross 1st and 2nd Classes during the Battle of France in May and June 1940. (*Deutsches Wehrkundearchiv*)

confirmed as Commanding General of his Army Corps. In January 1943 the Soviets attacked his command from both west and east and the fighting was tough. The Red Army pushed the Germans back and formed a corridor about 5 miles wide that enabled them to make a land connection with Leningrad, threatening the Germans. Leyser was transferred in November 1943 and appointed Commanding General of the XV. Mountain Corps in Croatia as part of the 2nd Panzer Army. On 20 July 1944 he took over as Commanding General of the XXI. Mountain Corps in Croatia as part of Army Group E. In early November his command retreated to Podgorica in Montenegro and by mid-November his corps tried to break through Danilivgrad and Nikšić toward Sarajevo but were stopped by Yugoslav partisans, supported by two British artillery units. By then end of November Leyser and his corps had to retreat and found it difficult to make any advancement. He was relieved of his command on 29 April 1945 and captured by US troops on 8 May. He was put on trial at the Nuremberg with twelve other high-ranking German officers accused of war crimes in the Hostages Trial from 13 May 1947 to 19 February 1948. Leyser was found guilty on two charges and was sentenced to ten years' imprisonment. After a review he was released on 3 February 1951.

Walter LICHEL

General der Infanterie

* 1 May 1885, Stolp
+ 10 December 1969, Bärnau

Walter Lichel entered the Army as a *Fahnenjunker* in November 1903 with Infantry Regiment 83, and was commissioned as a *Leutnant* in May 1905. He transferred into Infantry Regiment 147 in 1906 and then joined Infantry Regiment 144 in November 1909. In April 1914 he was promoted to *Oberleutnant* and in October he was Company Leader in Infantry Regiment 98, ending the war as a Battalion Leader. He remained in the *Reichswehr* after the war and by October 1932 he had risen to the rank of *Oberstleutnant* with Artillery Regiment 2. He was promoted to Oberst in September 1934 and from October was Course Director at the War School in Munich. He was Commander of Infantry Regiment 22 from October 1936 and was promoted to *Generalmajor* in February 1938. Towards the end of that year he was Commander of the 3rd Infantry Division. He was later awarded both classes of the Bar to the Iron Cross and in February 1940 he was promoted to *Generalleutnant*. (*Deutsches Wehrkundearchiv*)

Knight's Cross: Awarded on 18 September 1941 as *Generalleutnant* and Commander of 123rd Infantry Division while attached to II. Army Corps for actions during the opening phases of the invasion of the Soviet Union. From April 1941 he took his division to East Prussia for training before leaving for the Soviet Union as part of Army Group North in June. He saw action at Dvinsk and a number of other battles during the drive towards Leningrad, and during this time he was severely wounded and admitted to hospital in August 1941. He was presented with his Knight's Cross while still recovering and promoted to *General der Infanterie* in December 1942, but he never really recovered from his injury. From November 1944 he was named Commanding General of the Replacement XI. Army Corps and Commander of Military District XI, with his headquarters in Hannover. He was captured by Allied troops on 13 April and remained in captivity until 1947.

Karl CASPER
Generalleutnant

* 22 February 1893, Rehden, Graudenz
+ 25 August 1970, Munich

Karl Casper entered Army service in August 1914 at the start of the First World War with Infantry Regiment 129 and was commissioned as a *Leutnant* the following year. Transferred to Infantry Regiment 61, he was awarded both classes of the Iron Cross, and retired from the Army in March 1920. He then joined the police, rising to the rank of *Polizei-Major*, before rejoining the Army in October 1935 with Infantry Regiment 35. By the start of the Second World War he had been promoted to *Oberstleutnant* and served in Luxembourg and France, where he was awarded the Bar to the Iron Cross 1st and 2nd Classes. (*Deutsches Wehrkundearchiv*)

Knight's Cross: Awarded on 22 September 1941 as *Oberst* and Commander of Motorised Infantry Regiment 118, part of the 36th Motorised Infantry Division, in recognition of his regiment's breakthrough of the Soviet defensive ring near St Petersburg following tough combat north-west of Krasnogvardeysky. In a report it was said that Casper inspired his soldiers under his command, which led them to achieve an eventually decisive success with great courage. In October 1942 Casper was promoted to *Generalmajor* and took command of the 335th Infantry Division stationed in Brittany, France, as part of the coastal protection forces. In France he took his division to Marseille, where it remained until February 1943 when, as part of the 1st Panzer Army, it was sent to Ukraine on the Eastern Front. Promoted to *Generalleutnant* in August, Casper was wounded the following month. He was awarded the Wound Badge in Silver in October 1943 and returned to front-line duty from February 1944. He was now Commander of the 48th Infantry Division, part of the LXXXIX. Army Corps in Belgium, and stationed in Ostend for coastal protection. In August 1944 his division was transferred to Paris, where his command secured the bridges of the Seine and provided combat troops during the uprising. From mid-September his division was used to protect the mouth of both the Rivers Saar and Moselle. It was during this time that his division suffered heavy losses and it was withdrawn in November. From early 1945 it was attached to the 559th *Volksgrenadier* Division in Lower Austria. It was here that Casper surrendered to US troops on 9 May 1945 and he remained in captivity until May 1948.

Heinrich 'Heinz' GREINER

Generalleutnant

* 12 August 1895, Amberg, Bavaria
+ 19 November 1977, Rottach-Egern, Bavaria

Heinrich Greiner entered Army service with the Bavarian Infantry Regiment at the beginning of the First World War in August 1914, and was commissioned as a *Leutnant* in June 1915. He attended various training courses at this time and remained with the same regiment throughout the war. He was wounded in October 1917 and awarded the Iron Cross 1st and 2nd Classes. He remained in the Army after the war and entered Rifle Regiment 42 in August 1919. He attended various training programmes before being promoted to *Oberleutnant* in October 1923. He became an instructor at the Munich War School from October 1934, and was promoted to *Major* in March 1935. He was made Commander of the III. Battalion of Infantry Regiment 63 in November 1938 and saw action in Poland as part of the 27th Infantry Division. (*Deutsches Wehrkundearchiv*)

Knight's Cross: Awarded on 22 September 1941 as *Oberst* and Commander of Infantry Regiment 499 while attached to the 268th Infantry Division after distinguishing himself during the defensive battles of Yelnya, part of Smolensk in the Soviet Union. Greiner saw action during the battles near Vyazma and then he moved west when his regiment was hit by the Soviet winter. In early 1942 he took command of the 268th Infantry Division, seeing action during the fighting in Yukhnov as part of the 4th Army and later having to retreat due to the weather. Greiner was promoted to *Generalmajor* in March and the fighting dragged on throughout much of the year and during the early part of January 1943. Now with the rank of *Generalleutnant*, Greiner and his troops took part in the battles in the Spas–Demensk area. Soon after the beginning of the Soviet summer offensive in August his division suffered heavy losses and had to retreat to the Dnieper Region, and his command was disbanded. On 15 November Greiner took command of the 362nd Infantry Division stationed in the Rimini area of northern Italy, and from January 1944 his command was used in coastal protection on the Tyrrhenian Sea, part of the Mediterranean, off the western coast of Italy. From mid-February, while attached to the LXXVI. Panzer Corps, he took part in the defensive battles near Cisterna in central

Italy. Between May and June he led his command during the costly battles over the Aban Hills near Rome, and from August his command defended the Arno sector as part of the XIV. Panzer Corps.

Knight's Cross with Oakleaves: He became the 572nd recipient on 5 September 1944 as *Generalleutnant* and Commander of the 362nd Infantry Division, part of the I. *Fallschirm*-Corps, for his outstanding command of his division and a Battle Group composed of army and parachute troops near Velletri, Italy. His unit repelled a total of thirty-eight enemy tanks during successful counter-attacks and he was mentioned in the Armed Forces Daily Report of 2 June 1944. In mid-September his command prevented an enemy breakthrough at Firenzuola near Tuscany and he took part in heavy fighting against partisans in the Monte La Fine area. From October he saw action south of Bologna and shortly after November his command was rested. On 1 January 1945 he was transferred into the Reserves, but he was called up again in April, when he became Deputy Commander of the VII. Army Corps and Commander of Military District VII in Munich. He saw little action at this time and on 6 May his command surrendered to US troops. Greiner remained in American captivity until his release on 27 June 1947.

Friedrich Benno Georg HERRLEIN

General der Infanterie

* 27 April 1889, Ehrenbreitstein, Rhine Province
+ 28 July 1974, Giessen, Hesse

Knight's Cross: Awarded on 22 September 1941 as *Generalmajor* and Commander of the 18th Motorised Infantry Division, part of the I. Army Corps, for his leadership during the fighting in Bialystok and Minsk on the Russian Front. His command was badly mauled during the drive on Leningrad and at the beginning of the winter offensive. From February to October 1942 he entered the Reserves and then until October 1943 he was attached to the High Command of the Army. He was promoted to *Generalleutnant* on 1 September and from 15 to 25 May 1943 he was delegated with the leadership of the XXVIII. Army Corps while on the Soviet front as part of the 18th Army. On 12 October he was delegated with the leadership of the LV. Army Corps, which was in full retreat and was in the Dnieper region in early 1944. Herrlein was promoted to *General der Infanterie* in February 1944 and at the beginning of the Soviet summer offensive on 22 June 1944 his corps was part of the 9th Army and in

Friedrich Herrlein entered Army service in March 1910 as a cadet and from June that year was attached to the War School in Danzig. He was commissioned as a *Leutnant* in March 1911 and by June 1915 he was serving as an adjutant with Guard Reserve Regiment 2 with the rank of *Oberleutnant*. He was wounded in action in August 1916 and served with various regiments. He was awarded the Iron Cross 1st and 2nd Classes and ended the war with the rank of *Hauptmann*. He remained in the Army after the war and was promoted to *Major* in April 1931, serving as an adjutant and as a Company Commander. Promoted to *Oberstleutnant* in August 1934, he served as Commander of the I. Battalion attached to Infantry Regiment 65. He was given command of Infantry Regiment 116 from October 1936 and was promoted to *Oberst* in January 1937. He saw action during the opening stages of the war in September 1939 and was awarded the Bar to the Iron Cross 2nd Class. He then saw action during the Battle of France in 1940. (*Deutsches Wehrkundearchiv*)

a fighting retreat through the swampy Pripet Marshes, suffering heavy losses. From July his corps was transferred to Bialystok and a new front was formed as part of the 4th Army. From mid-January 1945 the Soviet winter offensive against East Prussia began. However, by the end of January the corps had to withdraw because of strong Soviet forces and Herrlein's command was pushed back towards Bartoszyce in Poland. During the last few weeks of the war he served as a general with special duties while attached to Army Group South. On 18 April 1945 he surrendered to the British and remained in captivity until 17 May 1948.

Friedrich-Wilhelm MÜLLER

General der Infanterie

*29 August 1897, Wuppertal-Barman, Westphalia
+ 20 May 1947, Athens, Greece

Knight's Cross: Awarded on 22 September 1941 as an *Oberstleutnant* and Commander of Infantry Regiment 105, part of the 72nd Infantry Division, for actions in the Soviet Union. During the battles near Nikolayev his regiment took part in the successful halt of the Soviet resistance at Warwarówka. He then proceeded to foil the Soviet attempts to inflict permanent damage to a bridge over the Bug River, and this achievement was of great significance not just for the corps but for the entire Army as they needed to be able to cross the river.

Friedrich-Wilhelm Müller volunteered for the Army in November 1914 and saw action from March 1915 with the 8th Company of Reserve Infantry Regiment 262. He was commissioned as a *Leutnant* in August 1916 and served as a Signals Officer and Company Leader, being captured by French soldiers just before the end of the war in November 1918. He was awarded both classes of the Iron Cross and when he returned from French captivity he joined the police in Münster, Germany, rising to the rank of *Polizei-Major* in March 1936. Soon after his promotion he entered the Army as a *Major*, served with the infantry and was promoted to *Oberstleutnant* in June 1939. From November 1938 he was Commander of the III. Battalion of Infantry Regiment 105, including at the beginning of the Western campaign. (*Deutsches Wehrkundearchiv*)

Müller continued to see action in the Soviet Union and was promoted to the rank of Oberst on 17 December 1941.

Knight's Cross with Oakleaves: He became the eighty-sixth recipient on 8 April 1942 as *Oberst* and Commander of the Infantry Regiment 105, and still part of the 72nd Infantry Division, for his recapture of Feodosia in the Crimea on the Black Sea, which was of great significance. On 1 August 1942 he was promoted to *Generalmajor* and took over as Commander of the 22nd Infantry Division. From November Müller led his division in Crete, where he took over the security of the island and this led to the conquest of the Islands of Kos, Samos and Leros. He was promoted to *Generalleutnant* in April 1943 and continued to command his infantry division until April 1944, when he was attached to the Army Personnel Office. From 8 May 1944 he took over as temporary leader of the V. Army Corps in the Crimea and briefly took command of the LIX. Army Corps in early June. He was promoted to *General der Infanterie* on 1 July and was named as Commandant of Fortress Crete, taking over from *Generalleutnant* Bruno Bräuer of the *Luftwaffe.* In April 1944 he took severe action after the kidnapping of *Generalmajor* Heinrich Kreipe, and ordered that every male inhabitant of the village where the general was kidnapped should be executed. In August he was responsible for the deaths of 164 Greek civilians and his infamy earned him the nickname 'The Butcher of Crete'.

Knight's Cross with Oakleaves and Swords: Awarded on 27 January 1945 to become the 128th recipient as *General der Infanterie* and Commanding General of the LXVIII. Army Corps, part of the 2nd Panzer Army, for his command achievements during the German retreat from the Balkans in late 1944. In October of that year he ensured that the vital supply city of Kraljevo in Serbia remained in German hands, and later as Commander of the LXVIII. Army Corps he managed to fend off all enemy attempts to eliminate the German troops in the Balkans. From 29 January 1945 Müller was Commander-in-Chief of the 4th Army in East Prussia and on 7 April he was captured by British troops and handed over to the Greek authorities, together with *General der Fallschirmtruppe* Bruno Bräuer. They were both tried for war crimes by a Greek Military Court in Athens, found guilty and sentenced to death. They were both executed by firing squad in Athens on 20 May 1947.

Georg von NEUFVILLE

Generalmajor z. V.

* 27 October 1883, Frankfurt am Main
+ 3 November 1941, Panovo, Soviet Union

Knight's Cross: Awarded on 22 September 1941 as *Oberst z. V.* and Commander of Infantry Regiment 195, part of the 78th Infantry Division, for his leadership and bravery during the battles at Bialystok and Smolensk in the Soviet Union. From September he saw action during the Battle of Moscow and he was seriously wounded near Mikhailovskoe about 50 miles from Moscow. He died from his wounds the following day in an aid station near Panovo, and was posthumously promoted to *Generalmajor z. V.*

Hans-Wolfgang REINHARD

General der Infanterie

* 11 December 1888, Hohenstein-Ernstthal
+ 18 January 1950, Karlsruhe- Baden

Knight's Cross: Awarded on 22 September 1941 as *General der Infanterie* and Commanding General of LI. Army Corps for actions in Kiev during the invasion of the Soviet Union as part of the 2nd Army. Later his Army Corps became part of the 6th Army, commanded by *General der Panzertruppe* Friedrich Paulus, who said of Reinhard, 'good and brave, cares about his troops'. From 1 July 1942 Reinhard was the Commanding General of the LXXXVIII. Army Corps in Utrecht in the Netherlands and was responsible for coastal defence. This was a peaceful command until the Allied breakout from Normandy and the advance on the Netherlands towards the end of August 1944. On 4 September his corps took part in the heavy defensive actions at Antwerp but by the end day the city was lost. His troops set up a defensive front on the Albert Canal and most of the bridges on the route were blown up. His corps engaged in heavy fighting with the Allies and on 14 September the Allies crossed the Maas-Scheldt Canal and a bridgehead was established. Three days later the Allies launched Operation Market Garden, the airborne invasion of Holland when Allied airborne units landed behind the German lines. There were some tough battles and on the 21st Reinhard's troops were engaged in defensive combat west and south-west of Eindhoven. The next day Allied gliders landed and heavier fighting took place. By the 17th, the Allies were trapped near the Arnhem bridge, suffering many casualties, and some troops were airlifted out, but others were taken prisoner. The whole operation was a failure for the Allies – they had lost approximately 17,000 troops either killed or taken prisoner and the Germans lost between 7,500 and 10,000 men. From December 1944 Reinhard entered the Reserves and from 2 February he was the Commanding General of Military District IV in Dresden. From 10 April until the end of the war he was on the reserve list.

Walther Oswin RISSE

Generalleutnant

* 13 December 1892, Geithain, Saxony
+ 21 June 1965, Hamburg, Lower Saxony

Knight's Cross: Awarded on 22 September 1941 as *Oberst* and Commander of Infantry Regiment 474, part of the 254th Infantry Division, for action in the fighting around Reval during the invasion of the Soviet Union. At this time his regiment broke the heavily fortified Soviet defence line along the Pirita River and pushed towards the north, gaining his division a new front by the evening of 24 August. From here it was possible to support the assault on the strongly defended high ground east of Reval and ensure its eventual fall by attacking German forces. He took part in the Siege of Leningrad and was heavily engaged with the enemy at Demyansk, seeing action mainly around the northern sector of the Eastern Front. On 25 September 1942 he was delegated with the leadership of the 225th Infantry Division while attached to Army Group North, and

Walther Risse volunteered as a sailor with 2nd Sailor Division in April 1914 and served as a Watch Officer with the rank of *Leutnant zur See* from November 1915. He was awarded both classes of the Iron Cross during the First World War and after it entered the Reich Water Protection Service. From December 1920 he was a member of the Protection Police in Hildesheim, and from January 1933 he saw service in Berlin, rising to the rank of *Major der Landespolizei* in June 1935. From October he was a *Major* in the Army and served as a Company Commander in the IV. Battalion of Infantry Regiment 4 until April 1937. Promoted to *Oberstleutnant* in April 1938, he was appointed Commander of Infantry Regiment 474 in Osnabrück in August 1939. He saw action in France and Belgium in 1940 and was awarded both classes of the Bar to the Iron Cross. He remained in France until the end of the year. (*Author's Collection*)

in November Risse was promoted to *Generalmajor.* His divisional command was confirmed and he later took part in the Siege of Leningrad, being heavily involved in the fighting during the Soviet winter offensive of 1942–43.

Knight's Cross with Oakleaves: He became the 704th recipient on 18 January 1945 as *Generalleutnant* and Commander of 225th Infantry Division, fighting as part of the 18th Army, for his leadership and bravery during the Third Battle of the Courland. He continued to see action in the Courland Pocket and during this time he lost nine grenadier regiments due to casualties. The war ended for him and his division in in the Courland in western Latvia, where he was taken prisoner by Soviet troops on 9 May 1945. He was tried by a Military Tribunal from July 1949 and in January 1955 was found guilty and sentenced to twenty-five years' forced labour. He was released in October 1955 after a general amnesty and repatriated to Germany.

Risse saw action on Lake Ilmen in March to May 1943, and was promoted to *Generalleutnant* in August 1943. In early 1944 Risse took part in the retreat to Narva in the Baltic States and fought at six battles of the Courland Pocket from October 1944. (*Deutsches Wehrkundearchiv*)

Hans Joachim Hermann SCHMIDT

General der Infanterie z.V.

* 28 April 1877,
+ 5 June 1948, Stuttgart

Hans Schmidt entered the Army with the 3rd Wurttemberg Infantry Regiment in July 1895 and in January 1899 he was commissioned as a *Leutnant.* He served as adjutant with the 3rd Wurttemberg Infantry Regiment from January 1906 and was promoted to *Oberleutnant* the following year. He entered the General Staff in March 1911 and was promoted to *Hauptmann* in October 1912. He served as a Battalion Commander in the 3rd Wurttemberg Infantry Regiment from 1915. Promoted to *Major* in April 1917, he served on the General Staff of the XXV. Panzer Corps and ended the war on the Staff of the 9th Infantry Division. He remained in the Army after the war and had risen to the rank of *Generalleutnant z.V.* in August 1939. He saw action at the beginning of the war as Commander of the 260th Infantry Division. (*Author's Collection*)

Knight's Cross: Awarded on 22 September 1941 as *Generalleutnant z.V.* and Commander of 260th Infantry Division for his part in the seizure of a bridgehead over the Desna River near Chernihiv in the Ukraine. His victory and others were of decisive importance for the rapid continuation of the operations in preventing the Soviets from establishing a solid defence line on the river. His division then had to fight on its own against fierce Soviet counter-attacks for days, and was not only able to crush these attacks but expanded the bridgehead further. As part of Army Group Centre his division took an active role in the successful attack and capture of Chernigov in the Ukraine and joined in the fighting in Kiev. It also took part in the attack on Moscow. Schmidt took command of the IX. Army Corps in January 1942 and was promoted to *General der Infanterie* the following month. By the spring of 1943 the Soviets began to push and the 3rd Panzer Army and the 4th Army were withdrawn. Schmidt took his corps back through Vyazma, where in September the front collapsed near Smolensk.

Knight's Cross with Oakleaves: He became the 334th recipient on 24 November 1943 as *Generalleutnant z.V.* and Commanding General of IX. Army Corps for his leadership during the hard and tough battles near and around Spas-Demensk and Nevel in the Soviet Union. From 21 July until 7 August 1944 he was appointed Commanding General of Military District V in Stuttgart and was then transferred to France, where he was appointed Commander of the Vosges Reconnaissance Staff. From mid-October 1944 he took command of the reconnaissance staff in the Danube area and from November was appointed Commander-in-Chief of the 24th Army. In early May 1945 he led a retreat through the Arlberg Tunnel to Strengen in Austria, where Schmidt and his staff surrendered to the commander of the 44th US Division and Schmidt was taken prisoner.

Hans-Heinrich SIXT VON ARNIM

Generalleutnant

* 6 November 1890, Stettin, Pomerania
+ 1 April 1952, Krasnogorsk, Moscow

Hans-Heinrich Sixt von Arnim joined the Army as a *Fahnenjunker* in February 1909 and was commissioned as a *Leutnant* in June 1910. At the beginning of the First World War he was adjutant of I. Battalion of the Royal Augusta Guard Regiment No.4 and was promoted to *Oberleutnant* in February 1915. He was wounded in May 1915. He served for a time with the War Ministry, was promoted to *Hauptmann* in October 1917 and remained in the Army at the war's end, having won both classes of the Iron Cross. He served with the Defence Ministry and as a staff officer with the 6th Division, and by October 1935 he was serving with the Army High Command with the rank of *Oberst*. In August 1939 he was Chief of the General Staff of the 5th Army with the rank of *Generalmajor* and from September 1939 was Commander of the 95th Infantry Division. (*Deutsches Wehrkundearchiv*)

Knight's Cross: Awarded on 22 September 1941 as *Generalleutnant* and Commander of 95th Infantry Division, fighting as part of the 6th Army, for his leadership during the tough battles on the southern sector of the Russian Front. Sixt von Arnim and his division were more or less in continuous action on the southern front from July 1941 until early 1942, fighting in Kiev, the Ukraine and Bryansk. His division lost most of their guns when the Soviets attacked the rear of the 2nd Army in mid-December 1941, and what was left continued to oppose the Soviet winter offensive. On 10 May 1942 Sixt von Arnim took command of the 113th Infantry Division while on the southern sector of the Russian Front. His division was part of the 6th Army and when this was surrounded at Stalingrad in November 1942, the 113th Infantry Division was destroyed on 20 January 1943. Sixt von Arnim was taken prisoner on the same day and died in a Soviet prison camp on 1 April 1952.

Wilhelm Emanuel BURGDORF

General der Infanterie

* 15 February 1895, Fürstenwalde an der Spree, Brandenburg
+ 1 May 1945, *Führer* Bunker, Berlin

Wilhelm Burgdorf entered Army service in August 1914 and served with Grenadier Regiment 12 throughout the First World War, being awarded both classes of the Iron Cross. He remained in the Army after the war, serving mainly with Infantry Regiment 8, and by the time Hitler came to power in January 1933 he held the rank of *Hauptmann*. He was an instructor at the War School in Dresden from September 1934 and was promoted to *Major* in November 1935. He saw action during the French campaign as Commander of Infantry Regiment 529. (*Deutsches Wehrkundearchiv*)

Knight's Cross: Awarded on 29 September 1941 as *Oberst* and Commander of Infantry Regiment 529 while attached to the 299th Infantry Division for the capture of Hill 234 on 9 July, this was an important hill as it was the lynchpin of the Soviet position on the eastern side of the Sluch River, and provided a decisive foothold for the division. Burgdorf remained commander of his regiment, which fought as part of the LV. Army Corps in the Soviet Union until April 1942. On 1 May he was named as Deputy Chief of the Army Personnel Office, working under *Generalmajor* Rudolf Schmundt. Burgdorf was promoted to *Generalleutnant* in October 1943 and he became Chief of the Army Personnel Office on 12 October after the death of Schmundt, who had been seriously wounded in the bomb blast at Hitler's headquarters at Rastenburg on 20 July 1944. On 14 October Burgdorf was sent by *Generalfeldmarschall* Keitel to see Rommel at his home and discuss his involvement in the assassination bomb plot to kill Hitler. He told Rommel that Hitler expected him to commit suicide and if he did he would be given a heroes' funeral and his involvement in the plot would be kept from the public. If, however, he chose a trial he must understand that he would be found guilty and his family would not be protected. Burgdorf left him cyanide and within an hour of their conversation the field marshal was slumped in the back of a staff car, dead. Burgdorf was appointed Chief Adjutant to Hitler and was promoted to *General der Infanterie* on 9 November 1944. He was a very good friend of Martin Bormann, and they would often drink together and get drunk and even danced together at a party at Rastenburg. Burgdorf was one of the witnesses to Hitler's Political Will and Testament and was in the bunker when Hitler shot himself. Burgdorf went the same way as his *Führer*; he shot himself on 1 May and his body was found by the Soviets.

Friedrich-Wilhelm von LOEPER

Generalleutnant

* 3 August 1888, Prieborn, Strehlen
+ 7 October 1983, Bückeburg

Knight's Cross: Awarded on 29 September 1941 as *Generalleutnant* and Commander of the 10th Motorised Infantry Division, part of the XXIV. Army Corps, for actions in the Soviet Union. He took part in the early stages of the invasion of the Soviet Union, crossing the Bug River, and he fought at Bobruisk, Smolensk, the Dnieper crossings, Kiev and during the Battle of Moscow, where Loeper was rewarded for his bravery and leadership. With the winter offensive of 1941–42 halted, he remained with his division in the central sector during the early defensive actions. In May 1942 he was appointed Commander of Motorised Division 178, which was basically a training division in Silesia, and from 5 April it became Panzer Division 17,8 which remained in Silesia part of Military District VIII. In August 1944 Loeper took command of Panzer Division *Tatra*, which had been formed in Slovakia when it looked as if that country might defect from the Axis. Its staff included veteran members of the 1st Panzer Division and was equipped with twenty-eight armoured vehicles and three Tiger tanks. Despite its lack of firepower, it performed well during the suppression of the Slovak Military Mutiny of 1944. From December it became the Field-Training Division *Tatra* and Loeper remained commander until January 1945. Then he helped to establish Division *Ludwig an der Oder*, which was hastily formed from 7,500 men from the Reich Labour Service and was to be used in Berlin against the Red Army. However, on 28 February Loeper retired from the Army and was briefly held by the Allies in July 1945.

Horst Hermann Julius Max STUMPFF

General der Panzertruppe

* 20 November 1887, Giessen, Hesse
+ 25 November 1958, Hamburg

Horst Stumpff entered the Army with Infantry Regiment 54 in March 1907 and was commissioned as a *Leutnant* the following year. He saw action during the First World War and served as a staff officer from February 1918, now with the rank of *Hauptmann*. He was awarded both classes of the Iron Cross during the war and remained in the Army when it ended. From 1924 he served with Infantry Regiment 4 and then from October 1929 he served as a trainer with the Infantry School in Dresden, now with the rank of *Major*. At the beginning of the Second World War he was serving as Commander of the 3rd Panzer Brigade with the rank of *Generalmajor* and was awarded the Bar to the Iron Cross 1st and 2nd Classes during the Polish campaign. (*Deutsches Wehrkundearchiv*)

Knight's Cross: Awarded on 29 September 1941 as *Generalleutnant* and Commander of 20th Panzer Division while attached to the LVII. Army Corps for actions in the Soviet Union. He led his division during the Minsk encirclement and took Vitebsk, and he fought during the Battle of Smolensk in July and August 1941. On 10 September he resigned his command and entered the Reserves, where he remained until April 1942 when he was appointed Inspector of Army Recruitment in Königsberg. From July 1944 he served as General with special duties attached to the Office of the General of Panzer Troops on 7 August, and was appointed General of Panzer Troops West with the Replacement Army. He was promoted to *General der Panzertruppe* in November 1944.

Heinrich Rudolf WITTKOPF

Generalmajor

* 15 August 1892, Hildesheim
+ 12 February 1946, Ostende, Belgium

Knight's Cross: Awarded on 29 September 1941 as *Oberst* and Commander of Infantry Regiment 530 while attached to 299th Infantry Division for actions during the Soviet invasion. On 1 July 1941 Soviet tank forces probed the German positions and were fought off, and the following day the Soviets launched tank attacks, which were not very successful. At approximately 1500 the Germans launched a counter-attack and Wittkopf and his regiment helped to destroy thirty-four Soviet tanks and six heavy guns. He saw action during the fighting at Zhitomir and Kiev and then at Kursk, and held a sector in the vicinity of Livny, east of Orel from January 1942. From March 1943 he served in the Reserve as an army consultant for the Inspector of Infantry for land fortifications and was promoted to *Generalmajor* in April 1944. In November he took command of the Infantry School in Döberitz and from April 1945 he was named as Commander of Special Division 402, and at the same time was Commandant of Greifswald until May 1945, when he was captured by British forces. He died on 12 February 1946 in Ostende, Belgium, while still in British captivity. He is buried in the largest War Cemetery in Western Europe in Lommel, Belgium, which contains almost 39,000 graves. Wittkopf rests in Block 62, Grave #197.

Traugott Johannes Gustav Otto HERR

General der Panzertruppe

* 16 September 1890, Weferlingen, Saxony-Anhalt
+ 13 April 1976, Wulfsfelde, Schleswig-Holstein

Traugott Herr entered Army service in April 1911 as a *Fahnenjunker* with Fusilier Regiment 35 and was attached to the War School in Glogau. He was commissioned as a *Leutnant* in August 1912 and was appointed adjutant of the II. Battalion of Fusilier Regiment 35 from the beginning of the war. He was promoted to *Oberleutnant* in November 1917. He saw action as a machine gun officer but was hospitalised from June 1918 and returned to his regiment a few months before the end of the war. He remained in the Army after the war and was promoted to *Hauptmann* in January 1926 while attached to the Staff of Infantry Regiment 9. Promoted to *Oberstleutnant* in October 1936, he was became an *Oberst* in August 1939 and was appointed Commander of Motorised Infantry Regiment 66 at the beginning of the war. (*Deutsches Wehrkundearchiv*)

Knight's Cross: Awarded on 2 October 1941 as *Oberst* and Commander of the 13th Rifle Brigade while attached to the 13th Panzer Division for actions on the Russian Front. It was awarded in particular for his role in the expanding of

On 31 October Herr was severely wounded by shrapnel in the base of the skull and was hospitalised and rested until mid-June 1943. On 29 June Herr, now with the rank of *Generalleutnant*, he was delegated with the leadership of the LXXVI. Army Corps. From 22 July it was redesignated the LXXVI. Panzer Corps, based in France. On 1 September 1943 Herr was promoted to *General der Panzertruppe* and took over as Commanding General of the LXXVI. Panzer Corps and saw action in Italy. (*Deutsches Wehrkundearchiv*)

the German bridgehead in Dnepropetrovsk during the summer of 1941, which he carried out despite grave misgivings. On 1 December Herr took over as Commander of the 13th Panzer Division and took part in the winter offensive of the 1st Panzer Army's drive on the Caucasus oilfields in 1942 at the point where it crossed the Terek River and pushed to within 15 miles of Grozny. For this he was promoted in April 1942 to the rank of *Generalmajor*.

Knight's Cross with Oakleaves: He became the 110th recipient on 9 August 1942 as *Generalmajor* and Commander of the 13th Panzer Division, part of the III. Panzer Corps, for his division's capture of Rostov in 1942. He was presented personally with the Oakleaves by Hitler at his headquarters at the Wolf's Lair in Rastenburg. Most of the division escaped isolation in the Kuban region before the Soviets retook Rostov, although part of it was cut off and had to be evacuated later via the Crimea.

Knight's Cross with Oakleaves and Swords: Awarded on 18 December 1944, the 117th recipient as *General der Panzertruppe* and Commanding General of the LXXVI. Panzer Corps while attached to the 10th Army. From the end of August until mid-November 1944 the Allies attempted to break through the front of the LXXVI. Panzer Corps near Rimini. However, according to German reports the Allies lost 651 tanks in the first four weeks, and the German front was pushed back but did not break. From 23 November Herr was given temporary command of the 14th Army, as part of Army Group C in Italy. In early December he was admitted to hospital for an operation on his head, probably to do with an old injury. He remained on sick leave until 16 February 1945, when he was delegated with the leadership of the 10th Army, again party of the Army Group C in Italy. He surrendered to British troops in Italy and was held in captivity until his release on 17 May 1948.

Karl KOETZ

Generalmajor

* 8 February 1908, Berlin-Neukölln, Brandenburg
+ 11 July 1977, Meran, South-Tirol, Italy

Karl Koetz joined the Army as a private with Infantry Regiment 9 in November 1925, and from November 1937 he served as a *Leutnant* and Company Commander with Infantry Regiment 106. He went on to serve as a Company Commander with two more regiments and was awarded the Iron Cross 2nd Class in June 1940 with Infantry Regiment 80 in France. From May 1941 he was Commander of II. Battalion of Infantry Regiment 463 and saw action during the opening stages of the invasion of the Soviet Union. (*Deutsches Wehrkundearchiv*)

Knight's Cross: Awarded on 2 October 1941 as *Hauptmann* and Commander of II. Battalion of Infantry Regiment 463 while attached to the 263rd Infantry Division for actions on the Russian Front. Between 17 and 18 August 1941 he saw action near the Yelyna Salient, facing a strong Soviet force that attempted to push back the Germans. During October he took part in the offensive fighting near Moscow, where he demonstrated his leadership and bravery as a young battalion commander in the battles of Bialystok, Smolensk and Vyazma. Together with the rest of the division, his command suffered heavy losses during the winter offensive of 1942–43 and during this time he was promoted to *Major*. On 1 July 1943 he was named as Commander of Infantry Regiment 195 part of the 78th Infantry Division and he took part in the Battle of Kursk.

Knight's Cross with Oakleaves: He became the 374th recipient on 24 January 1944 as *Oberstleutnant* and Commander of Grenadier Regiment 195, part of the 78th Infantry Division, during tough defensive battles by the Soviet Army between Vitebsk and Newel. His role in saving the division was rewarded with the Oakleaves and they were personally presented to him by Hitler at his headquarters in Rastenburg on 30 January 1944. Koetz was promoted to *Oberst* on 1 June and continued to command his regiment until the end of August, when on 1 September he was named as leader of the 349th *Volksgrenadier* Division. It had been reformed from the 349th Infantry Division and absorbed the 567th *Volksgrenadier* Division, first seeing action in East Prussia. Koetz took over command officially from 1 December 1944, when he was promoted to the rank of *Generalmajor*. On 4 April he transferred and was appointed Commander of the 21st Infantry Division in East Prussia, but two weeks later he was taken ill and left the front. In July he was taken prisoner by British troops and after interrogation was imprisoned until his release two years later.

Helmuth Kurt Karl SCHLÖMER

Generalleutnant

* 30 May 1893, Hausberge, Minden
+ 18 August 1995, Minden-Lübbecke

Helmuth Schlömer entered the Army as a *Fahnenjunker* in March 1913 and was commissioned as a *Leutnant* in June 1914. From May 1916 he served as a battalion adjutant and in September the following year he was promoted to *Oberleutnant*, ending the war as regimental adjutant. He remained in the Army after the war and by January 1935 was serving as an instructor at the War School in Munich with the rank of *Major*. In October 1936 he was promoted to *Oberstleutnant* and was serving as a Battalion Commander with Infantry Regiment 25 in Stettin, being promoted to *Oberst* in June 1939. In August he was appointed Commander of Infantry Regiment 5 and saw action in Poland, where he was awarded the Bar to the Iron Cross 1st and 2nd Classes. (*Deutsches Wehrkundearchiv*)

Knight's Cross: Awarded on 2 October 1941 as *Oberst* and Commander of Rifle Regiment 5 while attached to Rifle Brigade 12 for his leadership during the invasion of the Soviet Union and in particular for his part in the push to cut off the land connection to Leningrad. His troops played a major role in the final push through the heavily fortified and swampy ground towards the approach to the city. He later took command of the 7th Rifle Brigade while attached to the 7th Panzer Division and saw action in the battles in the Minsk Pocket. From April 1942 he was attached to the 3rd Infantry Division and was promoted to *Generalmajor* on the 20th. Nine days later he took command of the 3rd Motorised Infantry Division and continued to see action on the Russian Front.

Knight's Cross with Oakleaves: Awarded on 23 December 1942, to become the 161st recipient, as *Generalmajor* and Commander of 3rd Motorised Infantry Division as part of the XIV. Panzer Corps, while serving in the Soviet Union.

Primarily it was for his leadership at the Voronezh Bridgehead, where he led several counter-attacks and on the Don bend and during the defensive battles on the northern edge of the German lines at Stalingrad. From 18 January 1943 he was at the same time given leadership of the XIV. Panzer Corps and three days later he was promoted to the rank of *Generalleutnant*. On 29 January 1943 Schlömer was taken prisoner by the Soviets at Stalingrad and was not released until 24 October 1949.

Horst von WOLFF

Generalmajor

* 26 July 1886, Rosenberg, Silesia
+ 10 October 1941, near Voronki, Ukraine

Horst von Wolff joined the Army in February 1905 and was commissioned as a *Leutnant* the following year. He attended Potsdam Officer School from October 1910 until July 1913 and served during the First World War as a battalion adjutant until July 1916, during that time being promoted to *Hauptmann*. He then served as a Battalion Commander with the Reserve Infantry Regiment 109 and was awarded the Pour le Mérite on 28 November 1917. In February 1918 he transferred to the General Staff of the 220th Infantry Division and shortly after the end of the war he was discharged from the Army. He re-entered in August 1939 with the rank of *Oberstleutnant* and was attached to Infantry Regiment 94. Just four weeks later he was promoted to *Oberst* and from February 1941 he was Commander of Infantry Regiment 478. (*Deutsches Wehrkundearchiv*)

Knight's Cross: Awarded on 10 October 1941 as *Oberst* and Commander of Infantry Regiment 478 as part of the 258th Infantry Division for actions in the Soviet Union. On 30 September 1941 the 258th Infantry Division was ordered to send mobile reserves to the railway station at Dubrovka, which were sent under the command of Wolff. Once his group had arrived they were ordered to eliminate a Soviet penetration by attacking the northern flank and they pushed it back. Wolff began the thrust towards the Soviets and continued the assault the following day. The attack was a success and more than 800 prisoners were captured, as were twenty-one machine guns and mortars. The swift action by Wolff surprised the Soviets and prevented them from continuing their advance. On the day the Knight's Cross was agreed, the 10 October, Wolff was killed in action near Voronki in the Ukraine, and he was posthumously promoted to *Generalmajor*.

Curt Rudolf Theodor BADINSKI

Generalleutnant

* 17 May 1890, Grebenstein, Hofgeismar in Northern Hesse
+ 27 February 1966, Oldenburg, Lower Saxony

Knight's Cross: Awarded on 11 October 1941 as *Oberst* and Commander of Infantry Regiment 489 while attached to the 269th Infantry Division in recognition of his leadership during his regiment's advance through to the southern edge of Krasnogvardeysky on 9 September. His command was able to hold off several strong enemy attacks, carried out with the support of panzers, and he held this position. In February 1942, with six years' experience as a regimental commander, newly promoted *Generalmajor* Badinski was chosen to command the remnants of the 23rd Infantry Division, which was down to only 1,000 men. He led this division until 10 July, when he became ill, returning to duty in September. He then saw action in Bergen, Norway, as Commander of the 269th Infantry Division, and later became Territorial Section Commander in Bergen. In December he took over as Commander of the 276th Infantry Division in Germany. From January 1944 he saw action in Dax, France, and from mid-June took part in the heavy fighting around Normandy. His division became trapped in the Falaise Pocket on 20 August and was virtually destroyed. A small part did manage to break out but Badinski was taken prisoner by Allied troops the following day. He was at first taken to Prison Camp 2226 in Zedelgem in Belgium, and from 24 September 1944, he was kept at Camp Clinton, Mississippi, in the United States, where he remained until his release on 21 June 1947.

Curt Badinksi is seen here with Georg Lindemann, left. At the beginning of the Second World War Badinski took over as Commander of the 489th Infantry Regiment, with the rank of *Oberst*, leading it successfully during the Battle of France from May 1940. During 10–11 May Badinski led his regiment across the Meuse River and the Albert Canal at Ében-Émael, Belgium, and took Liège. During the second part of the campaign his regiment, together with the division, marched past Reims to the Dijon area and on to Lyon. (*Author's Collection*)

August Wilhelm Emil Hans BEHLENDORFF

General der Artillerie

* 13 August 1889, Allenstein, East Prussia
+ 16 March 1961, Baden-Baden in Baden-Württemberg

Knight's Cross: Awarded on 11 October 1941 as *Generalleutnant* and Commander of the 34th Infantry Division, part of the XII. Army Corps, for his part in successful breakthrough of the enemy south of Brest-Litovsk. The successful attack was mainly due to his efforts and leadership and the bridge over the River Muchawiez was captured undamaged and later used as a crossing point for the XXIV. Panzer Corps. His division fought as part of Army Group Centre and saw heavy action in Minsk and Smolensk. Behlendorff led his troops during the early part of the Battle of Moscow, and was promoted to *General der Artillerie* on 17 December 1941. In May 1942, now back in France, Behlendorff became the first Commanding General of the newly formed LXXXIV. Army Corps.

Hans Behlendorff entered the Army with Field Artillery Regiment 3 in September 1908, and was Commissioned as a *Leutnant* two years later. He saw action during the First World War as a Battery Commander, winning both classes of the Iron Cross. Promoted to *Oberleutnant* in February 1915, he was wounded in July 1916. From March 1917 he was adjutant with Special Purpose General Command 51 and was promoted to *Hauptmann* two months later. In October 1920 he joined the *Reichswehr* and was assigned to Artillery Regiment 3. From May 1928 he was with the staff of the IV. Battalion, with the same regiment. (*Deutsches Wehrkundearchiv*)

He took over the coastal protection of Normandy and had his headquarters in Saint-Lô, north-western France, covering the Orne Estuary and around the Channel Islands. In April 1943 he was transferred to the Reich War Courts but the command did not become effective as he went into the Reserves and retired on 31 December 1944.

Erhard Franz Josef RAUS

Generaloberst

* 8 January 1889, Wolramitz, Znaim, Austro-Hungary
+ 3 April 1956, Bad Gastein, Salzburg Austria

Erhard Raus served at the Cadet School in Königsfeld from 1905 and joined the Royal Silesian Infantry Regiment 'Kaiser' 1 in August 1909. He was commissioned as a *Leutnant* in May 1912 and was serving as Platoon Commander in Bicycle *Jäger* Battalion Nr. 1 at the start of the First World War. He was promoted to *Oberleutnant* in January 1915 and served as Company Leader with the Bicycle Company of *Feldjäger* Battalion 20 until the end of the war. He stayed with the Army after the war and served as a tactics instructor, and from September 1934 as Commander of the Infantry School with the rank of *Oberstleutnant*. In March 1938 he was promoted to *Oberst* and transferred from the Austrian Army into the German *Wehrmacht* with Infantry Regiment 50. At the beginning of the Second World War Raus was Chief of the General Staff of Military District Command XVII in Vienna, seeing action in the Soviet Union from June 1941 as Commander of the 6th Rifle Brigade. (*Author's Collection*)

Knight's Cross: Awarded on 11 October 1941 as *Oberst* and Commander of 6th Rifle Brigade while attached to 6th Panzer Division for his leadership during the advance on Leningrad during the summer of 1941. In a daring thrust on 13 and 14 July his battalion seized two undamaged bridges over the Plyussa and Luga Rivers and created a bridgehead. In capturing these bridges over a wide part of the river, Raus and his troops created a springboard that enabled the XXXXI. Army Corps to renew its drive on Leningrad. Raus helped to close the Vyazma Pocket and was delegated with the leadership of the 6th Panzer Division while *Generalleutnant* Franz Landgraf recovered from an illness. By 26 November he took over as permanent commander when it became apparent that its commander would not be returning. He led the division during the attack on Moscow as part of the V. Army Corps and from 25 December 1942 until 18 January 1943, and was in command during the attack on Bystraya in Belarus. This was followed by the defensive battle in the Donets region and from 5 to 31 January 1943 and he took part in the recapture of Kharkov. Promoted to *Generalleutnant* on 21 January, he took command of General Command *Raus* from February, part of Army Group B in Kharkov, and in April he was promoted to *General der Panzertruppe*.

Knight's Cross with Oakleaves: He became the 280th recipient on 22 August 1943 as *General der Panzertruppe* and Commanding General of the XI. Army Corps while attached to Army Detachment *Kempf* for actions during the fighting around Belgorod and Kharkov, preventing an enemy breakthrough. He was personally presented with the Oakleaves by Hitler at the headquarters in Vinnitsa, Ukraine, on or about 27 August. In November 1943 he was appointed Commanding General of the XXXXVII. Panzer Corps and as part of Manstein's 4th Panzer Army took part in the counter-attack near Kiev, where they were successful until the weather broke. From early December he was given leadership of the 4th Panzer Army, which became permanent from March 1944, and he continued to see action on the Eastern Front. From May he took over as Commander-in-Chief of the 1st Panzer Army as part of Army Group South, and in July his command became known as Army Group *Raus*. At that time the 1st Hungarian Army was placed under his command, and later he took command of the 3rd Panzer Army. On 20 September he was promoted to *Generaloberst* and saw heavy fighting north of Memel from October 1944, taking up a defensive position in East Prussia. From February 1945 he commanded eight divisions but had fewer than seventy tanks and held a 150-mile front on the Oder River, 40 miles from Berlin. In March 1945 he was summoned to see Hitler in his Bunker in Berlin and updated his Führer on the position. Although Ruas gave an excellent account of himself, Hitler took an instant dislike to him and he was sacked and replaced by *General der Panzertuppe* Hasso von Manteuffel. On 14 May Raus was captured by the Western Allies and taken prisoner, remaining in custody until his release in June 1947.

Rudolf Otto Hans Freiherr von WALDENFELS

Generalleutnant

* 23 September 1895, Ingolstadt
+ 14 August 1969, Rottach-Egern

Rudolf von Waldenfels entered the Army as a *Fahnenjunker* in August 1914 and after his training was assigned to the 6th Regiment of the Bavarian Army. He was commissioned as a *Leutnant* in July 1915 and served on many fronts. He was a Company Leader during the last months of the war and was awarded the Iron Cross 1st and 2nd Classes. He remained in the Army after the war and joined the cavalry. By November 1935 had been promoted to *Major* and was head of training at the Cavalry School in Ansbach. Promoted to *Oberstleutnant* in October 1938, he served as Commander of Reconnaissance Battalion 10 of the 10th Infantry Division during the Polish campaign. (*Deutsches Wehrkundearchiv*)

Knight's Cross: Awarded on 11 October 1941 as *Oberstleutnant* and Commander of Rifle Regiment 4 while attached to the 6th Panzer Division for his action on the Russian Front. On 8 August 1941 he led his unit during a breakthrough against tough enemy positions north of Leningrad, where Waldenfels and his men fought with great courage. During another attack on 13 August he and his men stormed through minefields and bunkers to capture Soviet trenches, and they were able to secure the area after six days of fighting. Promoted to *Oberst* near the end of 1941, Waldenfels took command of the 6th Rifle Brigade, part of the 6th Panzer Division now resting and refitting in France from April 1942. From November he was Commander of the Battalion Leaders School in Paris and on 22 August 1943 he took command of the 6th Panzer Division. He later fought at Kursk, Kharkov and in northern Ukraine, and was promoted to *Generalmajor* in November. By early 1944 the division had destroyed more than 1,500 Soviet tanks.

Knight's Cross with Oakleaves: He became the 476th recipient on 14 May 1944 as *Generalmajor* and Commander of 6th Panzer Division while attached to the 1st Panzer Army for the role his division played while trapped in the Kamianets–Podilskyi Pocket. Waldenfels flew to Hitler's Mountain Retreat at the Berghof on 31 May 1944, where he was personally presented with the Oakleaves and the following day was promoted to *Generalleutnant*. A few days later the 6th Panzer Division was transferred to Germany for rest and refitting, and from July he was back at the front with the division and took part in the attack on Vilnius to free a trapped German unit. In late 1944 his division was deployed to Poland and later saw action in Hungary, where he took part in the withdrawal to the Danube and towards Vienna. After weeks of heavy fighting his division surrendered to US troops on the southern sector of the Eastern Front and were handed over to the Soviets in May 1945. Waldenfels, like many officers, spent years in tough Soviet prison camps until his release in 1955.

Johannes Wilhelm BOHNSTEDT

Generalleutnant

* 5 October 1888, Schmarsow, Brandenburg
+ 11 August 1947, Hameln, Lower Saxony

Wilhelm Bohnstedt entered the Army in March 1909 with Infantry Regiment 52 and was wounded during the opening stages of the First World War as a young *Leutnant*. He was awarded the Iron Cross 2nd Class in October 1914 and received the Iron Cross 1st Class in August 1916, now with the rank of *Oberleutnant*. He now was serving with the Reserve Infantry Regiment and ended the war as *Hauptmann* and Commander of Reserve Infantry Regiment 271. He remained in the Army after the war and served as Commander of Infantry Regiment 51 during the invasion of Poland, where he was awarded both the Bar to the Iron Cross 1st and 2nd Classes. (*Deutsches Wehrkundearchiv*)

Knight's Cross: Awarded on 13 October 1941 as *Generalmajor* and Commander of the 32nd Infantry Division while attached to the II. Army Corps during an operation in the Soviet Union. At the end of July 1941 Bohnstedt was given orders to advance along the Cholm–Loknya Road, a swampy area west of Cholm, and capture the city. The enemy were tough and

Bohnstedt decided to shift the main effort of his division to the east bank of the River Lowyat. On 2 August his troops brought about the fall of the city. Bohnstedt commanded the 32nd Infantry Division until January 1942, when he was taken ill and entered the Reserves. He was promoted to *Generalleutnant* on 1 April 1942 and in May was appointed Inspector of Infantry until February 1945, when he was transferred as Military Replacement Inspector in Hannover. In April of that year he retired from active service and was captured by the Allies at the end of the war. He died in captivity in August 1947.

Sigfrid Karl HENRICI

General der Panzertruppe

* 10 May 1889, Soest in North Rhine-Westphalen
+ 8 November 1964, Bad Nauheim, Hesse

Sigfrid Henrici entered the Army in September 1907 as a *Fahnenjunker* with Field Artillery Regiment 11 and attended the War School in Metz. He was commissioned as a *Leutnant* in January 1909 and by the beginning of the First World War he was serving as adjutant of the Mounted Battalion of his regiment with the rank of *Oberleutnant*. In May 1918 he was Chief of Operations on the Staff of the Commander of Flying with the 18th Army and was promoted to *Hauptmann* in August that year. He retired from the Army in January 1920 and joined the police, rising to the rank of *Polizei-Oberst* in January 1935, while serving as Chief of the State Police with the Reich Ministry of Interior. In October he transferred into the Army with the rank of *Oberst* and joined the artillery, and during the invasion of Poland he served as Commander of Artillery Command 30. He was awarded the Bar to the Iron Cross 2nd Class on 20 September 1939, and the Bar to the Iron Cross 1st Class on 20 May 1940 during the invasion of France. (*Deutsches Wehrkundearchiv*)

Knight's Cross: Awarded on 13 October 1941 as *Generalleutnant* and Commander of the 16th Motorised Infantry Division while attached to the XXXXVIII. Panzer Corps for his distinguished leadership on the Russian Front.

He led troops during the seizure of a bridgehead over the Popovka River on 28 July 1941 and during the attack against Soviet forces south of Talnoje in the Ukraine, where his men contributed in halting the Soviet advances. From early December 1941 his division ceased its attack and held its position east of Kursk until May 1942, when it was relieved and refreshed. From July Henrici's division began to advance towards the Caucasus region and from August was ordered to advance towards the east, where it was later surrounded by Soviet forces but managed to breakout. In January 1943 Henrici was promoted to *General der Panzertruppe* and later part of his command was sent to relieve the troops at Stalingrad.

Knight's Cross with Oakleaves: Awarded on 9 December 1943 to become the 350th recipient as *General der Panzertruppe* and as Commanding General of the XXXX. Panzer Corps while attached to the 1st Panzer Army for his outstanding leadership during the defensive battle at Zaporozhye. The Oakleaves were personally presented by Hitler in December 1943 at his headquarters in Rastenburg. On 12 November he was delegated with the leadership of the 4th Panzer Army but fell ill just ten days later and was relieved of his command. He did not return to duty until 20 March 1944, when he was made commander of all troops in the Crimea and at the same time he was delegated with the temporary leadership of the 6th Army, which had been reformed after the defeat at Stalingrad. On 8 June he became seriously ill again and was admitted to Marienbad Hospital, where he stayed until early September. He was then appointed Commanding General of the XXXX. Panzer Corps in East Prussia and by early 1945 he was retreating towards Lower Silesia. On 9 May he surrendered to Soviet forces in Central Silesia and remained in captivity until his release on 6 October 1955.

Walter HEROLD

Generalmajor

* 18 August 1897, Weiden, Bavaria
+ 28 November 1944 near Bochnia, Silesia, Poland

Knight's Cross: Awarded on 13 October 1941 as *Oberstleutnant* and Commander of Motorised Artillery Regiment 10, part of the 10th Motorised Infantry Division, for his role in the support of his division during the defence of Propoisk in Minsk between 19 and 25 July 1941. Although the German defenders had been pushed to breaking point, they ultimately managed to

Walter Herold entered Army service in February 1915 as a war volunteer with Bavarian Artillery Regiment 8 and saw action on the Western Front. He was commissioned as a *Leutnant* in May 1917 and served with the artillery throughout the war, being awarded the Iron Cross 2nd Class. He remained in the Army after the war, attended various training courses and was promoted to *Oberleutnant* in April 1925. From 1929 he served as battalion adjutant with Artillery Regiment 7, and from October 1930 he served as regimental adjutant. In April 1932 he was promoted to *Hauptmann* and from October 1935 he served as Commander of the II. Battalion of Artillery Regiment 46. In April 1936 he was promoted to *Major* and in August 1939 he was made an *Oberstleutnant* and was serving as a Course Director at the Artillery School. In May 1940 he was appointed Commander of Artillery Regiment 10 and saw action during the invasion of France. (*Deutsches Wehrkundearchiv*)

push back the Soviet breakthrough, thanks to the support and leadership of Herold. Promoted to *Oberst* in October, he was transferred to Artillery School I in Berlin as an instructor in January 1942 and from April he was appointed Commander of Instruction Staff A at the Artillery School in Jüterbog. From February 1944 he was attached to the 2nd Panzer Division and on 7 May he took over as Commander of Motorised Grenadier Regiment 20, part of the 10th *Panzer* Grenadier Division. He took part in heavy fighting at Jassy in August 1944, when the division was almost destroyed, and the remnants marched to the Danube east of Oltenița in Romania. On 30 September Herold was given the leadership of the 10th Panzer Grenadier Division, which was reorganised and from mid-November had moved to south-west Poland for training. On 28 November during a routine patrol near Bochina in Poland, Herold was killed by partisans and was posthumously promoted to *Generalmajor*.

Ulrich KLEEMANN

General der Panzertruppe

* 23 March 1892, Bad Langensalza
\+ 1 January 1963, Oberursel

Knight's Cross: Awarded on 13 October 1941 as *Oberst* and Commander of 3rd Rifle Brigade while attached to the 3rd Panzer Division for actions during the invasion of the Soviet Union. His command pushed south of Smolensk and was able to cross various rivers, taking part in the Battle of Kiev, where his unit played

Ulrich Kleemann entered Army service in October 1911 as a *Fahnenjunker* with Dragoon Regiment 21 and was later attached to the Officer Riding School in Paderborn, where he was commissioned as a *Leutnant*. He saw action during the First World War with his regiment, was wounded in May 1915 and promoted to *Oberleutnant* in June 1916. He was awarded both classes of the Iron Cross during the war and remained in the Army after it. He attended cavalry school from January 1920 and transferred into Mounted Regiment 18, being promoted to *Rittmeister* in October 1923. He attended various courses over the next few years and was promoted to *Major* in August 1933. Three years later he was serving as Commander of Motorcycle Infantry Regiment 15 with the rank of *Oberstleutnant*. During the invasion of Poland he served as *Oberst* and Commander of Rifle Regiment 3. (*Deutsches Wehrkundearchiv*)

a major role in sealing off the pocket near Lokhvytsia. Kleemann was promoted to *Generalmajor* in November 1941 but was later wounded and became ill, giving up his command for several months. On 10 April 1942 he returned to combat in North Africa as Commander of the 90th Light *Afrika* Division and led his division during some of the worst fighting of the campaign, which included the capture of Tobruk and the invasion of Egypt. In September he was seriously wounded while leading an attack against British forces west of Alam Halfa Ridge. Kleemann remained in hospital until May 1943, when he assumed command of Assault Division *Rhodes* and on 10 June he was promoted to *Generalleutnant*.

Knight's Cross with Oakleaves: He became the 304th recipient on 16 September 1943 as *Generalleutnant* and Commander of Assault Division *Rhodes* and was awarded for actions in the area around the Aegean Sea near the southern Balkans. When Italy changed sides after the fall of Mussolini, Kleemann was given the task of disarming the remaining Italian forces in the Eastern Mediterranean area. He attacked the enemy forces with great skill, even though he was outnumbered by the Italians by a factor of 8 to 1. He was presented with the Oakleaves personally by Hitler at his headquarters the Wolf's Lair in Rastenburg in October 1943. Kleemann was appointed Commanding General of the LXXXXI. Army Corps on 18 September 1944, and was responsible for the forces in the Salonika area of Greece. Then on 11 October he took over as Commanding General of the IV. Panzer Corps and nine days later was promoted to the rank of *General der Panzertruppe*. From November his command was redesignated Panzer Corps *Feldherrnhalle* and he commanded this unit until the end of the war, seeing action during the fighting in Slovakia and Upper Austria. He surrendered to British troops on 8 May 1945 in Austria and remained in captivity until June 1947.

Friedrich 'Fritz' Wilhelm KOCH

General der Infanterie z. V.

* 15 January 1879, Odenkirchen, Rhine Province
+ 3 November 1961, Bonn

Friedrich Koch entered the infantry in September 1897 and was commissioned as a *Leutnant* two years later, serving as regimental adjutant of Infantry Regiment 15. Promoted to *Oberleutnant* in August 1909, he served on the General Staff at the start of the First World War with the rank of *Hauptmann*. He stayed in the Army after the war and from October 1919 he served with the Reich defence Ministry in Berlin with the rank of *Major*. From 1926 he served on the Staff of the 2nd Division as an *Oberstleutnant*. He retired from Army service in November 1931 and entered a veterans association. In 1936 he transferred into the SS, and from April 1937 he served as SS-Leader on the Staff of SS Upper Section West with the rank of *SS-Standartenführer*. When the Second World War began he became Commander of the 254th Infantry Division and was awarded both classes of the Bar to the Iron Cross during the Western campaign. (*Author's Collection*)

Knight's Cross: Awarded on 13 October 1941 as *General der Infanterie z. V.* and Commanding General of the XXXXIV. Army Corps while attached to the 17th Army for actions during the Battle of Uman on the Russian Front. His corps then advanced to the Dnieper area near Cherkassy and was later involved in the Battle of Kiev. It later took part in the advance on Kharkov, reaching the Donets at the end of October. From 11 November 1941 he was in the Reserves and he finally retired from Army Service on 31 May 1942, but remained a member of the SS. He was promoted to *SS-Brigadeführer* in November 1942 and from January 1943 he served in the ranks of *SS-Oberabschnitt* West with the rank of *SS-Gruppenführer* until the end of the war.

Karl Heinrich Georg Ferdinand KREIPE

Generalmajor

* 5 June 1895, Niederspeir, Sonderhausen
+ 14 June 1976, Northeim, Thüringen

Knight's Cross: Awarded on 13 October 1941 as *Oberstleutnant* and Commander of Infantry Regiment 209 while attached to the 58th Infantry Division in

Heinrich Kreipe was a war volunteer in August 1914, joined Field Artillery Regiment 52 and was commissioned as a *Leutnant* in December 1915. He was awarded the Iron Cross 1st and 2nd Classes during the war and he stayed in the *Reichswehr* after it and was promoted to *Oberleutnant* in April 1925. He served with Infantry Regiment 11 and from 1928 he was attached to Infantry Regiment 15 as a Company Leader. He was promoted to *Hauptmann* in February 1930 and from October 1935 served as a tactics instructor at the War School in Hannover, being promoted to *Major* in November 1935. At the beginning of the Second World War in September 1939 Kreipe was an *Oberstleutnant* and Commander of Infantry Regiment 209 and he saw action in France. (*Deutsches Wehrkundearchiv*)

recognition of his leadership and bravery during the drive towards Leningrad. The Knight's Cross was presented to Kreipe by the Commanding General of the XXXVIII. Army Corps, *General der Infanterie* Friedrich-Wilhelm von Chappius. Kreipe remained in Leningrad until May 1942, when he transferred back to Germany and took up some teaching and administration posts. He returned to the Eastern Front in June 1943 as Leader of the 70th Infantry Division in the North Caucasus area of southern Russia and on 1 September he was promoted to *Generalmajor.* In February 1944 he took over command of the 22nd Air Landing Infantry Division, operating on Crete. On the night of 26 April he left his headquarters in Archanes and as usual he was driven to his well-guarded residence. He was met by two German military policemen, who were in fact SOE agents from Britain, Major Leigh Fermor and Captain Bill Moss. They asked for his papers and jumped into the car and threatened the general with a pistol. Moss then drove the car for an hour and half through twenty-two controlled road blocks in Heraklion. They abandoned the car and set off on a cross-country march, supported by Greek resistance, and were soon being hunted by German patrols. However, they crossed the mountains and reached the southern side of the island. Eventually, on 14 May they were picked up from a beach near Rodakino and taken to Egypt. *Generalmajor* Kreipe was interrogated and sent to a POW camp in Canada. He was later transferred to a camp in Wales, being released in October 1947.

Wilhelm THOMAS

Generalleutnant

* 8 October 1892, Minden, Germany
+ 24 August 1976, Hameln, Lower Saxony

Knight's Cross: Awarded on 13 October 1941 as *Oberst* and Commander of Motorised Infantry Regiment 71 while attached to the 29th Motorised Infantry Division for actions during the Bialystok and Minsk encirclements in the early months of the invasion of the Soviet Union. From mid-September 1941 Thomas was in the Reserves and in February 1942 was appointed Commander of the Officer Candidates at the Dresden Military School. Promoted to *Generalmajor* in May 1942, he served as Commander of the 321st Infantry Division and saw heavy action in the Soviet Union from November. Thomas was promoted to *Generalleutnant* in July 1943 and from March 1944 was attached to *Wehrmacht* Commander Bohemia and Moravia (Czechoslovakia). From April he commanded Special Division Nr. 539 in Prague, which consisted of local defence units with replacement and training battalions. On 18 November he took command of the 203rd Infantry Division, a unit that had been redesignated from a security division to an Infantry Division, which he organised. On 26 December he transferred as Commander of the 286th Infantry Division, which had also gone through the reorganisation from a security division. He was in hospital from 26 January 1945 and was then attached to the Inspector of Recruitment Office in Hannover from March, later becoming the Inspector of the Recruitment Office. He went into Allied captivity from 23 June 1945 and was released two years later.

Gottfried Ludwig WEBER

Generalleutnant

* 31 January 1899, Breslau, Silesia
+ 16 August 1958, Villach, Carinthia, Austria

Knight's Cross: Awarded on 13 October 1941 as *Major* and Commander of I. Battalion of Infantry Regiment 162 while attached to the XXXXII. Army Corps for actions on the Russian Front. On 2 August 1941 his regiment was advancing along the Järva Road when he got a report of a Soviet regiment advancing on them from the south. Weber immediately took a battalion and swiftly plunged into the middle of the Soviet troops. They were able to kill

Gottfried Weber entered the Army as a *Fahnenjunker* in June 1917, served during the First World War and was commissioned as a *Leutnant* in May 1918. He left the Army after the war and rejoined as a *Hauptmann* in October 1934 as Commander of the 2nd Company of Infantry Regiment 23 in Rastenburg. He stayed with Infantry Regiment 23 until August 1939, when he transferred to Infantry Regiment 162 as a Battalion Commander. He saw action during the invasion of Poland, where he was awarded the Iron Cross 1st and 2nd Classes. (*Deutsches Wehrkundearchiv*)

most of them and so the rear area and flanks of the German divisions were cleared. On 17 October he was decorated with the Knight's Cross by his divisional commander, *Generalleutnant* Siegfried Haenicke during a ceremony on the field. From January he saw action in Volkhov near Leningrad and was promoted to *Oberstleutnant* in February, continuing to take part in defensive fighting around Lake Ladoga and Lake Ilmen. On 20 April he was appointed Commander of Infantry Regiment 176 and took part in the fighting on the northern sector of the Eastern Front, where he was also given temporary command of three different infantry divisions between March and June 1943. During this time he was promoted to *Oberst* and from 15 November he took command of the 12th *Luftwaffe* Field Division. In February 1944 he was promoted to *Generalmajor*.

Knight's Cross with Oakleaves: He became the 490th recipient on 9 June 1944 as *Generalmajor* and Commander of 12th *Luftwaffe* Field Division while attached to the 18th Army for his part in halting the Soviet advance near Pskov in the spring of 1944. He was decorated with the Oakleaves on 20 June personally by Hitler during a ceremony at the Berghof on the Obersalzburg. Weber was promoted to *Generalleutnant* in August 1944 and from April 1945 was given the leadership of the XVI. Army Corps in the Courland. He was captured by the Soviets at the end of the war and was not released from captivity until October 1955. When he returned to Germany he served with the *Bundeswehr*, rising to the rank of *Generalmajor* and ending his career as Inspector of Infantry.

Ernst Friedrich DEHNER

General der Infanterie

* 5 March 1889, Hersbruck, Middle Franconia, Bavaria
+ 13 September 1970, Wiesbaden, Hesse

Ernst Dehner entered Army service in October 1908 as a volunteer and after attending War School in Munich he joined Bavarian Infantry Regiment 14 as a *Leutnant*. He was wounded in September 1914 and awarded both classes of the Iron Cross. From August 1916 he was in French captivity as a prisoner of war. He remained in the Army after the war and served in various regiments, holding the rank of *Major* in February 1931. At the outbreak of war he was serving as Commander of Infantry Regiment 87 and was awarded both classes of the Bar to the Iron Cross while serving in Poland. (*Deutsches Wehrkundearchiv*)

Knight's Cross: Awarded on 18 October 1941 as *Generalmajor* and Commander of the 106th Infantry Division while attached to the V. Army Corps and during August and the beginning of September 1941 his division repelled numerous Soviet armoured attacks. On one occasion during this time Dehner managed to reach a command post of a particularly threatened regiment, and from there he oversaw various countermeasures against the attacks. He personally dispatched anti-aircraft and heavy Panzers against enemy tanks and sealed off the existing front-line gap through his counter-attacks, which prevented a Soviet breakthrough. On 13 October Dehner received word that he was to be awarded the Knight's Cross for his tireless actions in leading his division. From May 1942 he led his division in northern France and in October Dehner was promoted to *Generalleutnant*. The following month he took command of the LXXXII. Army Corps in France, where it was used for coastal protection at the Pas-de-Calais. He was promoted to *General der Infanterie* in December 1942, and from July 1943 he was Commanding General of the LXIX. Army Corps. In January 1944 the corps was used against partisans. In August he was attached to the Military Commander in France and appointed Commander of Army Area South France and General Command Dehner until January 1945. He was then attached to Army Group A for Special Duties but in May he was taken prisoner and remained in Allied captivity until 1947. He was then arrested and tried as part of the 'South-East' Trial and was sentenced to seven years' imprisonment in 1948. However, he was released early from Landsberg Prison in 1951.

Martin Gustav Adolf GRASE

General der Infanterie

* 3 May 1891, Schlochau, Pommerania
+ 4 August 1963, Freiburg im Breisgau, Baden-Württemberg

Martin Grase entered the Army in March 1909 as a cadet, was commissioned as a *Leutnant* in August 1910 and was assigned to Grenadier Regiment 4 in October 1913. He served as a leader with a machine gun company at the beginning of the First World War and was awarded the Iron Cross 2nd Class in September 1914. He was wounded in March 1915 and promoted to *Oberleutnant* in January 1916, being appointed machine gun officer on the staff of Infantry Regiment 374 in September. He was awarded the Iron Cross 1st Class in December 1916 and was serving with the 16th Landwehr Division at the end of the war. (*Author's Collection*)

Knight's Cross: Awarded on 18 October 1941 as *Oberst* and Commander of Infantry Regiment 1, part of the 1st Infantry Division, for holding a key position at Kingisepp near Leningrad in August 1941. His action played a crucial role to ensure contact remained between the 18th Army and the 4th Panzer Group in mid-August, which allowed the latter to continue its advance

Grase remained in the Army after the war and was promoted to *Hauptmann* in May 1922. Shortly after he was appointed Commander of the 15th Company with Infantry Regiment 2. He was promoted to *Major* in 1933 and from October 1935 he served as Commander of the III. Battalion of Infantry Regiment 30 with the rank of *Oberstleutnant*. Promoted to *Oberst* in February 1938, he was serving as adjutant with Army Command 16 at the outbreak of the Second World War. He saw action during the invasion of Poland and in France and was awarded the Bar to the Iron Cross 1st and 2nd Classes. (*Author's Collection*)

towards Leningrad. Shortly before Grase was presented with his Knight's Cross he was promoted to *Generalmajor* and in January 1942 he was appointed Commander of the 1st Infantry Division. Later that year the commander of the 18th Army, *Generaloberst* Georg Lindemann, said of Grase that during the fighting in Leningrad, 'his determination in front-line combat was so frequent that he was more of a soldier than a commander'.

Knight's Cross with Oakleaves: He became the 248th recipient on 23 May 1943 as *Generalleutnant* and Commander of the 1st Infantry Division while attached to the XXVI. Army Corps for his demonstration of outstanding devotion to duty as well as first-rate leadership qualities while engaged in heavy fighting with Soviet troops. He held on to an important bridgehead at Luga near Leningrad after days of constant attacks by Soviet troops, and showed great leadership during the Second Battle of Lake Ladoga between January and April 1943. In fact, his division had the distinction of being the only command to hold on to the position it occupied before the battle began. The Oakleaves were presented to Grase by Hitler at his headquarters at the Wolf's Lair in Rastenburg sometime in June or July 1943. From August Grase was delegated with the leadership of the I. Army Corps and with his promotion to *General der Infanterie* in December 1943 his command was confirmed and he later saw action in Nevel in the Soviet Union as part of the 16th Army. From January 1944 he took over as the Commanding General of the XXVI. Army Corps but only briefly as he entered *Führer* Reserve a month later. On 18 July 1944 he was appointed *Wehrmacht* Commander in Belgium and Northern France, and from September he took command of a military police unit *Feldjäger* Corps III. It was formed in Vienna and answered to *Generalfeldmarschall* Wilhelm Keitel, responsible for capturing deserters. Grase surrendered to Allied troops in May 1945 and remained in captivity until 20 July 1947.

Kurt HERZOG

General der Artillerie

* 27 March 1889, Quedlinburg, Harz in the west of Saxony-Anhalt
+ 8 May 1948, Soviet Prison Camp, Vorkuta

Knight's Cross: Awarded on 18 October 1941 as *Generalleutnant* and Commander of the 291st Infantry Division while attached to the XXXVIII. Army Corps for his actions during the initial attack on Leningrad. The division played a key role in the invasion, pushing back the Soviets across the line at Peterhof, which enabled the German heavy artillery to be positioned in range of the Petersburg tank factory and the Kronstadt fortress as well as the Soviet battleships nearby. Herzog was presented with his Knight's Cross by the Commanding General of the XXXVIII. Army Corps, *General der Infanterie* Friedrich-Wilhelm Chappius. He fought during the Battle of Volkhov between January and March 1942 and continued to see action during the Siege of Leningrad as part of the 18th Army. He had proven to be an excellent divisional commander and in recognition of his abilities he was promoted to *General der Artillerie* on 1 September 1942, the same day he was appointed Commander of the XXXVIII. Army Corps. From January 1944 the Leningrad front collapsed as a result of the Soviet winter and Herzog and his Corps had to break away from Volkhov and retreat west. Throughout June and July the Soviet offensive began to advance at a quicker pace and by mid-July they had broken through the German defences. Herzog had to retreat again to avoid encirclement, and by September and into early October his corps took part in the retreat via Riga to the Courland, where there was heavy fighting. By the beginning of 1945 the fighting had eased and Herzog took some leave on 9 January in order to get his family to safety and out of reach of the advancing Red Army.

Knight's Cross with Oakleaves: He became the 694th recipient on 12 January 1945 as *General der Artillerie* and Commanding General of the XXXVIII. Panzer Corps, part of the 16th Army, for the defensive success of his corps during the Third Battle of Courland. Herzog was presented with the Oakleaves personally by Hitler in the Bunker in Berlin. Herzog returned to his command on 15 March, which soon became isolated on the Eastern Front in Latvia. He had no chance to escape Soviet captivity and he surrendered his Army Corps to the Red Army on 8 May 1945. He spent the remainder of his life in various Soviet prison camps and he died in Camp Vorkuta on 8 May 1948.

Walter KUNTZE

General der Pioniere

* 23 February 1883, Prizerbe, Rathnow
+ 1 April 1960, Detmold

Walter Kuntze entered Army service in March 1902 as a *Fahnenjunker* with Pioneer Battalion 5 and from October 1905 he was attached to the Military Technical Academy in Berlin with the rank of *Leutnant*. He served with the 2nd Field Company of Pioneer Battalion 26 at the beginning of the war with the rank of *Hauptmann* and was severely wounded a few days into the conflict. He served as Chief of Operations on the Staff of the 4th Cavalry Division from May 1917 until the last weeks of the war and remained with the Army when it was over. He was promoted to *Oberstleutnant* in February 1929 and by May 1935 was serving as Leader of the 6th Division with the rank of *Generalmajor*. In August of the following year he was promoted to *Generalleutnant* and was serving as Commanding General of the XXIV. Army Corps during the invasion of Poland. (*Deutsches Wehrkundearchiv*)

Knight's Cross: Awarded on 18 October 1941 as *General der Pioniere* and Commanding General of the XXXXII. Army Corps while attached to the 16th Army for actions in Leningrad on the Soviet Front. From 26 October he took over the leadership of the 12th Army and saw action in the Balkans. At the same time he served as *Wehrmacht* Commander South East. During his time in the Balkans he was responsible for the execution of men and teenage boys in the Kragujevac massacre, when Serbian civilians were murdered in reprisal for an attack on German troops. It was ordered that one hundred Serbs were to be shot for every German soldier killed, and the executions continued well into 1942. A total of 4,750 were shot in Belgrade, 2,300 in Kragujevac and another 1,700 hostages were killed in Kraljevo. From July he transferred into the Reserves and on 15 September 1942 was appointed Head of Training Matters with the

Replacement Army In March 1945 he was appointed Commanding General of the Replacement III Army Corps and Commander in Military District III, Berlin. He surrendered to British troops on 2 May 1945 at Mecklenburg and was handed over to the Americans, who sentenced him to life imprisonment in February 1948 for the crimes committed in the Balkans. However, he was released from Landsberg Prison on 10 February 1953 due to ill health.

Max LEMKE

Generalmajor

* 7 April 1895, Schwedt, Andermünde
\+ 29 May 1985, Hannover

Knight's Cross: Awarded on 18 October 1941 as *Major* and Commander of Reconnaissance Battalion 17, part of the 17th Infantry Division, for his leadership during the thrust towards Moscow at the time of the invasion of the Soviet Union. After the Soviet winter offensive his battalion, as part of the 17th Infantry Division, was sent to France in the summer of 1942 to rest. In September Lemke was promoted to *Oberstleutnant* and towards the end of January 1943 he was named as Commander of the 25th Panzer Grenadier Regiment and saw action once again on the Russian Front as part of the 12th Panzer Division. He was promoted to *Oberst* in September 1943 and continued to see action in Russia in Orel and later in Leningrad and East Prussia. In October 1944 he attended the 15th Divisional Leaders Course in Hirschberg and in January 1945 he was delegated with the leadership of the 7th Panzer Division in Danzig, where it later became trapped as part of Army Group North. On 9 February Lemke was transferred and given leadership of the *Fallschirm*-Panzer Division 1 '*Hermann Göring*'. The division saw fighting in the central sector of the Eastern Front in East Prussia during the Vistula battles and suffered heavy casualties. Lemke was promoted to *Generalmajor* on 20 April 1945 and he managed to escape Soviet capture and surrendered to Western Allies on 12 May, remaining a prisoner until his release five weeks later.

Kurt Wilhelm Gustav Erdmann von der CHEVALLERIE

General der Infanterie

* 23 December 1891, Berlin
+ 18 April 1945, region of Kolberg, Pomerania

Knight's Cross: Awarded on 23 October 1941 as *Generalleutnant* and Commander of the 99th Light Division while attached to the XXIX. Army Corps for his leadership during the decisive assault on Kiev on 17 September 1941. It was Chevallerie's command and leadership and his personal intervention that created the decisive impetus that enabled his division to reach its attack objective. On 15 November 1941 his command was reclassified the 7th Mountain Division and he remained in command during its transition period and entered the Reserves in December 1941. On 1 February 1942 Chevallerie was promoted to *General der Infanterie* and appointed Commanding General of the LIX. Army Corps.

Kurt von der Chevallerie entered Army service in February 1910 with Guards Grenadier Regiment 5 and from October 1914 he was attached to the War School. He served in the infantry at the start of the war, was wounded in July 1915 and was promoted to *Oberleutnant* the following month. Awarded both classes of the Iron Cross, he entered the *Reichswehr* as a *Hauptmann* after the war and served with Infantry Regiment 4 from October 1920. By October 1935 he held the rank of *Oberst* with Infantry Regiment 87 and from December 1939 he was Commander of the 83rd Infantry Division with the rank of *Generalmajor*. (*Author's Collection*)

Knight's Cross with Oakleaves: *General der Infanterie* Chevallerie became the 357th recipient on 19 December 1943 as Commanding General of the LIX. Army Corps while attached to the 4th Panzer Army when he distinguished himself during the fighting around Nizhyn and north of Kiev during September to November. At this time his mission was to tie down enemy forces and prevent any breakthrough of the German front line to buy time for the forces making ready for a counter-attack. The Oakleaves were presented to him by Hitler at his headquarters in Rastenburg on 13 February 1944. In June Chevallerie took command of the 1st Army in France, taking part in the fierce fighting against the Allies in the area around the Atlantic coast. He failed in his mission when he found himself completely outnumbered by a strong Allied force, and then shortly after was placed on the Reserve List by Hitler. In January 1945 he was captured by Soviet troops and disappeared, but later it was revealed that he had been executed.

Karl EGLSEER

General der Gebirgstruppe

* 5 July 1890, Bad Ischl, Gmunden, Austria
+ 23 June 1944, Rettenegg, Austria

Karl Eglseer entered the Austrian Army in August 1908 and saw action during the First World War as part of Infantry Regiment 87 and was wounded twice, ending the war as a *Hauptmann*. He transferred into the military police in November 1918 but later returned to the Army and was promoted to *Major* in 1927. (*Deutsches Wehrkundearchiv*)

Karl Eglseer was from September 1936 Chief of Staff to the 6th Division, and from March 1938 was Commander of the division with the rank of *Oberst*. From October 1940 he commanded the 4th Mountain Division and was awarded the Iron Cross 1st and 2nd Classes on 30 April 1941. (*Author's Collection*)

Knight's Cross: Awarded on 23 October 1941 as *Generalmajor* and Commander of the 4th Mountain Division while attached to the XXXXIX. Army Corps for his leadership during the Battle of Uman in the Ukraine against the Soviet 6th and 12th armies. At the beginning of 1942 he took part in the defensive battles in the Donets Region and later saw action during the Battle of Rostov-Bataysk on the Eastern Front. In early February Eglseer was promoted to *Generalleutnant* and was attached to the Staff of the Chief Training Officer of the High Command of the Army until 20 March. He was then appointed Commander of the 114th Jäger Division and saw action in Croatia. On 10 December he was delegated with the Leadership of XVIII. Mountain Corps and from January 1944 he took part in the offensive to liberate Leningrad as part of the 18th Army, but was pushed back on both sides and failed to advance as much as he wanted. He was promoted to *General der Gebirgstruppe* on 1 March 1944 and was appointed officially as Commanding General of the XVIII. Mountain Corps. On 21 and 22 June Eglseer attended a conference at Hitler's Mountain Retreat on the Obersalzburg, together with *General der Infanterie* Thomas-Emil Wickede, Commanding General of the X. Army Corps; *Generalleutnant* Franz Rossi, Commandant of Fortress Petsamo in Finland; and *Generaloberst* Eduard Dietl, Commander-in-Chief of the 20th Mountain Army. On 23 June they all flew back to Germany on board a Junkers Ju 52 aircraft that crashed near Rettenegg, Austria, and all on board were killed.

Bruno Richard Karl BIELER

General der Infanterie

* 18 June 1888, Gumbinnen, East Prussia
+ 22nd March 1966, Dorfmark, Lower Saxony

Bruno Bieler entered Army service as a *Fähnrich* with Fusilier Regiment 33 in March 1907 He attended the War Academy and was commissioned as a *Leutnant* in August 1908. In December 1916 he transferred to the Staff of XXV. Reserve Corps, and in November 1917 he was promoted to the rank of *Hauptmann* and transferred to the General Staff of Commander-in-Chief East. Bieler remained in the Army after the war and from February 1919 served with the General Staff, later being transferred into the Defence Ministry. From October 1923 he was Company Commander with Infantry Regiment 7, and in April 1927 Bieler transferred into the 3rd Division. He was promoted to *Oberstleutnant* in October 1932, and transferred to Military Region Command in Allenstein the following year. (*Deutsches Wehrkundearchiv*)

Knight's Cross: Awarded on 26 October 1941 as *Generalleutnant* and Commander of the 73rd Infantry Division, part of the LIV. Army Corps, for his bravery and leadership on 12 August during surprise attacks by enemy forces. It was his command post that was in the immediate proximity of enemy forces in the area west of the River Bug, and thanks to his personal leadership on the battlefield the enemy was successfully pushed back two days later. From 30 October he was delegated with the leadership of the XXXXII. Army Corps, seeing action during the conquest of the Crimean Peninsula as part of Army Group South. He took part in the advance to the Kerch Peninsula, was promoted to *General der Infanterie* on 17 December and appointed Commanding General of VI. Army Corps in January 1942. He fought as part of the 9th Army near Rzhev in the Soviet Union, but became ill on 9 April 1942, being admitted to hospital in Bad Nauheim. After his recovery he was appointed Commanding General of LXXXVI. Army Corps, which had been formed in France in November and Bieler was its first commander. The corps was responsible for coastal security in south-west France from Bordeaux to the Spanish border. On 4 February 1943 he was once again taken ill and hospitalised in Baden-Baden and later in Freiburg. He was named as Commander of northern France in May 1943, but was still recovering in hospital and never took up the command. From early August he was attached to the Staff of Replacement General Command XI. Army Corps, and from the 21st he was appointed as commander. However, during this time he was admitted to hospital yet again, being admitted to the Army Reserve Hospital in Bad Pyrmont. In September he was forced to retire at the end of April 1945 due to ill health.

Willi Albin MOSER

General der Artillerie

* 2 November 1887, Breslau
+ 18 October 1946, Soviet Prison Camp near Kaliningrad Oblast

Knight's Cross: Awarded on 26 October 1941 as *Generalleutnant* and Commander of 299th Infantry Division while attached to the XXIX. Army Corps for actions on the Russian Front. From the very beginning of the campaign his division was almost continuously engaged in fighting at Zhitomir and Kiev, in the Donets and at Kursk. Moser was promoted to *General der Artillerie* in December 1942 and took over as Commanding General of the Higher Commando LXXI. in Norway. From 26 January 1943 his command became known as the LXXI. Army Corps and was mainly used as an occupation force and for coastal protection in northern Norway. From February 1945 he was briefly Commander of Military Polcie Corps I and then in April took over as Commander of Corps Group Moser, part of the 4th Army in Silesia, seeing action against the Soviets. On 9 May he surrendered to Soviet troops and was sent to NKVD Camp 27 in Krasnogorsk, where he died of tuberculosis on 16 December 1946. He is buried in the Širokorečenskoje Cemetery in Russia, grave No. 20.

Karl STRECKER

General der Infanterie

* 20 September 1884, Radmannsdorf, West Prussia
+ 10 April 1973, Riezlern, Austria

Knight's Cross: Awarded on 26 October 1941 as *Generalleutnant* and Commander of 79th Infantry Division while attached to the LI. Army, part of the 6th Army, for his part in the Battle of Kiev, where several Soviet armies

Karl Strecker trained as a cadet at Gross-Lichterfeld from 1896 until 1901 and joined the Cadet Corps of the Royal Prussian Army in March 1905 with the rank of *Leutnant*. At the beginning of the First World War he served as adjutant and Legal officer of II. Battalion of 1st Alsatian Germany Order Infantry Regiment No. 152 with the rank of *Oberleutnant*. He was promoted to *Hauptmann* in July 1915 and from May 1917 he was assigned to the General Staff of Railway Transport Battalion West with the 52nd Infantry Division. The photo shows, left to right: Carl Rodenburg, *Generalmajor* Martin Lattmann, Karl Strecker and Werner Sanne. (*Author's Collection*)

were surrounded and destroyed. On 1 April 1942 Strecker was promoted to *General der Infanterie* and appointed Commanding General of the XVII. Army Corps, seeing action in Belgorod. On 1 June he took over command of the XI. Army Corps and during this time it was referred to as Group *Strecker*. After the start of the German summer offensive it fought as part of the 6th Army at the Battle of Stalingrad. From early 1943, together with the VIII. Army Corps Commanded by *Generaloberst* Walter Heitz, it took over the defence of the northern section of the front. However, on 1 February Strecker's corps were virtually annihilated by the Soviets and he was taken prisoner. He was not released until 9 October 1955.

Gottwalt Theodor Walther GRAESSNER

General der Infanterie

* 31 January 1891, Magdeburg, Saxony
\+ 16 July 1943, Field Hospital in Troppau, Silesia

Erwin Osswald is pictured left with Walther Graessner, who entered Army service in March 1909 with Infantry Regiment 98 and was commissioned as a *Leutnant* two years later. He saw action during the First World War and was promoted to *Oberleutnant* in January 1916. He ended the war as a staff officer and remained in the Army. By April 1931 he had risen to the rank of *Major* and was on the Staff of the 1st Division. In October 1935 he was appointed Chief of Operations on the Staff of the 14th Division and was promoted to *Oberst* in January 1936. By October 1939 he had risen to the rank of *Generalmajor* and was appointed Commander of the 298th Infantry Division the following month. (*Author's Collection*)

Knight's Cross: Awarded on 27 October 1941 as *Generalleutnant* and Commander of the 298th Infantry Division while attached to the XVII. Army Corps for actions near Hrubieszów and later in Kiev during the invasion of the Soviet Union. Graessner saw further action near Izium, a city on the Donets River, and in early December 1941 fell ill and was transferred into the Reserves. On 18 February 1942 he was given the leadership of the XII. Army Corps and from June after his promotion to *General der Infanterie* he was named as Commanding General of the XII. Army Corps. He then saw action in the area north-east of Spas-Demensk and then west of Yukhnov. He was wounded in mid-February 1943 and transferred into the Reserves but he died from his wounds in July of that year in a field hospital in Troppau, Silesia.

Heinrich 'Heinz' THOMA

Generalleutnant

* 26 April 1891, Nuremberg
+ 30 October 1948, Prison Camp near Tscherenee, Soviet Union

Heinrich Thoma entered the Army in July 1910 as a *Fahnenjunker* and was commissioned as a *Leutnant* in October the same year, serving as a Battalion Commander during the first two years of the First World War. He was interned in Holland, returned to Germany in September 1919 and stayed in the Army. He was promoted to *Hauptmann* in July 1921. From October 1935 he served as Commander of II. Battalion of Infantry Regiment 19 and in August 1937 he was promoted to *Oberst*. He was appointed Commander of Infantry Regiment 85 in November 1938 and led this unit during the early stages of the invasion of Poland at the start of the Second World War. (*Deutsches Wehrkundearchiv*)

Knight's Cross: Awarded on 27 October 1941 as *Generalmajor* and Commander of Infantry Regiment 519 while attached to the 296th Infantry Division for actions on the Russian Front. His regiment was stationed in France until the spring of 1941 and was then transferred as part of Army Group Centre to the Soviet Union, seeing action during the fighting at Zhitomir, Kiev and Orel, where Thoma was awarded the Knight's Cross. He was transferred to the *Führer* Reserve in September 1941, and from 1 to 9 June 1942 he was briefly appointed Commander of Division 413 in Nuremberg. On 3 August he was appointed Commander of Division Nr. 432 in Kattowitz, Poland, and took command of all replacement units in Silesia. They were engaged in operations against the Soviets from early 1945. Thoma was captured by Soviet troops in May 1945 and he died in a Soviet prison camp near Tscherensee on 30 October 1948. He is buried today in the German War Grave Cemetery Row 5, Grave No. 2, in Cherntsy, Russia.

Wilhelm WEGENER

General der Infanterie

* 29 April 1895, Treebatsch-Beeskow, Brandenburg
+ 24 September 1944, Wolmar an der Düna, Latvia

Wilhelm Wegener was a war volunteer and joined the Army with Grenadier Regiment 9 in September 1914, being commissioned as a *Leutnant* in January 1915. He was awarded the Iron Cross 1st and 2nd Classes early in the war and was captured by British forces in July 1916. He stayed in the Army after the war and served with Infantry Regiment 4 in various companies. He later served as adjutant and was promoted to *Oberleutnant* in July 1925. From August 1931 he served as Company Commander with the rank of *Hauptmann*. From November 1934 he served as adjutant of Infantry Regiment 25 and in November 1939 he was serving in Poland on the Staff of the I. Army Corps with the rank of *Oberstleutnant*. He was awarded the Bar to the Iron Cross 1st and 2nd Classes, and from June 1940 he was serving as Commander of Infantry Regiment 94. (*Deutsches Wehrkundearchiv*)

Knight's Cross: Awarded on 27 October 1941 as *Oberst* and Commander of Infantry Regiment 94 while attached to 32nd Infantry Division for his outstanding combat performance during the Battle of Staraya Russa. On 24 July 1941 three Soviet divisions attacked the German 32nd Infantry Division on the left flank while it was marching and the attackers were largely repelled. However, groups of Soviet soldiers managed to infiltrate between the German columns in order to cause damage and confusion and they were hunted down and killed by Wegener's regiment.

Knight's Cross with Oakleaves: He became the sixty-sixth recipient on 19 January 1942 while still *Oberst* and Commander of Infantry Regiment 94 while attached to 32nd Infantry Division for actions near Demyansk on the Russian Front. In January 1942 the Soviets launched an attack and captured the village of Medyanki held by the Germans, and Wegener's regiment launched a counter-attack and was able to push the Soviets from the town after bitter house-to-house fighting. Wegener was presented with the Oakleaves on 12 May 1942 by Hitler at his Wolf's Lair headquarters. On 1 June he was promoted to *Generalmajor* and took command of the 32nd Infantry Division. He saw action during the battles around Demyansk, where his command was tied down in battle from January 1942 to February 1943. Wegener was promoted to *Generalleutnant* on 1 February and during evacuation from the Demyansk Pocket he took part in the heavy fighting south of Staraya Russa. In September Wegener took over as Leader of the L. Army Corps and saw heavy action in the area around Leningrad. He was officially appointed Commanding General of his Corps on 1 December, when he was promoted to *General der Infanterie.*

Knight's Cross with Oakleaves and Swords: Awarded on 17 September 1944 to become the ninety-seventh recipient as *General der Infanterie* and Commanding General of the L. Army Corps for his excellent leadership during August in holding back Soviet attacks in the Madona area of the Eastern Front. Wegener was never presented with the Swords because while on his way to Corps headquarters near Riga in Latvia on 24 September 1944 he was killed when his staff car was attacked by a Soviet fighter plane.

Karl August GÜMBEL
Generalleutnant

* 24 June 1888, Finstringen, Lorraine
+ 28 October 1970, Heidelberg, Baden-Württemberg

Karl Gümbel entered Army service in October 1907 as a volunteer with Jäger Regiment 8 and attended War School in September 1909. He was a *Leutnant* in June 1910 and was attached to a machine gun detachment at the beginning of the First World War. From February 1916 until November 1917 he served with a sniper unit and was promoted to *Oberleutnant*. He remained in the Army after the war but from 1920 he transferred into the police, rising to the rank of *Polizei-Oberstleutnant* in September 1935. He transferred back into the Army in October that year and was assigned as Battalion Commander with Infantry Regiment 110 with the rank of *Oberst*. At the beginning of the Second World War he was Commander of Infantry Regiment 118 and saw action in Poland. (*Author's Collection*)

Knight's Cross: Awarded on 30 October 1941 as *Oberst* and Commander of Infantry Regiment 516, part of the 295th Infantry Division, for actions during the invasion of the Soviet Union. Gümbel saw action from July in Uman in the Ukraine, later in the Dnieper region and from October in Poltava. From November he saw action in Artemovsk. From early December

1941 he was delegated with the leadership of the 295th Infantry Division and with his promotion to *Generalmajor* in February 1942 his command was made official. In May he briefly commanded the 257th Infantry Division as part of the XXXXIV. Army Corps, and from 5 June he took over as Commander of the 182nd Infantry Division 182. Now serving on the Atlantic coast in the Saint-Nazaire and Lorient area in France, from September he helped to create the newly formed 348th Infantry Division, part of the occupations force in Dieppe and Calais. Gümbel was promoted to *Generalleutnant* in January 1943 and remained on occupation duty in France until February 1944. From March he took over as Commander of Division 152 in Stettin, Germany, and by April most of his command had been incorporated into the 83rd Infantry Division. On 10 May he surrendered and went into Allied captivity, where he remained until his release in July 1947.

Otto-Maximilian HITZFELD

General der Infanterie

* 7 May 1898, Schlugsee-Blasiwald, Baden
\+ 6 December 1990, Dossenheim, Baden-Württemberg

Otto Hitzfeld wearing the Oakleaves. He entered the Army on 18 January 1915 as a war volunteer and from July 1915 he served in the field as an officer candidate. From May 1917 he was adjutant of the III. Battalion of Infantry Regiment 142, and was wounded and hospitalised from May 1918. He remained in the Army after the war and served as an adjutant and later weapons officer. Promoted to *Oberleutnant* in July 1925, he attended various courses and in April 1932 was promoted to *Hauptmann*. He had been transferred into Mounted Regiment 3, then spent almost eighteen months at the Infantry School in Dresden. He was promoted to *Major* in April 1936, and the following year he was appointed Tactics Instructor at the War School in Dresden. (*Author's Collection*)

Knight's Cross: Awarded on 30 October 1941 as *Oberstleutnant* and Commander of Infantry Regiment 213, part of the 73rd Infantry Division, for his leadership during the German breakthrough of the Perekop Isthmus in the Ukraine. During heavy fighting on 24 and 25 September Hitzfeld led his regiment through Soviet defences, which later triggered a general collapse in that area.

Knight's Cross with Oakleaves: He became the sixty-fifth recipient on 17 January 1942 as *Oberstleutnant* and still Commander of Infantry Regiment 213 in recognition of the outstanding performance of his regiment during the massive Soviet assault during the fighting in the Crimea. Hitzfeld was presented with the Oakleaves by Hitler at his headquarters in Rastenburg in March 1942. On 15 August Hitzfeld was wounded and in a Berlin hospital for four days, then returning home to recover. On 20 January 1943 he took over as Leader of the 102nd Infantry Division, seeing action on the Soviet Front in Rzhev. In April he was promoted to *Generalmajor* and his command was confirmed and took part in defensive battles south-west of Orel. He was promoted to *Generalleutnant* on 8 November 1943 and after two weeks on leave he was appointed Commander of the Infantry School in Döberitz on 20 November. On 1 November 1944 he was given temporary command of the LXVII. Army Corps and was based in Belgium as part of the 15th Army. On 1 March 1945 he was promoted to *General der Infanterie* and confirmed as Commanding General of the LXVII. Army Corps in the area near Kassel. At the same time, between 2 to 8 April he was appointed Leader of the 11th Army.

Hitzfeld was promoted to *Oberstleutnant* in August 1939 and made Battalion Commander with Infantry Regiment 158. He was awarded the Bar to the Iron Cross 2nd Class in August 1940 for actions during the French campaign. He is seen here post-war wearing the Knight's Cross with Oakleaves and Swords. This was never made official during the war and was awarded by the Knight's Cross Association quoting the Dönitz Directive, which was not legally valid. (*Author's Collection*)

Knight's Cross with Oakleaves and Swords: Awarded on 9 May 1945 to become the 158th recipient as *General der Infanterie* and Commanding General of the LXVII. Army Corps for his part in the defence of the area around the West Wall. In April he was responsible for establishing a resistance front in the Kassel area and in the southern Harz Mountain area. However, there is no recommendation from the field and no act of bravery had been noted to justify the award of the Swords. It seems that the Award Commission of the Knight's Cross considered the matter in 1981 and approved the award as a result of the 'Dönitz Directive', which is not legally valid. On 1 March 1945 Hitzfeld was promoted to *General der Infanterie* and on 19 April he was captured by US troops and spent just over two years in captivity before being released in May 1947.

Erwin JOLLASSE

Generalleutnant

* 8 December 1892, Hamburg
+ 14 March 1987, Tutzing, Bavaria

Erwin Jollasse entered Army service with Infantry Regiment 68 in October 1911 and was commissioned as a *Leutnant* two years later. He served as a Platoon Leader during the opening stages of the First World War and was wounded in September 1914. He then served as a battalion adjutant and Company Leader and was promoted to *Oberleutnant* in August 1916. He was wounded again in April 1917. The following month he became an instructor with the Flying Observer School West and ended the war as an orderly officer with the General Command of VI. Army Corps. He left the Army after the war and returned as a full =0time member with the rank of *Hauptmann* in May 1934. He served as Company Commander with Infantry Regiment 64 and later saw action during the French campaign of 1940 as Commander of Infantry Regiment 52. (*Deutsches Wehrkundearchiv*)

Knight's Cross: Awarded on 2 November 1941 as *Oberst* and Commander of Rifle Regiment 52 while attached to the 18th Panzer Division for actions on the Russian Front. The Knight's Cross was personally presented on 7 November by the Commander of the 18th Panzer Division, *General der Panzertruppe* Walther K. Nehring. On the morning of 17 November Jollasse was injured in a fall. He had to have an operation and was sent home, returning to the front in January 1942. In June the division was reorganised, renamed the Panzer Grenadier Brigade 18 and saw action on the southern sector of the Eastern Front, where Jollasse took part in the initial advances on Stalingrad. From 20 July he was delegated with the leadership of the 18th Panzer Division while keeping his command of the Panzer Grenadier Brigade. On 27 April 1943 he was wounded and evacuated from the front to recover, and from 15 June he attended the 5th Divisional Leaders Course. On 22 July 1943 he was named as Commander of the 9th Panzer Division and saw action near Kursk and then north of Orel. Soon after the German defeat began. By the end of September his division had reached the Dnieper and on 1 October Jollasse was promoted to *Generalmajor* and pushed his command towards Dnepropetrovsk. In June he was then transferred to the southern sector of France and from early August he moved to Belgium. On the 10 August Jollasse was once again on sick leave and from September he was in hospital. He returned to duty on 25 January 1945 as Commander of Division 408, which he led briefly until March when he was named as Commander of the 344th Infantry Division, part of 1st Panzer Army, seeing action in Upper Silesia. He was promoted to *Generalleutnant* on 20 April, and at the same time was appointed Commander of Battle Group *Jollasse*. His Battle Group was almost destroyed but he managed to break through south of Spremberg on 22 April and from the beginning of May he led the remainder of his troops through the Black Elster Forest in Eastern Germany. There, on 8 May, he surrendered to Allied troops.

Stephan Georg Julius RITTAU

Generalleutnant

* 27 December 1891, Wongrowitz, Posen
+ 22 August 1942, Martinowo, Rzhev, Soviet Union

Stephan Rittau entered the Army with *Jäger* Battalion 'Graf Yorck von Wartenburg' in East Prussia in March 1911 and was commissioned as a *Leutnant* the following year. He served during the First World War as a Platoon Leader with a Bicycle Company attached to the 8th Cavalry Division and was promoted to *Oberleutnant* in January 1916. He served on the General Staff during the last year of the war and was awarded both classes of the Iron Cross. He stayed in the Army after the war and by October 1935 had risen to the rank of *Oberstleutnant* and was serving as Commander of the I. Battalion of Infantry Regiment 7 in Breslau. In March 1938 he was promoted to *Oberst* and was serving on the Staff of the 7th Infantry Regiment, and from February 1939 he was Commander of Infantry Regiment 102. (*Deutsches Wehrkundearchiv*)

Knight's Cross: Awarded on 2 November 1941 as *Generalmajor* and Commander of 129th Infantry Division while attached to LVI. Army Corps for actions at Bialystok, Smolensk and Vyazma in the Soviet Union. His division helped establish the Kalinin bridgehead on the upper Volga in October and held it against repeated counter-attacks. During these battles two of his grenadier battalions suffered such heavy losses that they were reorganised into bicycle companies. Later that year Rittau and his division faced the Soviet winter offensive as part of the 9th Army and took part in the defensive battles around Rzhev. He was promoted to *Generalleutnant* on 1 August 1942. Unfortunately however, Rittau was killed by partisans just three weeks later in Martinovo, Rzhev.

Friedrich 'Fritz' Mathias Felix FRANEK
Generalleutnant

* 16 July 1891, Vienna, Austro-Hungary
+ 8 April 1976, Vienna, Austria

Friedrich Franek entered the Austrian Army in August 1910 with Infantry Regiment 41 and served during the First World War as an *Oberleutnant* and Platoon Leader, and later as a company commander with Infantry Regiment 63. He saw service with the General Staff during the last months of the war and was promoted to *Hauptmann* in November 1918. He remained in the Army after the war and transferred into the Germany Army in March 1938, serving as an *Oberstleutnant* with Infantry Regiment 32. From April 1939 he served as Commander of the I. Battalion of Mountain Jäger Regiment 98 and was awarded the Bar to the Iron Cross 2nd Class in October 1939 and the Iron Cross 1st Class a month later. (*Deutsches Wehrkundearchiv*)

Knight's Cross: Awarded on 4 November 1941 as *Oberst* and Commander of Infantry Regiment 405 while attached to the 121st Infantry Division for his bravery and leadership during an attack across the Izhora River in north-western Russia. His regiment created a bridgehead that would be decisive for the breakthrough and push towards Leningrad. On 12 September 1941 Franek pushed forward towards the river and was wounded twice in the head by rifle rounds, and was hospitalised. He returned to active duty on 1 March 1942, with leadership of the 196th Infantry Division while stationed in Trondheim in Norway. Franek was promoted to *Generalmajor* in April 1942, and a year later was promoted to *Generalleutnant*. On 1 January 1944 he was appointed Commander of the 44th *Reichs* Grenadier Division *Hoch und Deutschmeister* and saw action during the fighting at Monte Cassino in Italy. From 26 June 1944 he served as Commander of the 73rd Infantry Division in Mius on the Eastern Front as part of the 9th Army until May 1944, when the division was virtually destroyed. At the end of July he saw action during the Lublin–Brest Offensive and joined the battle with the Soviet 2nd Guards Tank Army at Garwolin, in eastern Poland, where he was taken prisoner on 29 July, being released four years later.

Botho von FRANTZIUS

Generalmajor

* 9 August 1898, Sawdin, Eastern Prussia
+ 11 December 1942, near Nevel, Pskov Oblast, Soviet Union

Botho von Frantzius entered Army service on 23 October 1916 as a *Fahnenjunker* with Dragoon Regiment 10, where he stayed for the entire war. Commissioned as a *Leutnant* in June 1918, he served with Mounted Regiment 2 from May 1920 and was promoted to *Oberleutnant* in July 1925. From October 1931 he served as Squadron Chief in Mounted Regiment 2 and three years later was transferred to Mounted Regiment 10 with the rank of *Rittmeister*. He served as Commander of Reconnaissance Battalion 161 shortly after the end of the Polish campaign in October 1939 and saw action during the French campaign, where his command remained as part of the occupation forces in Brittany. (*Deutsches Wehrkundearchiv*)

Knight's Cross: Awarded on 4 November 1941 as *Oberstleutnant* and Commander of Grenadier Regiment 504 of the 61st Infantry Division after he distinguished himself during the fighting and subsequent conquest of the Baltic Islands of Muhu, Ösel and Dagö. From 24 January until 15 February 1942, Frantzius served as Acting Deputy Commander of Infantry Regiment 176 and then served as Deputy Commander of Infantry Regiment 504. From 15 March he was appointed Commanding Officer of his Regiment, and was promoted to *Oberst* the following month. His Infantry Regiment was reclassified a Grenadier Regiment in October 1942. He fought as part of the 291st Infantry Division on the Russian Front near Nevel, where on 10 December he was shot and killed during an attack. He was posthumously promoted to *Generalmajor* and is buried at the German War Cemetery in Sebezh, a town in the Sebezhsky District of Russia.

Walther Karl Otto HAHM

General der Infanterie

* 21 December 1894, Neudorf-Sulau, Lower Silesia
+ 11 August 1951, Heide, Schleswig-Holstein

Walther Hahm entered the Army in August 1914 as a war volunteer and served with Reserve Infantry Regiment 214. He was awarded the Iron Cross 2nd Class in December 1914 but was taken ill in July 1915 and was in hospital for almost two months. He was commissioned as a *Leutnant* in June 1915 and became adjutant of II. Battalion of Infantry Regiment 23 four months later. In April 1917 he became adjutant of his regiment and was awarded the Iron Cross 1st Class in September of that year. He remained in the Army after the war and attended various courses. By November 1935 he held the rank of *Major* and was the Instructor at the War School in Munich. He was promoted to *Oberstleutnant* in August 1938 and saw his first action of the Second World War in France in 1940, where he was awarded the Bar to the Iron Cross 1st and 2nd Class. From December he was named as Commander of Infantry Regiment 480 and led this regiment during the opening stages of the war against the Soviet Union. He was promoted to *Oberst* in August 1941. (*Deutsches Wehrkundearchiv*)

Knight's Cross: Awarded on 15 November 1941 as *Oberst* and Commander of Infantry Regiment 480, part of the 260th Infantry Division, for his leadership during the successful destruction of an enemy tank regiment west of Bobruisk on the Russian Front. The enemy was attacking the southern flank of the 2nd Army, which broke the momentum of the offensive operation and could have potentially led to serious operational consequences for the German advance. Hahm continued to see action on the Eastern Front during the fighting near Taganrog, a port city in south-west Russia that was the birthplace of the playwright Anton Chekhov. On 1 April 1942 Hahm was promoted to *Generalmajor* and from May to June he saw action in Kharkov–Izyum in eastern Ukraine and during the battles in the Don area from July. On 1 January 1943 he was promoted to *Generalleutnant* and in mid-January most of the 113th Infantry Division was destroyed at Stalingrad but Hahm and his regiment managed to escape as they were outside the main pocket. By early February his regiment had been reorganised and loaded on to trains and relocated to the Saint-Quentin and Rouen area of northern France. In April his command, together with a newly formed division, began to move back to the Eastern Front, where it replaced the 129th Infantry Division north-east of Smolensk. By early August the division was hit by heavy Soviet attacks, but managed to push back the enemy and maintain a front line; however, by November Hahm and his regiment had to make their escape once again. He returned to Germany, where he was named Commander of the 389th Infantry Division from April 1944, seeing action as part of Army Group North.

Knight's Cross with Oakleaves: He became the 676th recipient on 9 December 1944 as *Generalleutnant* and Commander of the 389th Infantry Division while attached to the 16th Army. He was awarded the Oakleaves in recognition of his bravery during the heavy fighting east of Riga. In mid-November Hahm was transferred to the staff of Commander-in-Chief West and from December was delegated with the Leadership of the LXXXII. Army Corps. He was promoted to *General der Infanterie* on 30 January 1945 and his command was made official. He had attempted to retake the West Wall but without success. Tough battles followed with US troops throughout March and by the 18th the LXXXV. Army Corps had been lost. By early April Hahm's own command was withdrawn and retreated, and by 11 April it had been split by heavy fighting in Bamberg. His command was pushed back towards the US lines and finally on 8 May 1945 he surrendered to US troops, remaining in captivity until 1947.

Harald Siegwart Hans Lutze von HIRSCHFELD

Generalmajor

* 10 July 1912, Saxe-Weimar-Eisenach
\+ 18 January 1945, near Tarnow, south-eastern Poland

Knight's Cross: Awarded on 15 November 1941 as *Oberleutnant* and Chief of the 7th Company of the II. Battalion attached to Mountain *Jäger* Regiment 98 for his leadership during the attack and defence of the village of Alexandrovka on the Russian Front. During September the Soviets encircled the village and then launched repeated attacks against Hirschfeld and his company. The defenders of the village successfully fended off these attacks due to their bravery and leadership of their commander *Oberleutnant* Hirschfeld. He was always present at the hotspots of the battle, where he would inspire his men during the counter-attacks to destroy the enemy forces that were attacking the village. The regiment managed to hold its position until January 1942 and in April Hirschfeld was promoted to *Hauptmann* and named as Leader of the II.

Harald von Hirschfeld entered the Army in October 1935 with Mountain Infantry Regiment 99 and was commissioned as a *Leutnant* in September 1937. He attended various courses and from November 1938 he served as adjutant of the II. Battalion of Mountain Infantry Regiment 98, later becoming an Orderly Officer. From July 1939 he was Platoon Leader with the 16th Anti-tank Company of his regiment, and was awarded the Iron Cross 2nd Class during the invasion of Poland. In January 1940 he was temporary Commander of the 1st Mountain Anti-tank Replacement Company and was promoted to *Oberleutnant* in June 1940. By November he was an Orderly Officer with the staff of the 1st Mountain Division. (*Deutsches Wehrkundearchiv*)

Battalion of Mountain Infantry Regiment 98 from 26 April. In May he took part in several attacks on the enemy and broke through the Soviet positions. He was part of the German attack that surrounded and destroyed three Soviet armies at Barvinkove in the Ukraine towards the end of May 1942. From early August Hirschfeld was appointed Leader of a Battle Group attached to the 1st Mountain Division and saw action in the Caucasus.

Knight's Cross with Oakleaves: He became the 164th recipient on 23 December 1942 as *Hauptmann* and Leader of the II. Battalion of Mountain *Jäger* Regiment 98 for his leadership during the Battle of Barvenkovo in May 1942. He launched an attack with his battalion that penetrated the enemy artillery positions and he was able to capture several batteries during close combat. On the evening of 17 August 1942, during the fighting in the Caucasus his battalion stormed the important 9,200ft-high Kluchor Pass. Under his outstanding leadership, his battalion broke through twelve enemy defensive positions while storming more than 350 bunkers in the process during two weeks of hard fighting. He was personally presented with the Oakleaves by Hitler at the Wolf's Lair on 9 January 1943. He was promoted to *Major* on 21 January and remained in the Reserves until June, when he was attached to a department in the Army High Command. From October he became Commander of the 98th Mountain Infantry Regiment and was involved in coastal protection in Greece until November, when he was transferred to northern Greece and promoted to *Oberstleutnant* in December. From early 1944 his command was used against partisans in Bosnia and Croatia and from March he took part in the invasion and occupation of Hungary. From May until July he was deployed to Yugoslavia and was promoted to *Oberst* in July 1944. In August he attended the 13th Divisional Leaders Course and attended various commander training briefings the following month. On 22 September 1944 he was granted leadership of the 78th Assault Division, and he was confirmed as Commander in December and promoted to *Generalmajor* on 15 January 1945. Three days later he was seriously wounded during an air attack near Tarnow, south-eastern Poland, when a bomb exploded right next to him. He died later that same day and was posthumously promoted to the rank of *Generalleutnant* on 10 February 1945.

Helwig Fedor Johannes LUZ

Generalleutnant

* 28 June 1892, Buttenheim, Bamberg
+ 28 April 1980, Krün, Upper Bavaria

Helwig Luz entered the Army as a *Fahnenjunker* in July 1912, attended War School and was commissioned as a *Leutnant* in August 1914. He served as a Platoon Leader at the beginning of the First World War and was promoted to *Oberleutnant* in December 1917, being awarded both classes of the Iron Cross. Just before the end of the war he fell from a horse and was in hospital at the Armistice. He remained in the Army after the war and was attached to the 17th Mounted Regiment from 1919 until 1932. He was promoted to *Rittmeister* in November 1924. Promoted to *Major* in April 1934, he served in the Reich Defence Ministry as a department head and was promoted to *Oberstleutnant* in August 1936. In December 1939, with the rank of *Oberst*, he was appointed Commander of the 110th Rifle Regiment and he was awarded the Bar to the Iron Cross 1st and 2nd Classes in France in June 1940. (*Deutsches Wehrkundearchiv*)

Knight's Cross: Awarded on 15 November 1941 as *Oberst* and Commander of Rifle Regiment 110, part of the 11th Panzer Division, for his leadership and bravery during the defensive battle of Smolensk on the Russian Front. From December Luz was Commander of the 11th Rifle Brigade and they were on the defensive, seeing action during the fighting near Moscow. In March and April he was involved in the fierce battles near Vyazma and in June he took part in the terrible battles in the area of Army Group Centre. He was promoted to

Generalmajor in April 1942 and from 11 to 24 May he was given temporary command of the 11th Panzer Division. At the beginning of July he was appointed Commander of the 11th Panzer Grenadier Brigade and saw action at Orel and Voronezh. He then entered the Reserves until February 1943, when he was appointed Commander of the Demobilisation Office. He headed a small staff contingent responsible for the disbandment and reorganisation of the 6th Army after Stalingrad and after it was almost destroyed in June 1944 during the Battle of Romania. In April he was promoted to *Generalleutnant* and from June he was Commander of the 199th Infantry Division, based at the time in Narvik in Norway, where it was on garrison duty. It was earmarked for the Eastern Front and was sent to Oslo in March 1945 as part of the XXXIII. Army Corps, and then in April it was sent to Denmark. On 2 May Luz surrendered his command to the Americans at Havelberg and he was kept in Allied captivity until 26 June 1947.

Heinrich 'Heinz' MEYER-BUERDORF

General der Artillerie

* 13 December 1888, Kassel, Hesse-Nassau
+ 1 May 1971, Kassel, Hesse

Heinrich Meyer-Buerdorf entered the Army in March 1908 and was attached to Foot Artillery Regiment Nr. 13 in Ulm. He was commissioned as a *Leutnant* in August 1909. Meyer-Buerdorf was adjutant of the I. Battalion of Foot Artillery Regiment 16 at the beginning of the First World War and was promoted to *Oberleutnant* in January 1915. He later served with Foot Artillery Regiment 18 and later with Foot Artillery Regiment 4, and he was promoted to *Hauptmann* in January 1917. He stayed in the *Reichswehr* after the war and by 1935 he held the rank of *Oberstleutnant* and was serving as Higher Artillery Officer while attached to the Office of the Inspector of Artillery. He was promoted to *Oberst* in January 1936 and by October 1939 was serving as Commander of the Staff Headquarters of Artillery Regiment 720 in Germany. (*Deutsches Wehrkundearchiv*)

Knight's Cross: Awarded on 15 November 1941 as *Generalleutnant* and Commander of 131st Infantry Division while attached to the XXXXIII. Army

Corps for actions in the Soviet Union. He saw action on most fronts in Russia, most notably in Bialystok, Gomel, Kiev, Bryansk and Moscow, and his division suffered heavy casualties during the Soviet winter offensive of 1941–42. He later saw action in the Spass-Demyansk, Bryansk and Mogilev battles in 1942 and 1943. From February 1944 he served as General of Artillery attached to the Commander-in-Chief West *Generalfeldmarschall* Gerd von Rundstedt and later *Generalfeldmarschall* Günther von Kluge. During the latter stages of the war he was General of Artillery while attached to the Commander-in-Chief South *Generalfeldmarschall* Albert Kesselring. Meyer-Buerdorf was promoted to *General der Artillerie* on 20 April 1945 and surrendered to the Allies on 8 May 1945.

Erwin Max Clemens Heinrich Ernst Harry VIEROW

General der Infanterie

* 15 May 1890, Berlin
+ 1 February 1982, Tecklenburg

Erwin Vierow entered the Army in September 1908 and was commissioned as a *Leutnant* two years later. From June 1912 he served as an adjutant and Court Officer with Infantry Regiment 64. He was promoted to *Oberleutnant* in January 1915 and served as a regimental adjutant until December 1916. He was then an Ordnance Officer with the 6th Infantry Division. Promoted to *Hauptmann* in April 1917, he served on the General Staff until the end of the war. He stayed in the Army after the war and held the rank of *Oberst* in September 1934. At that time he was serving as Commander of Infantry Regiment Gieβen, which was renamed Infantry Regiment 36 from October 1935. In October 1936 he was Commander of Infantry Regiment 105 and a year later he served as Chief of the General Staff of the General Command XI. Army Corps. He served as Commander of the 96th Infantry Division from September 1939 and in January the following year he was promoted to *Generalleutnant*. (*Author's Collection*)

Knight's Cross: Awarded on 15 November 1941 as *General der Infanterie* and Commanding General of the LV. Army Corps while attached to the 6th Army for his leadership during the Battle of Kiev and during the fighting on the Dnieper Front. From late October his command was ordered to form two bridgeheads across the Una River south of Kharkov and then attack the city. From 14 February 1943 he was Commander of the XX. Army Corps but only briefly as after clearing the front near Rzhev Vierow he was transferred into the *Führer* Reserve. From July 1943 he was Commander of Military Administrative District A in north-western France and in June 1944 he was Commanding General of the General Command Somme. In September he was captured by British troops and sent to a prisoner of war camp in Clinton, Mississippi.

Ludwig MERKER

Generalleutnant

* 1 September 1894, Künzelsau, Württemberg
+ 14 March 1964, Tübingen, Baden-Württemberg

Ludwig Merker entered the Army in 1914 and served as a *Fahnenjunker* with Infantry Regiment Nr. 180, being commissioned as a *Leutnant* in August 1916. He was captured by British troops in September 1916 and spent the rest of the war a prisoner. He remained in the Army after the war and returned to Germany and joined the *Reichswehr* in December 1919, being promoted to *Oberleutnant* in 1923. He served in various units and from October 1935, now with the rank of *Major*, he was Commander of the I. Battalion of Infantry Regiment 35. Promoted to *Oberstleutnant* in October 1937, he was appointed Commander of Infantry Regiment 215 on 26 August 1939. (*Author's Collection*)

Knight's Cross: Awarded on 18 November 1941 as *Oberst* and Commander of Infantry Regiment 215, part of the 78th Infantry Division, for actions in the Soviet Union. He distinguished himself during the fighting at Bialystok and Smolensk, and later went on to see heavy fighting in the battles of Bialowieza and the Yelnya bend. Merker had served in France on occupation duty until April 1941 and from June he saw action as part of Army Group Centre during the invasion of the Soviet Union. On 10 September 1942 he took over the leadership of the 35th Infantry Division on the Russian Front and the division had suffered heavy casualties, losing more than 2,500 men – about 1,000 due to frostbite! On 1 October Merker was promoted to *Generalmajor* and his command of the division was confirmed. It remained in the Ghatsk sector until early 1943. On 20 April Merker was promoted to *Generalleutnant* and in the spring he took part in the Rzhev withdrawal and saw heavy action in the defensive fighting in the central sector that summer and into the winter. From early November 1943 until March 1944 he was away from the front in the Reserves and was then attached to the General Staff of Army Group Centre (probably wounded as he left the front for such a long time and returned to staff duties). From mid-July until mid-August 1944 he served on the Eastern Front as Senior Field Commander 399 and then from 23 September he was Commandant of Vienna. He left Vienna in early April 1945 and returned to Germany and surrendered to Allied troops on 6 May.

Egbert Martin PICKER

Generalleutnant

* 15 February 1895, Nuremberg
+ 27 March 1960, Ingolstadt, Bavaria

Knight's Cross: Awarded on 18 November 1941 as *Oberst* and Commander of Mountain *Jäger* Regiment 98 while attached to the 1st Mountain Division for operations against the 12th Army of the Soviet Union on the night of 7 August 1941. His command sealed off the Soviet penetration and brought the attack

Egbert Picker entered the Army in August 1914 with the Replacement Battalion of Infantry Regiment 11 and was commissioned as a *Leutnant* in May 1915. He served as Platoon Leader from December 1915, then as a Company Leader and finally as an adjutant, and was awarded the Iron Cross 1st and 2nd Classes. He remained in the Army after the war and served with various infantry units. He was Instructor at the War School in Dresden from April 1934, and in December 1935 he was attached to the War School in Hannover with the rank of *Major*. He served as Battalion Commander with Mountain Jäger Regiment 100 from July 1937, and from October he served in a similar position with Mountain Jäger Regiment 98 and was appointed its Commander from May 1940. (*Deutsches Wehrkundearchiv*)

by the Soviet 12th Army to a halt. As a result of his efforts the encirclement around the enemy remained unbroken and the following day the enemy troops were wiped out. He took part in the Battle of Mius from October to December 1941 and was involved in trench warfare until mid-February 1942, when his division was transferred to the Mius area. On 25 March he was taken ill and rested until he returned to operations in May, taking part in the Battle of Kharkov and then the advance on the Donets. In September he was taken ill once again but returned in early 1943 with the XXXIX. Mountain Corps and then attended the 4th Divisional Leader Course. Promoted to *Generalmajor* in August, Picker took command of the 3rd Mountain Division, seeing action as part of the 6th Army in the Donets region, and later saw action in area around Zaporizhzhia and Volnovakha, both in the Ukraine. From November 1943 he was attached to Military District V, Stuttgart, as Commander of the Training and Education Staff, and from July 1944 he was Commander of German Communication Command 183 with the Italian Alpine Division *Monte Rosa*. At the same time between January and February 1945 he was delegated with the deputy leadership of the 148th Infantry Division and took part in the Po River campaign. He was promoted to *Generalleutnant* on 20 April, just before he surrendered to American troops and was in custody until March 1947.

Friedrich Maximilian SIEBERT

General der Infanterie

* 6 July 1888, Ludwigshafen
+ 13 March 1950, Würzburg

Knight's Cross: Awarded on 18 November 1941 as *Generalleutnant* and Commander of 44th Infantry Division while attached to the LI. Army Corps and as part of the 6th Army for his leadership during the initial advance on southern Russia at the start of the Soviet campaign. He later saw further action from 1941 until early 1942 in the Ukraine, at Zhitomir, Kiev, and Kharkov during the initial advance toward the Caucasus, until he was attached to the 6th Army for the drive on to Volga. From mid-August 1942 he was appointed Commander of the 57th Infantry Division, seeing action on the southern sector of the Soviet Union and taking part in the Battle of Voronezh in 1942. From 20 February 1943 he was delegated with the leadership of the XIII. Army Corps and continued to see action in the Soviet Union. He was promoted to *General der Infanterie* on 1 May and his command was confirmed. After the counteroffensive at Kharkov he took part in the Battle of Kursk. In September

Friedrich Siebert entered the Army as a cadet in July 1907 and was commissioned as a *Leutnant* two years later. He was a battalion adjutant from September 1913, and when the First World War began he was serving in the field as adjutant of Infantry Regiment 3. Promoted to *Oberleutnant* in May 1915, he was appointed Deputy Court Officer in October 1916 and became brigade adjutant a year later. He was promoted to *Hauptmann* in March 1918 and was awarded both classes of the Iron Cross during the war. He stayed in the Army after the war and served as an instructor at the War School in Dresden from October 1934. He was promoted to *Oberst* a year later, and at the beginning of the Second World War he was serving in Poland as Commander of the 44th Infantry Division with the rank of *Generalmajor*. (*Author's Collection*)

1943 he entered the Reserves and from November was assigned as General with Special Duties to the High Command of the Army. From March 1944 until the end of the war he was attached to the High Command of the Armed Forces and became Chief of the Army Patrol Service until the end of the war. [insert photo No: 154]

Arnold SZELINSKI

Generalleutnant

* 30 August 1891, Hohenstein, East Prussia
+ 9 December 1943, Kirovograd, Ukraine

Knight's Cross: Awarded on 18 November 1941 as *Oberst* and Commander of Infantry Regiment 525, part of the 298th Infantry Division, for actions in the Soviet Union. He saw action in the drive to Kiev, in the Battle of Kharkov and during the fighting in the southern sector of the Eastern Front. In January 1942 he was delegated with the leadership of the 298th Infantry Division and was promoted to *Generalmajor* in February 1942, seeing action during the Stalingrad campaign, when he officially took over as divisional commander. He entered the Reserves at the end of December 1942, was promoted to *Generalleutnant* on 21 January 1943, and from April took command of the 376th Infantry Division.

Friedrich Siebert, right, is seen here with his brother Ludwig wearing the uniform of a SA-Obergruppenführer. Note the Golden Badge of the Nazi Party. (*Author's Collection*)

The division was created in Holland and it took several months to bring it up to strength. It was equipped with captured Soviet guns, and was finally ready to be sent to the Soviet Union in November 1943. Szelinski led it during the Battle of Kirovograd, during which he was killed on 9 December 1943.

Curt Otto Rudolf Wilhelm GALLENKAMP

General der Artillerie

* 17 February 1890, Wesel, Rhine Province
+ 13 April 1958, Wiesbaden, Hesse

Knight's Cross: Awarded on 19 November 1941 as *Generalleutnant* and Commander of the 78th Infantry Division while attached to IX. Army Corps for actions in the Soviet Union. He took part in the opening days of the invasion and saw action near the Berezina and the Dnieper River and in the area around Mogliev in Belarus. During August and September 1941 his division took part in heavy fighting around Moscow and then saw action near Yelnya and later near the Ugra River in Smolensk and in the Vyazma area. From early

Curt Gallenkamp is seen here with SS-*Brigadeführer* Lothar Debus Higher Police Leader East. Gallenkamp entered Army service with Field Artillery Regiment 7 in March 1909 and was commissioned as a *Leutnant* the following year. He was transferred into Field Artillery Regiment 15 in October 1913, and shortly after the beginning of the war he was wounded and hospitalised. While recovering he was promoted to *Oberleutnant* in February 1915. He was attached to the Staff of the 105th Infantry Division from November 1916, was promoted to *Hauptmann* in December the following year and served as a Company Leader with Infantry Regiment 338. He was transferred to the General Staff a few months before the end of the war and remained in the Army after it. By November 1934 had been promoted to *Oberst*. From March 1938 he was attached to the General Staff of the III. Army Corps with the rank of *Generalmajor* and first saw action during the French campaign as Commander of the 78th Infantry Division. (*Deutsches Wehrkundearchiv*)

March 1942 he was attached to the general Staff of Army High Command 1 and later Army High Command 7. Gallenkamp was promoted to *General der Artillerie* on 1 April 1942 and from the end of May was Commanding General of the newly formed LXXX. Army Corps in western France. It was created by renaming the commander of German troops in Denmark and was used for coastal protection in western France. Gallenkamp surrendered to British troops in France on 12 April 1945 and was tried as a war criminal, charged with the deaths of British commandos and an American pilot. He was found guilty in February 1947 and sentenced to death but his sentence was commuted to life imprisonment and he was released in 1952.

Otto Wilhelm SCHELL

Generalmajor

* 9 July 1895, Altendorf, Hattingen, Rhine Province
+ 2 September 1944, near Jassy, Moldavia in Romania

Knight's Cross: Awarded on 19 November 1941 as *Major* and Commander of III. Battalion of Infantry Regiment 39, part of the 26th Infantry Division, for his bravery during the early stages of the invasion of the Soviet Union. He distinguished himself during the fighting between Moscow and Leningrad and was heavily involved in the beginning of the winter offensive. Schell was promoted to *Oberstleutnant* in January 1942 and from 28 March took command of Infantry Regiment 413, seeing action during the defensive battles near Rzhev and during the Battle of Smolensk. Between 15 and 22 August he was also temporary commander of the 161st Infantry Division, and was promoted to *Oberst* on 18 December 1942. On 24 January 1943 he took command of Grenadier Regiment 364, which was attached to the 161st Infantry Division, and fought at Kharkov, where the division suffered heavy losses at Dnepropetrovsk in the autumn. He took command of Grenadier Regiment 993 in December 1943 and served in the Bologna area in northern Italy, where he was responsible for building up its strength and fighting power. In early June until 9 July he was assigned to the 8th *Jäger* Division for training and on 10 July Schell was delegated with the leadership of the 320th Infantry Division and saw action once again on the Russian Front. In August his division was encircled by the Soviets near Bessarabia, Romania, and was destroyed, along with most of the 6th Army. Schell, who had been promoted to *Generalmajor* on 1 September, was killed the following day near Jassy, Romania.

Oskar BLÜMM

Generalleutnant

* 20 June 1884, Zwiesel, Regen
+ 12 December 1951, Ursberg near Thannhausnen, Swaba, Bavaria

Knight's Cross: From June 1941 Blümm led his division during the invasion of the Soviet Union, sweeping across southern Russia, and saw action during the battles at Brody, Uman, Krivoy Rog and Kharkov. On 23 November 1941 he was awarded the Knight's Cross as *Generalleutnant* and Commander of the 57th Infantry Division while attached to the LV. Army Corps for the part he and

Oskar Blümm was a good soldier and was awarded both classes of the Iron Cross. He was promoted to *Hauptmann* in September 1916. During the last months of the war he served as adjutant of the 22nd Bavarian Infantry Brigade before being taken ill and hospitalised four days after Germany's defeat. He left hospital in February 1919 and transferred back into Infantry Regiment 5 before joining the *Freikorps*. In February 1933 he was appointed Commander of the III. Battalion of Infantry Regiment 21 and in October 1934 was appointed Commander of the newly formed Infantry Regiment Bayreuth, being promoted to *Oberst* in February 1935. On 26 August 1939 Blümm took command of the newly formed 57th Infantry Division and joined in the heavy fighting in southern Poland. He took part in the Western campaign, crossing into Luxembourg and southern Belgium, where his division blunted the attempts made by the French General Charles de Gaulle to annihilate the German bridgehead at Abbeville. (*Author's Collection*)

his division played in the major victory near Poltava in the Soviet Union. His command eliminated the city's tank-supported garrison and took over its control and later captured the bridge over the River Vistula. From 28 June until 24 July 1942 he took part in the opening phase of the German summer offensive in the Battle of Voronezh on the River Don. His division fought as part of *Generaloberst* Hermann Hoth's 4th Panzer Army but the Germans soon found themselves fighting in the streets, house by house with flamethrowers. It was a situation not unlike what would be seen at Stalingrad a few months later. When the battle ended the Germans were still bogged down by a strong Soviet force and both sides had suffered terrible loses. The Germans had suffered 19,000 killed and 95,000 wounded, while the Soviets had lost 200,000 troops, 80,000 more had been captured and almost 198,000 wounded. However, Soviet forces recaptured the city in February 1943. In November 1942 Blümm was transferred and took over command of Division 407, which had been reformed and made up from older troops from Bavaria. It was not until 1943 that it took part in combat training, but had many problems, shortage of supplies and weapons and inexperienced troops. It was disbanded in September 1944 and later reformed at the 407th Replacement Division, still with Blümm in command. In March 1945 it was engaged in the construction of defensive positions in southern Germany and a month later Blümm was ordered to hold the Bavarian city of Augsburg at all costs. However, within a few days the Americans arrived and he surrendered his division.

Franz MATTENKLOTT

General der Infanterie

* 19 November 1884, Grünberg, Silesia
+ 28 June 1954, Braunlage, Lower Saxony

Knight's Cross: Awarded on 23 November 1941 as *Generalleutnant* and Commander of 72nd Infantry Division as part of the XXX. Army Corps for actions in the Crimea. He saw action during the invasion of France in 1940 and spent three months in Brittany and three months in Paris, before being sent to Romania in January 1941. He led his division during the fighting in the Balkans campaign, fighting in Greece from the spring and then crossing into the Soviet Union, where he saw action during the opening stages of the Siege of Sevastopol. He was promoted to *General der Infanterie* in January 1942 and appointed Commanding General of the XXXXII. Army Corps. From May was involved in the conquest of the Kerch Peninsula in the Crimea. Between June and August that year he took part in the capture of the Fortress of Sevastopol and the latter stages of the Siege of Sevastopol. From April 1943 he transferred to the middle section of the Eastern Front as part of Army Detachment Kempf and later took part in the summer offensive at Kursk. From 12 to 30 November he took part in the Battle of Kiev and from December his command was pushed back by the Soviets, preventing further German successes in the south of the Soviet Union. By 26 December Zhitomir had been lost and his corps had been pushed back to the Dnieper in the Myronivka area in the Ukraine. By the end of January 1944 the corps was trapped in the Cherkassy

Franz Mattenklott entered the infantry in December 1903 and was commissioned as a *Leutnant* in May 1905. From July 1910 he served as adjutant of I. Battalion of Infantry Regiment 67 and just before the beginning of the First World War he was promoted to *Oberleutnant.* He served with his regiment until December 1916, when he joined the General Staff with the rank of *Hauptmann*. He ended the war as Operations Officer with Infantry Division 86, and he remained in the Army after the war, part of the General Staff. Promoted to *Major* in February 1928, he was appointed Tactics Leader of the Infantry School in Dresden and in October 1932 was promoted to *Oberstleutnant*. Appointed Commander of Infantry Regiment 25 in October 1935 with the rank of Oberst, he was promoted again in March 1938 to *Generalmajor* and was appointed Commander of the 72nd Infantry Division in time for the invasion of Poland. (*Deutsches Wehrkundearchiv*)

Pocket and when it finally broke out at the beginning of March the unit was crushed and those remaining, including Mattenklott, were sent back to Germany. From June 1944 he was appointed Deputy Commanding General of VI Army Corps Headquarters and Commander of *Wehrkreis* VI, Münster. He was taken prisoner by Allied forces on 21 April 1945 and remained in captivity until his release on 4 July 1947.

Martin Ernst Gerhard WANDEL

General der Artillerie

* 15 April 1892, Berlin
+ 14 January 1943, Rossosh, Soviet Union

Martin Wandel entered the 3rd Company of Field Artillery Regiment 21 in February 1910 and was commissioned as a *Leutnant* in August the following year. He served as Ordnance Officer on the staff of the 12th Infantry Division from November 1914 and was promoted to *Oberleutnant* in August the following year while serving as adjutant of Field Artillery Regiment 233. He served on the Staff of the VI. Army in 1918 and was promoted that year to *Hauptmann.* He was a recipient of both the Iron Cross 1st and 2nd Classes. He remained in the Army after the war and was promoted to *Major* in October 1931. From October 1935 served as Chief of Staff of the Inspector of Artillery with the rank of *Oberstleutnant*. When the Second World War began he was serving as an *Oberst* and as Chief of Staff of the General of Artillery. (*Deutsches Wehrkundearchiv*)

Knight's Cross: Awarded on 23 November 1941 as *Generalmajor* and Commander of 121st Infantry Division, part of the XXVIII. Army Corps, for actions on the Russian Front. In October his division was down to just 40 per cent of its strength but remained in action during the attack on Leningrad and later saw action during the Battle of Mga and during the Battle of Volkhov. From 10 November he entered the Reserves and was promoted to *Generalleutnant* on 16 November. From December he took the leadership of the XXIX. Panzer Corps. He saw action in the River Don area and on 14 January he was killed when his command post at Rossosh was overrun by the Soviet Army. He was posthumously promoted on 21 January to the rank of *General der Artillerie.*

Kurt Oskar Heinrich Ludwig Wilhelm von TIPPELSKIRCH

General der Infanterie

* 9 October 1891, Berlin-Charlottenburg
+ 10 May 1957, Lüneburg

Kurt von Tippelskirch joined the Army in 1911 as a *Leutnant* and served for just a few weeks during the First World War before being captured by the French. He returned to Germany in 1919 and stayed in the Army, being promoted to *Oberleutnant* in September and joining Infantry Regiment 29. He joined the Army Statistics Department of the Troop Office in Berlin in April 1924 and by February 1933 had been promoted to *Oberstleutnant*. On 15 October 1935, now with the rank of *Oberst*, Tippelskirch was Commander of Infantry Regiment 27 in Rostock and from October 1936 was appointed Chief of Department 3 of the General Staff of the Army. Promoted to *Generalmajor* in April 1938, he served as Senior Supply Officer IV and Deputy Chief of Staff for Intelligence in the Army General Staff, and was promoted to *Generalleutnant* in June 1940. (*Deutsches Wehrkundearchiv*)

Knight's Cross: Awarded on 23 November 1941 as *Generalleutnant* and Commander of 30th Infantry Division, part of the X. Army Corps, for his excellent leadership during the attack on Leningrad. The battle lasted a week and after repelling the Soviets south of Lake Ilmen, and despite his troops' weakened condition, Tippelskirch was able to inspire and push his men forward and defeat a major Soviet attack. He was presented with the Knight's Cross by the Commanding General of the X. Army Corps, *General der Artillerie* Christian Hansen. At the beginning of 1942 he led his division during the encirclement at Demyansk but was flown out of the Pocket on 27 August before it fell. Two days later Tippelskirch was promoted to *General der Infanterie*, and on 11 September 1942 he was appointed German General assigned to the Italian 8th Army. On 16 February 1943 he was appointed Commanding General of the XII Army Corps and took part in the fighting at Spass–Demensk, Bryansk and Mogilev–Minsk.

Knight's Cross with Oakleaves: He became the 539th recipient on 30 July 1944 as *General der Infanterie* and Deputy Commander-in-Chief of the 4th Army for his command during Operation Bagration, the military campaign fought between 22 June and 19 August 1944 in Soviet Byelorussia. On 18 July, before being advised of the award of the Oakleaves, he was involved in an aircraft crash and hospitalised for a few days. He entered the Reserves until 29 October, when he took over the temporary leadership of the 1st Army. It was at that time that he was well enough to travel to Hitler's headquarters in Rastenburg to receive his Oakleaves. From 6 December 1944 he became Leader of the 14th Army on the Italian Front, where he launched a surprise offensive that severely disrupted the Allies' preparation of their offensive to liberate Italy. In April 1945 he took command of the 21st Army and at the same time was named as Commander of Army Group Vistula. He surrendered to British forces near Lübeck on 2 May 1945 and was released from imprisonment two years later.

Wilhelm Ernst Gottlieb FALLEY

Generalleutnant

* 25 September 1897, Metz, Lorraine
+ 6 June 1944, Chateau de Bernaville-Picauville, Normandy, France

Knight's Cross: Awarded on 26 November 1941 as *Oberstleutnant* and Commander of Infantry Regiment 4, part of the 32nd Infantry Division, for actions on the Eastern Front. He led his regiment against strong enemy positions near the fortifications near Sarjanka, which were bitterly defended. His regiment suffered a heavy assault and secured an important victory after many losses. From January 1942 he led his regiment during many tough battles in the area around Demyansk, and was promoted to *Oberst* the following month before being relieved. From August 1942 Falley was appointed Commander of School V for Officer Candidates of Infantry in Döberitz and from September 1943 he was delegated with the leadership of the 36th Infantry Division, seeing action near Smolensk as part of the XXXXI. Army Corps. In October he took temporary command, for five days only, of the 330th Infantry Division, and from 5 October he took leadership of the 246th Infantry Division and saw action in Orsha, a city in Belarus. Promoted to *Generalmajor* on 1 December 1943, his command was confirmed and he continued to see action on the Eastern Front until the end of April 1944, when he was transferred as Commander of the 91st Air Landing Division in France. He was promoted to *Generalleutnant* on 1 May and on 6 June, at the start of the Allied landings in Normandy, was on his way to Rennes in Brittany when he noticed a mass of aircraft in the sky above him. He ordered his driver to turn round and head back to his headquarters near Bernaville. On the way back he encountered a group of landed American paratroopers, who opened fire on his staff car and he was killed along with his adjutant, *Major* Bartuzat. Falley was later buried and his body now lies at the German War Cemetery in Orglandes, Normandy, in Plot 10, Row 2, Grave No. 207.

Dr med.dent Karl MAUSS

General der Panzertruppe

* 17 May 1898, Plön, Schleswig-Holstein
+ 9 February 1959, Hamburg

Knight's Cross: Awarded on 26 November 1941 as *Oberstleutnant* and Commander of II. Battalion of Rifle Regiment 69 while attached to the 10th Panzer Division for his part in the encirclement of Minsk and Smolensk. On the night of 6–7 October 1941, Mauss and his battalion captured the most important bridges and exits leading out of Vyazma. They then cleared the city of Soviets, creating provisional defensive positions towards the west. His actions ensured that the Vyazma Pocket could be closed off to the south. All attempts made by the Red Army to retake the position failed. Mauss and his men fought with courage and determination before the fighting halted just 15 miles from Moscow. On 7 February 1942 he took over command of Rifle Regiment 33, part of the 4th Panzer Division, and saw heavy action on the Russian Front. He was promoted to *Oberst* in April. From November 1942 he was delegated as leader of the 4th Panzer Division and saw action at Orel and Kursk. In mid-July 1943 he took command of Panzer Grenadier Regiment 33 and continued to see action in the Dnieper region during the Soviet summer offensive while still attached to the 4th Panzer Division.

Karl Mauss joined the Army as a war volunteer in August 1914 with Infantry Regiment 162, and was commissioned as a *Leutnant* in May 1915. He served as a Platoon and Company Leader, and even trained to be a pilot. He left the Army shortly after the war but returned in September 1934 as *Hauptmann* with the staff of the 4th Infantry Regiment. From March 1935 he served in Infantry Regiment 6 in Lübeck and from October 1935, now with the rank of *Hauptmann*, he served in Hamburg with Infantry Regiment 69. (*Author's Collection*)

Knight's Cross with Oakleaves: He became the 335th recipient on 24 November 1943 as *Oberst* and Commander of Panzer Grenadier Regiment 33 while still attached to the 10th Panzer Division for continued actions on the Russian Front. He particularly distinguished himself in February 1943, playing a major role in saving the VII. Army Corps from annihilation and later in March he contributed to the attack made by the 4th Panzer Division that involved the capture of Sevsk. The Oakleaves were presented to him by Hitler on 6 December 1943 at the *Führer's* headquarters in Rastenburg, East Prussia. In January 1944 he was appointed Commander of the 7th Panzer Division and was promoted to *Generalmajor* three months later.

Knight's Cross with Oakleaves and Swords: Awarded on 23 October 1944 to become the 101st recipient as *Generalmajor* and Commander of the 7th Panzer Division while attached to the XXVIII. Army Corps in recognition of his leadership. On 23 March 1944 the division was encircled by the Soviets and took command of a group of Panther tanks belonging to the 1st SS-Panzer Division and attacked towards the south. It was able to make contact with troops of the 1st Panzer Army and secured a victory. Mauss was promoted to *Generalleutnant* in October while commander of the 7th Panzer Division and from November was heavily engaged in action during the Battle of Raseiniai in Lithuania.

In October 1939 he was Commander of II. Battalion of Infantry Regiment 69 with the rank of *Major* and was later awarded both classes of the Iron Cross. Mauss is seen here clearly wearing his Knight's Cross with Oakleaves and Swords on patrol in an armoured vehicle. (*Author's Collection*)

Knight's Cross with Oakleaves, Swords and Diamonds: He became the 26th recipient on 15 April 1945 as *Generalleutnant* and Commander of the 7th Panzer Division while attached to the VII. Panzer Corps after he distinguished himself during the fierce defensive fighting in Latvia and Lithuania between 5 and

10 November 1944. He was described as a brave divisional commander who always led from the front and who inspired his men during the fierce fighting, during which his command was able to destroy the bulk of the enemy tanks. It resulted in a decisive success and a breakthrough to East Prussia, with the flexible leadership and personal bravery of Mauss decisive in the success of the division. He was heavily engaged during the Soviet winter offensive of 1944–45 near the Vistula and his division was trapped in Danzig as part of Army Group North. On 23 March 1945 Mauss was seriously wounded when an artillery shell exploded next to him and he had to have his left leg amputated. He spent days lying on a stretcher in a field hospital still giving out orders to his men. He was eventually evacuated by torpedo boat to a hospital in Copenhagen, where on 5 May he was taken prisoner by British troops.

Hans Hellmuth PFEIFER

Generalleutnant

* 18 February 1894, Altenburg, Saxe-Altenburg
\+ 22 April 1945, near Finale, Sovona in Italy

Hellmuth Pfeifer entered the Army as a *Fahnenjunker* in March 1912 and was commissioned as a *Leutnant* in August 1913. He saw action at the beginning of the First World War as a battalion adjutant, then as a Company Leader and was awarded the Iron Cross 1st and 2nd Classes. He was promoted to *Oberleutnant* in October 1916 and served as a regimental adjutant and later as an Ordnance Officer on the Staff of the 111th Infantry Division. He left the Army after Germany's defeat but rejoined in July 1934 with the rank of *Hauptmann* and was appointed Company Commander with Infantry Regiment 37. From October 1935 he served as Commander of a machine gun company with Infantry Regiment 58 and was promoted to *Major* in August 1936. From October 1937 he was assigned to the Department of Foreign Affairs and in September 1939 he was appointed Commander of the III. Battalion of Infantry Regiment 185 and was promoted to *Oberstleutnant* in December of that year. (*Deutsches Wehrkundearchiv*)

Knight's Cross: Awarded on 26 November 1941 as *Oberstleutnant* and Commander of Infantry Regiment 185 while attached to the 87th Infantry Division for actions on the Russian Front. Pfeifer led his division during the Battle of Moscow and at Bialystok, Smolensk and Vyazma during the Soviet winter. His leadership was recognised in December 1941 when he was promoted to *Oberst*, and in June during the fighting near Rzhev on 18 November 1942 he was seriously wounded. Once he had recovered he attended a divisional leader's course from July 1943 and was promoted to *Generalmajor* two months later. On 6 July he was delegated with the temporary leadership of the 332nd Infantry Division and saw action briefly during the Kursk offensive as part of the 4th Panzer Army. On 3 August he was once again wounded and spent time in hospital and spent the next two months in the Reserves recovering, and in December he was appointed Commander of the 65th Infantry Division, which had been reorganised after its terrible mauling by the British in October 1943. In January 1944, Pfeifer and his division was rushed to Anzio as part of the I. *Fallschirmjäger* Corps and remained in Italy until Rome fell, and he was promoted to *Generalleutnant* in June 1944.

Knight's Cross with Oakleaves: He became the 574th recipient on 5 September 1944 as *Generalleutnant* and Commander of the 65th Infantry Division for his leadership during his skilful withdrawal battles in July and August 1944 during the Italian campaign near Arno, Anzio, Aprilia, and Velletri. He was personally presented with the Oakleaves by *SS-Reichsführer* Heinrich Himmler at Trossingen, a town in Baden-Württemberg, Germany, on 16 December 1944. When Rome fell his division took part in the retreat from Anzio and later fought in the Battles of the Gothic Line and Po River. He remained at the Italian Front until 22 April 1945, when Pfeifer was killed near Finale, Italy. He is buried today at the Futa Pass military cemetery in the Tuscan-Emilian Apennines, in block 49, grave no: 177.

Alois WEBER

Generalmajor

* 26 July 1903, Kastl, Bavaria
+ 19 June 1976, Freising, Bavaria

Knight's Cross: Awarded on 26 November 1941 as *Major* and Commander of I. Battalion of Infantry Regiment 19 of the 7th Infantry Division for his achievements and leadership during the fighting at Godunovo in the Soviet Union. As part of the German efforts to construct a bridgehead nearby his troops managed to seize Hill 204 despite armoured attacks from Soviet forces. Weber then held his position for two days against heavy attacks with minimal support and played a major role in the defence of the German crossings over the Protva River. Consequently the expansion of the bridgehead followed, for which he was again recognised for his success. He was promoted to *Oberstleutnant* on

Alois Weber entered the Army with a training battalion of Infantry Regiment 21 in October 1921 and was commissioned as a *Leutnant* in July 1934. He was then appointed Commander of the 11th Company of Infantry Regiment 19 and was promoted to *Oberleutnant* in December 1935. From November 1938 he took command of the 9th Company with the same regiment and was awarded the Iron Cross 1st and 2nd Classes during the Polish campaign of September 1939. He was appointed Battalion Commander with his regiment in August 1940 and was promoted to *Major* in February 1941. (*Deutsches Wehrkundearchiv*)

28 June 1942 and from 1 July he took command of the Army NCO School at Marienburg. He remained there until December 1943, when he took command of Grenadier Regiment 61.

Knight's Cross with Oakleaves: He became the 579th recipient on 10 September 1944 as *Oberst* and Commander of Grenadier Regiment 61 for his distinguished leadership between December 1943 to August 1944 and success in the attack and defence between the Bug and Narew Rivers. From 19 October he attended the 12th Divisional Leaders Course at Hirschberg and was decorated with the Oakleaves in November 1944 by *SS-Reichsführer* Heinrich Himmler at Posen. On 30 January 1945 he was promoted to *Generalmajor* and was appointed Commanding General of the 78th Volksgrenadier Division, which he led in Galicia. Weber was wounded in action on 29 December and was away from the front line until February 1945, when he was appointed Commander of the 362nd Infantry Division. The division saw fighting near Bologna, Italy, where it was shattered by the last Allied offensive in Italy. He was taken prisoner by the Western Allies on 23 April 1945 in the area of the Po Valley and was released in 1947.

Gerhard BERTHOLD

Generalleutnant

* 12 March 1891, Scharzenburg in Saxony near the German-Czech border
+ 14 April 1942, Saizeva-Gora in Mahilyowskaya near Minsk in Belarus

Knight's Cross: Awarded on 4 December 1941 as *Generalmajor* and Commander of the 31st Infantry Division while attached to the XXXXIII. Army Corps in recognition of his leadership during the offensive battle near Bryansk in the

Soviet Union. On 6 October 1941 Berthold received a message about the Soviet tank attack in his sector and he immediately drove to his forward headquarters through heavy artillery and machine gun fire to take personal command of the area. The Soviet tanks were successfully driven back and the successful defence of the area was attributed to the superior bravery of Berthold, the divisional commander. Berthold saw action as part of the 2nd Army in the central sector of the front, seeing action in Bialystok and Minsk. On 20 January 1942, Berthold was delegated with the leadership of the XXXXIII. Army Corps, part of the 4th Army, on the northern part of the Soviet front, seeing action near Demyansk. Only a month later he was transferred and was appointed Commander of the 31st Infantry Division and took part in the defensive battles as part of Army Group Centre in Saizeva-Gora in Mahilyowskaya near Minsk in Belarus, where he was killed in action.

Herbert Erich Adolf Wilhelm von BÖCKMANN

General der Infanterie

* 24 July 1886, Bremen
+ 10 March 1974, Baden-Baden, Württemberg

Herbert von Böckmann entered the Army in March 1905 with Grenadier Regiment 109 as an officer candidate, being commissioned as a *Leutnant* in August the following year. He served as a staff officer during much of the First World War, rising to the rank of *Hauptmann* by the end of it. He remained in the Army after the war. He was promoted to *Oberstleutnant* in June 1933 and became chief of the training department from September 1934. He became Chief of the General Staff of the I. Army Corps from November 1938 and was promoted to *Generalmajor* in January 1939. (*Deutsches Wehrkundearchiv*)

Knight's Cross: Awarded on 4 December 1941 as *Generalleutnant* and Commander of the 11th Infantry Division as part of the I. Army Corps after leading both the 11th and 21st Infantry Divisions in a push along the Volkhov River. On 28 October he led his forces during a breakthrough of the enemy positions, capturing more than 500 combat bunkers and Soviet troops. Böckmann commanded the 11th Infantry Division until the end of January 1942, and after spending about six weeks in the Reserves he was delegated with the leadership of the L. Army Corps. From March he led his corps as part of the 18th Army, in the area around

Leningrad, and was promoted to *General der Infanterie* the following month but was put back in the Reserves in July 1942. On 31 January 1943 the chief of the Army Personnel Office proposed that Böckmann be retired from the Army for the reason, 'he cannot adapt to the changing requirements of a modern army'. As a result Böckmann was retired from the Army on 31 March that same year.

Eduard HAUSER

Generalleutnant

* 22 June 1895, Erlangen, Bavaria
+ 16 July 1961, Garmisch-Partenkirchen, Bavaria

Eduard Hauser entered the Army in August 1914 at the beginning of the First World War and was assigned to Bavarian Infantry Regiment 17. He was commissioned as a *Leutnant* in May 1915 and was awarded the Iron Cross 2nd Class in June 1915 and the Iron Cross 1st Class in September 1917, just before he was captured by the British. He remained in the Army after the war, and attended various courses. He was promoted to *Oberleutnant* in July 1925 and by November 1935 he held the rank of *Major* and was adjutant of Panzer Brigade 1. At the beginning of the Second World War he was serving on the staff of the General Command of the XIX. Motorised Army Corps. (*Deutsches Wehrkundearchiv*)

Knight's Cross: Awarded on 4 December 1941 as *Oberst* and Commander of Panzer Regiment 25, part of the 7th Panzer Division, for actions on the Soviet Front. On 3 October 1941 Hauser led his regiment across the heavily defended Dnieper River, capturing the bridge at Gluschova shortly before it was blown up. Two days later he led his regiment during the capture of the village of Kamenev, and this success was made possible through the skill and initiative of Hauser. The next day his regiment stormed past the Vyazma position and his swift action guaranteed the fall of the city. The 7th Division as a whole suffered heavy losses and from May 1942 was sent to France to rest and refit, from November taking part in the occupation of Vichy France. From February 1943, after the fall of Stalingrad, he took part in the fighting near Rostov and during the Battle of Kharkov. Hauser was delegated with the leadership of the 13th Panzer Division from September 1943, and with his promotion to *Generalmajor* in December he became official divisional commander.

Knight's Cross with Oakleaves: Awarded on 26 January 1944, to become the 376th recipient as *Generalmajor* and Commander of the 13th Panzer Division while attached to the LII. Army Corps for his successful leadership during the battles near Melitopol in the Ukraine. Between 10 October and 22 December 1943, Hauser led his Panzer Division through nine successful counter-attacks, in which the division suffered heavy losses. However, he also captured sixteen Soviet armoured vehicles, fifty-two artillery pieces of all kinds, thirty trucks and took 350 prisoners. During the last counter-attack, Hauser became a casualty himself and was evacuated to hospital. He was presented with the Oakleaves by Hitler at the Berghof on 24 February 1944. He was promoted to *Generalleutnant* on 20 July and appointed Commandant of the Fortifications near Lötzen in north-east Poland. In November he was appointed Commander of Special Purpose Division Staff 605 and fought as part of the 4th Army on the Eastern Front. From March 1945 he served as Fortress Commandant of Pillau and managed to escape Soviet forces with some of his men on the last ship out of the port on 25 April. He was admitted to the Bad Tölz hospital on 9 May 1945 and was taken prisoner by US forces. He remained in US captivity until 14 June 1947.

Hugo HÖFL

Generalleutnant

* 16 June 1878, Regensburg, Bavaria
+ 13 April 1957, Weipertshausen, Bavaria

Hugo Höfl entered Army service as a *Fahnenjunker* in July 1897 and was commissioned as a *Leutnant* two years later. He served as battalion adjutant with Infantry Regiment 20 from October 1905, and was promoted to *Oberleutnant* four years later. From October 1911 he was attached to the Bavarian War Academy. Promoted to *Hauptmann* in January 1914, he was second adjutant with Infantry Regiment 2 at the start of the First World War. He later served with Infantry Brigade 3 and then as an Orderly Officer with the Staff of the 14th Bavarian Infantry Division. He remained in the Army after the war, being promoted to *Major* in October 1919 and serving with the Central Office of the Bavarian General Staff. From January 1920 he served as Tactics Instructor at the Army Infantry School and was promoted to *Oberstleutnant* in April 1924. Five years later he was promoted to *Oberst* and shortly after he retired from the Army. He then served with the Turkish Army and in December 1935 he rejoined the German Army and was promoted to *Generalmajor* in June 1936. (*Deutsches Wehrkundearchiv*)

Knight's Cross: Awarded on 4 December 1941 as *Generalleutnant* and Commander of the 206th Infantry Division while part of the XXIII. Army Corps for actions in East Prussia and the Russian Front. At the end of 1941 his division retreated to an area north-west of Rzhev, where he was heavily involved in trench warfare over the next few months. On 14 July 1942 Höfl transferred to become Commander of the newly formed 39th Infantry Division and as part of the 15th Army took part in training in Vlissingen in the Netherlands. From December he was delegated with the leadership of the LXXXIX. Army Corps and as part of the 15th Army during training in Antwerp. On 30 April Höfl retired from active service.

Erich JASCHKE

General der Infanterie

* 11 May 1890, Danzig, Pommerania
+ 18 October 1961, Hamburg

Erich Jaschke entered Army service as a *Fahnenjunker* in June 1909 with Infantry Regiment 132 and was commissioned as a *Leutnant* in November 1910. In August 1914, with the war only days old, he was wounded but remained at the front and was promoted to *Oberleutnant* in March 1916. From May 1916 he was leader of a machine gun troop and later served as regimental adjutant. During the last months of the war he served with Infantry Regiment 11 and was wounded in October and hospitalised. He was promoted to *Hauptmann* in October 1922 and attended various courses. He was attached to the Reich Defence Ministry from 1935, now with the rank of *Oberstleutnant*. From February 1938 he was Chief of Staff of the Inspector of Infantry and from March 1941 he was named as Commander of Motorised Infantry Regiment 90, now with the rank of *Oberst*. (*Author's Collection*)

Knight's Cross: Awarded on 4 December 1941 as *Oberst* and Commander of Motorised Infantry Regiment 90, part of the 20th Motorised Infantry Division, for distinguished service during the advance towards Tikhvin near Leningrad in the Soviet Union. He was presented with the Knight's Cross by the Commander of the 20th Motorised Infantry Division *Generalleutnant* Hans Zorn. He was promoted to the rank of *Generalmajor* on 17 December and from January 1942 Jaschke was delegated with the leadership of the 20th Motorised

Infantry Division, seeing action in Volkhov near Leningrad. He took over as Commander in January 1943 when he was promoted to *Generalleutnant* and continued to command this division on the Russian Front until January 1943. On 1 March he was delegated with the leadership of the LXXXII. Army Corps for just nine days while responsible for coastal protection in the Pas-de-Calais. From March he took over the leadership of the LV. Army Corps, seeing action in the area near Orel and from April moved to Bryansk, temporarily under the command of the 2nd Panzer Army. On 1 May Jaschke was promoted to *General der Infanterie* and from June until August saw action in the Battle of Orel.

Knight's Cross with Oakleaves: He became the 295th recipient on 7 September 1943 as *General der Infanterie* and Commanding General of the LV. Army Corps after he continued to prove himself as a commander in crucial situations and tough battles, especially during the fighting for Orel in mid-1943. Jaschke was personally presented with the Oakleaves by Hitler at the *Führer*'s headquarters in Rastenburg. From October 1943 until the end of the war he was attached to the staff of the High Command of the Army in Berlin. He surrendered to the Americans on 9 May 1945 and remained in US captivity until his release on 30 June 1947.

Max Heinrich Wilhelm PFEFFER

General der Artillerie

* 12 June 1883, Geldern, Rhine Province
+ 3 January 1946, Prison Camp Voikova near Ivanovo, Soviet Union

Max Pfeffer entered the Army in October 1902, attended Military Technical Academy and was commissioned as a *Leutnant* in January 1904. In October 1910 he became a battalion adjutant and from 1913 an *Oberleutnant*. At the beginning of the First World War in 1914 he was adjutant of the Commander of Ammunition in the VII. Army Corps, and from December he held the rank of *Hauptmann*. In January 1915 he became a Battery Chief and in August 1916 he served as a Brigade adjutant, ending the war as an adjutant of the Artillery Commander of the 13th Infantry Division. He remained in the Army after the war and by October 1933 had been promoted to the rank of *Oberst* and was on the Staff of Artillery Leader VI in Münster. In October 1934 he was appointed Commander of Artillery Regiment 16 and in October 1936 he was promoted to *Generalmajor* and took command of Artillery Regiment 26. At the beginning of the Second World War he held the rank of *Generalleutnant* and was Artillery Commander 44. (*Author's Collection*)

Knight's Cross: Awarded on 4 December 1941 as *Generalleutnant* and Commander of 297th Infantry Division while attached to the LV. Army Corps for actions in the Soviet Union. From June 1941 his division fought as part of Army Group South and Pfeffer saw action at Zhitomir, Uman, Kiev, Kharkov and Rostov. From 1942 his division fought with the 6th Army during the Battle of Kharkov, later during the clearing of the Izyum Pocket and in the drive across the Don. In January 1943 Pfeffer was promoted to *General der Artillerie* and from 17 January 1943 took command of the IV. Army Corps at Stalingrad. He was captured there on 31 January and held in a prison camp at Voikova near Ivanovo, where he died on 3 January 1945. He lies today at the German War Cemetery in Tschernzy, location – Grave No. 29.

Alfred-Hermann REINHARDT

Generalleutnant

* 15 November 1897, Affalterbach-Backnang, Württemberg
+ 14 January 1973, Öhringen, Baden-Württemberg

Alfred-Hermann Reinhardt entered the Army with the 5th Württemberg Grenadier Regiment from January 1916, where he remained for the entire war. In December 1920 he entered the police and was commissioned as a *Polizei-Leutnant* from April 1921, serving as a Platoon Leader and an instructor and trainer. From 1925 he served as adjutant of the Police School in Stuttgart and the Police Emergency in Tübingen, and he was promoted to *Polizei-Hauptmann* in November 1932. In November 1935 he entered the *Wehrmacht* with the Staff of Infantry Regiment 55 and with the rank of *Hauptmann*. From August 1939 now with t,he rank of *Major*, Reinhardt was appointed Commander of the III. Battalion of Infantry Regiment 490. Promoted to *Oberstleutnant* in March 1940, he was appointed Commander of I. Battalion of Infantry Regiment 421. (*Deutsches Wehrkundearchiv*)

Knight's Cross: Awarded on 4 December 1941 as *Oberstleutnant* and Commander of Infantry Regiment 421, part of the 125th Infantry Division, for his efforts and achievements during the Battle of Kiev. Through the capture of Tarasovka in the Soviet Union by his regiment on 20 September 1941 the Germans were able to prevent a large amount of Soviet soldiers from escaping the Kiev Pocket.

Reinhardt later took part in the capture of Rostov and saw action during the Caucasus campaign. In January 1942 he was promoted to *Oberst*, and for a time served as the military administrator of the Kuban area. In late 1942 he was reunited with his regiment.

Knight's Cross with Oakleaves: He became the 306th recipient on 28 September 1943 as *Oberst* and Commander of Grenadier Regiment 421 while attached to the 125th Infantry Division in recognition of his leadership and bravery during the battles for the Kuban Bridgehead in July 1943. His regiment had been sent to the front line to take part in the counter-attack on 25–26 July, and after some tough battles the old German line along the Kama River was retaken. Reinhardt was presented with the Oakleaves by Hitler on 29 October 1943 at the Wolf's Lair in Rastenburg. From September he attended the 7th Divisional Leader Course and between 20 and 30 November he was deputy Commander of Infantry Regiment 73 on the Russian Front. He served briefly as deputy Commander of the 370th Infantry Division and on 1 February 1944 was promoted to *Generalmajor* and appointed Commander of the 98th Infantry Division, and as part of the V. Army Corps saw action in the Crimea. In the summer of 1944 his division was transferred to Zagreb in Yugoslavia, where it was rested and refitted, returning to combat in Italy in September.

Knight's Cross with Oakleaves and Swords: Awarded on 24 December 1944 as *Generalleutnant* and became the 118th recipient as Commander of 98th Infantry Division while attached to the XIV. Army Corps for actions on the Adriatic coastal areas and in the Bologna area of Italy. The Swords were probably presented to Reinhardt in January 1945 by Hitler at his Adlerhorst headquarters in Bad Nauheim, Hesse. He saw action in Italy from September, where he led his division at San Savino and in the Battle of the Rimini Line, and from January 1945 he saw further action during the fighting north-west of Bologna. A month later his command was now designated the Volksgrenadier Division and formed part of the LXXVI. Panzer Corps in the Ardennes. He fought in the Po River campaign and ended the war in Italy, where he surrendered to US troops in the Alps on 8 May 1945. He was released in July the same year.

Theodor TOLSDORFF
Generalleutnant

* 3 November 1909, Lehnarten, East Prussia
+ 25 May 1978, Barmen in Dortmund, North Rhine-Westphalia

Knight's Cross: Awarded on 4 December 1941 as *Oberleutnant* and Commander of 14th Panzer Defence Company while attached to 1st Infantry Division for actions on the Russian Front. On 21 November 1941 he led a breakthrough near the Vyborgskaya Bridgehead and then a counter-attack against Soviet forces, despite being wounded three times. He was later treated in hospital and was away from combat duty until 20 April 1942, returning to combat with the same company shortly after being promoted to *Hauptmann*. However, on 20 September he was wounded once again when he lost half of his foot in an explosion and was hospitalised, returning to action in January 1943 as Commander of the I. Battalion of Fusilier Regiment 22.

Tolsdorff had a unique career in the Army. He volunteered for duty in October 1934 as a *Leutnant* and in less than eleven years rose to the rank of *Generalleutnant*. He was also awarded Germany's highest award for bravery, at the age of 35! He was one of only twenty-seven members of the *Wehrmacht* to be awarded the Knight's Cross with Oakleaves, Swords and Diamonds. (*Deutsches Wehrkundearchiv*)

Knight's Cross with Oakleaves: He became the 302nd recipient on 15 September 1943 as *Major* and Commander of I. Battalion of Füsilier Regiment 22 while still attached to 1st Infantry Division for action on Lake Ladogo in July and August 1943. His battalion fought against a large Soviet force and managed to hold them back for fourteen days, with Tolsdorff leading from the front. For this he was awarded the Oakleaves and was presented with the award personally by Hitler in September at his home on the Obersalzburg, the Berghof. On 18 November Tolsdorff was delegated with the leadership of Fusilier Regiment 22, seeing further action on the southern sector of the Soviet Front. He was wounded once again on 22 November 1943 and hospitalised until June 1944.

Knight's Cross with Oakleaves and Swords: Awarded on 18 July 1944, to become the eightieth recipient, as *Oberstleutnant* and Commander of Grenadier Regiment 1067 and Leader of Battle Group Tolsdorff in Vilnius. Tolsdorff took over command of a scratch force and made it into a Battle Group that broke through to the garrison at Vilnius and succeeded in rescuing 3,000 wounded German soldiers. He and his men distinguished themselves during the defence of the city, so much so that Tolsdorff was named 'The Lion of Vilnius' by German propaganda. He was personally presented with the Swords by Hitler at his headquarters at Rastenburg in August 1944, and was promoted to *Oberst*. On 15 September he was delegated with the leadership of the 340th Volksgrenadier Division and oversaw the formation of the newly formed division in East Prussia. In mid-November the unit transferred to the Aachen area to defend against US forces trying to cross the Rhine. On 30 January 1945 Tolsdorff was promoted to *Generalmajor* and his command of a division was confirmed.

In December 1952 Tolsdorff was arrested and charged with the execution of *Hauptmann* Holzey on 3 May 1945. As a result of the hearing he was sentenced to two and a half years' imprisonment. The finding was later overturned by a Federal Court and a retrial was ordered, and in June 1960 Tolsdorff was found not guilty. (*Deutsches Wehrkundearchiv*)

Knight's Cross with Oakleaves, Swords and Diamonds: He became the twenty-fifth recipient on 18 March 1945 as *Generalmajor* and Commander of 340th *Volksgrenadier* Division, part of Army Group B, in recognition of his excellent leadership during the Battle of the Bulge, where his troops successfully seized and held a river crossing. The presentation of the Diamonds was made by Hitler in the Bunker of the Reich Chancellery in Berlin in late March 1945, and by that time Tolsdorff had been promoted to *Generalleutnant*. He ended the war as Commander of the LXXXII. Army Corps in the Amberg area of Bavaria, seeing action against the Americans. He surrendered to US forces of the 101st Airborne on 8 May 1945 and was released from captivity two years later.

Eugen-Heinrich BLEYER

Generalleutnant

* 20 November 1896, Mainz, Hesse
+ 18 March 1979, Bad Tölz, Bavaria

Eugen-Heinrich Bleyer entered the Army on 13 August 1914 as a *Fahnenjunker* with Infantry Regiment 117. He attended an officer training course at Döberitz from November before being transferred into Infantry Regiment 186 as a newly commissioned *Leutnant* in May 1915. He was wounded in battle in October and hospitalised. He returned to his regiment in July 1916 as an adjutant, and later served briefly in the *Freikorps*. At the beginning of the Second World War, with the rank of *Oberstleutnant*, he served as Commander of II. Battalion of Infantry Regiment 355, seeing action during the Saar Offensive against the French. From 15 March 1940 he served with Infantry Regiment 630 as a Battalion Commander, later seeing action on the Siegfried Line. In March 1941 he was appointed Commander of Infantry Regiment 379, part of the 169th Infantry Division, and served on occupation duty in France. (*Deutsches Wehrkundearchiv*)

Knight's Cross: Awarded on 14 December 1941 as *Oberstleutnant* and Commander of Infantry Regiment 379 while attached to the 169th Infantry Division for his leadership and skill on the Arctic Front in 1941. This was awarded particularly for his intervention and pushing back Soviet forces near Keinuvaar during the Battle of Salla in Finland. Bleyer was promoted to *Oberst* in January 1942, and after the division was pushed back by Soviet forces he remained in Lapland with his regiment until April 1943. Shortly after attending the 4th Divisional Leaders Course in May 1943, Bleyer took over the leadership of the 258th Infantry Division in October. He was promoted to *Generalmajor* in December and his command of the division was confirmed. Bleyer led the division in the Mius and Dnieper retreats and fought on the Nikopol Bridgehead, and from March 1944 took part in the withdrawal from the lower Dnieper bend. In July he was promoted to *Generalleutnant* and from September he was attached to Army Group South. From October he was Commander of the 181st Infantry Division. He took part in the heavy fighting on the southern sector of the Eastern Front until the end of the war. Bleyer was captured by Yugoslavian forces and a large number of his troops were murdered by Yugoslav Communist partisans after they had surrendered. Bleyer was sentenced to death by a Yugoslav court but his sentence was commuted to eighteen years' imprisonment in June 1950. He was granted an amnesty and released in May 1952, whereupon he returned to Germany.

Walter FRIES

General der Panzertruppe

* 22nd April 1894, Gusterhain, Dillkreis, Hessen-Nassau
+ 6 August 1982, Weilbug an der Lahn

Walter Fries entered Army service in October 1912, seeing action during the First World War with Infantry Regiment 88. Commissioned as a *Leutnant* in January 1915, he served as a Company Leader and was awarded both classes of the Iron Cross. After the war he joined the police, rising to the rank of *Polizei-Major* in September 1934, and then transferred back into the Army in March 1936 with the rank of *Major*. From October 1936 he served as Commander of II. Battalion of Motorised Infantry Regiment 15, and was promoted to *Oberstleutnant* in March 1938. He saw action in Poland, where he was awarded the Bar to both the Iron Cross 1st and 2nd Classes. (*Author's Collection*)

Knight's Cross: Awarded on 14 December 1941 as *Oberst* and Commander of Motorised Infantry Regiment 87 while attached to the 36th Motorised Infantry Division after the storming of the Duderhof Heights, part of Leningrad, which laid the foundation for the attack on the city itself. Fries was an excellent regimental commander who inspired his troops and whose initiatives brought crucial success to his command. Fries took part in various defensive battles from January 1942 until July 1942, when he had to withdraw to more favourable defensive positions near Trisseli, Barsuki and Prilepy. From December he was transferred to the Reserves for a well-deserved rest and from January 1943 he served as Commander of the Staff at the Infantry School in Döberitz. On 23 June he was appointed Commander of the newly formed 29th Panzer Grenadier Division, which had been formed from the 29th Infantry Division in France after its annihilation at Stalingrad. It was soon moved to Italy and then to Sicily, where Fries was promoted to *Generalmajor* in June, taking part in the defence against the Allied landings the following month. With the loss of Sicily very possible, his division was moved to mainland Italy in mid-August 1943, and later when American troops went ashore near Salerno his division was used to seal off the American bridgehead. From November 1943 until January 1944 Fries saw action during the defence of the area south of Monte Cassino, and was promoted to *Generalleutnant* on New Year's Day 1944.

Knight's Cross with Oakleaves: He became the 378th recipient of the Oakleaves on 29 January 1944 as *Generalleutnant* and Commander of the 29th Panzer Grenadier Division, part of the XIV. Army Corps, for his actions and bravery during the landing in Sicily by the Allies. His command was involved in near ceaseless combat and he was mentioned twice in the daily *Wehrmacht* Reports. His division fulfilled its missions even under the most difficult of circumstances during heavy combat in Sicily, during the battle of Salerno and the defence of the southern Italian front. He was personally commended by *Generalfeldmarschall* Albert Kesselring, the Commander-in-Chief South-west, and the Oakleaves were personally presented to Fries by Hitler at the Berghof on 19 March 1944.

Knight's Cross with Oakleaves and Swords: Awarded on 11 August 1944 to become the eighty-seventh recipient as *Generalleutnant* and while still serving as Commander of the 29th Panzer Grenadier Division for his command and bravery during the heavy fighting west of Lake Trasimero and in Florence, Italy. Furthermore he led numerous and successful counter-attacks during this time and alongside the bravery of his troops the successes and achievements were down to his leadership. Hitler presented Fries with the Swords during a ceremony at his Wolf's Lair headquarters in Rastenburg. In September 1944 he took over the leadership of the XXXXVI. Panzer Corps stationed in Warsaw and after his promotion to *General der Panzertruppe* on 1 December his command was confirmed. On 20 January 1945, Fries was unjustly relieved of his command by Hitler for his failure to prevent Soviet forces from breaking out of the Baranov Bridgehead on the River Vistula, south of Warsaw. He was arrested and tried by court martial before the Reichs War Court in Torgau from 24 March, and was accused of retreating without orders – a serious offence. He was represented by *General der Panzertruppe* Otto von Knobelsdorff, who argued well for Fries and he was acquitted of all charges in April but was never reassigned – although the war would be over in a matter of weeks.

Alfons HITTER

Generalleutnant

* 4 June 1892, Höchstadt, Altkirch in Alsace North-Eastern France
+ 11 March 1968, Thomasberg, North Rhine-Westphalia

Alfons Hitter entered Army service in October 1911 with the Reserves, and was officially called up for front-line duty in August 1914 with the 6th Battery of Reserve Foot Artillery Regiment 10. He was awarded both classes of the Iron Cross during the war and retired from Army service in December 1918. He rejoined the Army in June 1922, given the rank of *Leutnant* and was attached to the Artillery School until October 1924. He served with Artillery regiment 3 until September 1930, he rose to the rank of *Hauptmann* and was appointed Commander of the 1st Battery of Artillery Regiment 5. He was promoted to *Major* in September 1934 and soon after was appointed Commander of I. Battalion of Artillery Regiment 52. When the Second World War began he was serving with Special Purpose Artillery Regiment Staff 613 and was awarded both classes of the Bar to the Iron Cross in 1940. (*Deutsches Wehrkundearchiv*)

Knight's Cross: Awarded on 14 December 1941 as *Oberst* and Commander of Artillery Regiment 178 of the 78th Infantry Division for his outstanding defensive support during the fighting in the Yelnya Salient from 30 August until 8 September 1941, part of the Battle of Smolensk against the Soviet Army. At the beginning of February 1942 Hitter was Commander of Artillery Command 112 and from mid-February to May he was attached to the *Führer* Reserve. On 3 May 1942 he was appointed Leader of the 206th Infantry Division, taking over as commander during a fighting retreat north-west of Rzhev during heavy trench fighting. In August 1942 Hitter was promoted to *Generalmajor* and his command of the division was confirmed and he continued to see action on the Russian Front and on 1 March 1943 he was promoted to *Generalleutnant*.

Knight's Cross with Oakleaves: He became the 488th recipient on 4 June 1944 as *Generalleutnant* and Commander of the 206th Infantry Division while attached to the LIII. Army Corps for continued actions on the Russian Front. In particular during the period between December 1943 and January 1944, when he succeeded in preventing a Soviet breakthrough near Vitebsk. Hitter was presented with the Oakleaves by Hitler at his Bavarian retreat, the Berghof on the Obersalzburg, towards the end of 1944. On 25 June Hitter was appointed Commander of Fortress Vitebsk, but he could not hold back the Soviet forces and just three days later his command was captured by the Soviets and he was imprisoned until 9 October 1955.

Paul LAUX

General der Infanterie

* 11 November 1887, Weimar, Thüringia
+ 3 September 1944, Field Hospital 158 in Riga, Latvia

Paul Laux entered Army service as a *Fahnenjunker* with Infantry Regiment 134 in February 1907 and was commissioned as a *Leutnant* in August 1908. At the start of the First World War he was an adjutant with I. Battalion of his regiment and was promoted to *Oberleutnant* within weeks. From 1916 until the end of the war he served as a general staff officer with XXVII. Reserve Corps and was promoted to *Hauptmann* in August 1916. He remained in the Army after the war and served in various staff posts. In October 1935 he was appointed Commander of Infantry Regiment 24 with the rank of *Oberst*. At the beginning of the Second World War he held the rank of *Generalmajor* and was Senior Quartermaster of the 1st Army. He was awarded the Bar to the Iron Cross 1st and 2nd Classes in 1940. (*Deutsches Wehrkundearchiv*)

Knight's Cross: Awarded on 14 December 1941 as *Generalleutnant* and Commander of 126th Infantry Division while attached to the XXXIX. Army Corps for his leadership during the seizure and expansion of a bridgehead over the Volkhov River at Kusino in the Soviet Union. Despite the terrain and bad weather, Laux and his division were able to secure the jump-off area for the successful attack on Tikhvin, a town near Leningrad. An official announcement stated, 'The success of the attack was largely due to the leadership, energy and commitment of the 126th Infantry Division and its commander Generalleutnant Laux.' In October 1942 he was appointed Leader of Corps *Laux*, a unit formed from the 8th *Jäger* and 81st Infantry Divisions, which he led as part of the 16th Army at Demyansk. It was a brief command as from 28 November 1942 he was named as Commander of the II. Army Corps and on 1 December he was promoted to *General der Infanterie*. He remained in the same area and continued in combat in Demyansk until the end of February 1943, when his corps was used for defensive fighting in the Cholm and Nevel areas.

Knight's Cross with Oakleaves: He became the 237th recipient on 17 May 1943 as *General der Infanterie* and Commanding General of the II. Army Corps as part of the 16th Army for his leadership during the defence of the Demyansk Salient during two large Soviet offensives in 1942. The Oakleaves were presented to him by Hitler on 28 August 1943 at the Wolf's Lair in Rastenburg. The fighting in the areas around Cholm continued until February 1944, and then from 1 April Laux was delegated with the leadership of the 16th Army. He continued to see defensive fighting in the areas around Cholm, Pustoshka and Pskov until July 1944. Later the southern wing of Army Group North, which included the 16th Army, had to retreat along the Dvina to Riga, where they were cut off from the Red Army. On 30 August Laux, while making a reconnaissance flight in his private aircraft, crashed and was seriously wounded. He was rushed to Field Hospital 158 in Riga, where he died of his wounds on 2 September 1944. He is buried today at the German War Cemetery in Ogre, Riga, in Latvia.

Gustav Adolf Heinrich WAGNER

Generalmajor

* 23 September 1890, Bischofsburg, East Prussia
\+ 26 May 1951, Goslar, Lower Saxony

Gustav Wagner volunteered to join the Army in October 1909 as a *Gefreiter* and was part of the *Jäger* Battalion 'Graf Yorck von Wartenburg' No: 1 in East Prussia. He saw action at the start of the First World War with this unit and was wounded in action on 23 August. He also saw action during the Battle of Tannenburg and served through the war as a non-commissioned officer. He had won both classes of the Iron Cross and saw service in the *Reichswehr* after the war, being commissioned as a *Leutnant* in September 1919. He commanded various machine gun units and a training battalion, and from October 1935, now with the rank of *Major*, he was Commander of III. Battalion of Infantry Regiment 44. Promoted to *Oberstleutnant* in April 1937, he saw action in Poland during the Second World War. (*Deutsches Wehrkundearchiv*)

Knight's Cross: Awarded on 14 December 1941 as *Oberst* and Commander of Infantry Regiment 44 while attached to the 11th Infantry Division in recognition of his regiment's breakthrough of the Soviet bunker line at Kirishi just west of Volkhov. There his regiment destroyed 533 hostile enemy bunkers and in doing so helped with the rapid collapse of Soviet resistance in the area and he was revered by his men as 'Iron Gustav'. As part of the 11th Infantry Division Wagner took part in the early stages of the Siege of Leningrad and remained in command of his regiment until 30 October 1942. On 31 December 1942 he took Commander of Special Division 540, which had been formed in Moravia area of the Protectorate (formerly Czechoslovakia), where it was formed of older men, and directed local defence. He was promoted to *Generalmajor* on 1 October 1943. Wagner joined the ranks of the Reserve once again in mid-October, was taken ill in mid-1944 and hospitalised for a time. He went into Allied captivity from May 1945.

Joachim Hans Herbert WITTHÖFT

General der Infanterie

* 23 September 1887, Marienwerder, West Prussia
+ 7 July 1966, Dalheim-Rödgen, North Rhine-Westphalia

Joachim Witthoft joined the Army as a *Fahnenjunker* in December 1906 with Infantry Regiment 71 and was commissioned as a *Leutnant* in August 1907. At the beginning of the First World War he served as adjutant of the II. Battalion of Reserve Infantry Regiment 82 and was promoted to *Hauptmann* in October 1915. He later served as Company Commander and as an adjutant, and was awarded both classes of the Iron Cross. When the war ended he entered the police, where he remained until April 1936, when he transferred back into the Army with the rank of *Oberst*. He served as Commander of Infantry Regiment 6 and from October 1938 served as *Generalmajor* and Infantry Commander 26 in Düsseldorf. From August 1939 he served as Commander of the 86th Infantry Division and saw action during the invasion of France and Belgium. (*Deutsches Wehrkundearchiv*)

Knight's Cross: Awarded on 14 December 1941 as *Generalleutnant* and Commander of the 86th Infantry Division of the XXVII. Army Corps for his demonstration of great bravery and decisiveness along with his division, which achieved great battlefield success. Particularly noteworthy were his actions during Operation Volga Reservoir on 15 and 16 November 1941, where he distinguished himself through his bravery and leadership. In March 1942 he was promoted to *General der Infanterie* and was serving as Commanding General of the XXVII. Army Corps, which was heavily involved in the defensive fighting near Rzhev. From July he served as Commanding General of Security Troops and Commander of Army Area B, and from February 1943 he was Commander of Army Area South. In September he was briefly Military Commander in northern Italy, and from October served as Commander of the Security Area of the Alpine Foothills. In May 1944 he was serving as Commander of the Venetian Area and in August was relived of this post and transferred to the Reserves until mid-March 1945, when he was appointed Special Representative of the Supreme

Commander West, *Generalfeldmarschall* Gerd von Rundstedt. From April he served in a similar post of the Commander North-west *Generalfeldmarschall* Ernst Busch with its headquarters near Lüneburg Heath, where on 8 May 1945 he surrendered to British troops.

Ernst HAMMER

Generalleutnant

* 20 October 1884, Falkenau an der Eger, Bohemia, Austria
+ 2nd December 1957, Vienna, Austria

Ernst Hammer entered the Imperial Austrian Army in October 1903 as a volunteer and then from February 1908 he was adjutant of the II. Battalion of Foot Artillery Regiment 4 with the rank of *Leutnant*. He saw action during the First World War as part of the Austrian Army and was promoted to *Hauptmann* in September 1915, being awarded both classes of the Iron Cross. He remained in the Army after the war and from March 1938 he transferred into the German Army with the rank of *Generalmajor*. He was placed at the disposal of the Commander-in-Chief of the Army from November, and from April 1939 he served as Artillery Commander 32. (*Deutsches Wehrkundearchiv*)

Knight's Cross: Awarded on 20 December 1941 as *Generalleutnant* and Commander of the 75th Infantry Division for actions on the Russian Front as part of the 6th Army. Later his division crossed the Bug River and fought its way through the Ukraine via Dubno and the Teterev to the combat area around Kiev. After the Battle of Kiev the division turned to the Donets in the area south of Belgorod and fought there until June 1942, later taking part in the German offensive in the Volga area. On 20 October 1942 Hammer was named as Commander of Division 190, where he controlled replacement training units for X. Military District in Hamburg. On 4 September 1944 his division was renamed the 190th Infantry Division and was hastily mobilised and sent to the Western Front, where it fought against the US 82nd Airborne Division near Nijmegen. He saw action on the northern flank of the western front until November and then spent five months in north-west Germany, seeing action in Goch in Westphalia, Kleve in the Lower Rhine area and in Venlo in the Netherlands. From March he saw action against a large Allied ground offensive north of the Rhine, but on 4 April his division ceased to exist after it was absorbed by the recently created Infantry Division *Ulrich von Hutten*. Hammer and his staff had to get back to Germany and while trying they were captured by US troops in the Ruhr Pocket on 13 April 1945. Hammer was released from captivity in April 1947.

Norbert HOLM

Generalmajor

* 16 December 1895, Hamburg, Lower Saxony
+ 3 June 1962, Wohltorf, Hamburg

Norbert Holm entered Army service as a war volunteer with Infantry Regiment 76 in August 1914 and was commissioned as a *Leutnant* in November 1915. He saw service with the same regiment throughout the war and ended it as a machine gun officer. He stayed with the Army after the war and was promoted to *Oberleutnant* in November 1923, serving as a Company Leader. He was transferred to the Troop Office and from March 1936 he was appointed Chief of Operations in the General Staff of the 12th Division with the rank of *Major*. He was transferred to the Staff of the 23rd Infantry Regiment from October 1937 and with the rank of *Oberstleutnant* and was appointed Commander of the III. Battalion of Infantry Regiment 90. From February 1940 he was Commander of Infantry Regiment 196. (*Deutsches Wehrkundearchiv*)

Knight's Cross: Awarded on 20 December 1941 as *Oberst* and Commander of Motorised Infantry Regiment 156 while attached to the Motorised 16th Infantry Division for actions in southern Russia. At the end of January 1942 he entered the Reserves and on 27 May he became Commander of Infantry Regiment 579 and was once again assigned to the Russian Front. There on 17 July 1943 he was involved in a large-scale attack, which he survived and soon after entered the Reserves once again. From 15 August he was appointed Chief of Investigation Staff with Army Group Ukraine and from 30 August he was delegated with the Leadership of the 304th Infantry Division on the Mius-Front in the Soviet Union, as part of the 6th Army. He was briefly Commander of Infantry regiment 579 for eleven days in October and once again entered the Reserves. From March 1944 he was attached to the 214th Infantry Division as a regimental leader. From 12 May he was given leadership of the 357th Infantry Division, part of the 1st Panzer Army on the Eastern Front, and he became official Commander when he was promoted to *Generalmajor* in August 1944. On

16 September Holm was arrested by the Gestapo and the reasons are unknown but it seems that it was probably something to do with his service and possible friendship with *Generalfeldmarschall* Rommel's Chief of Staff, who had been shot for his part in the plot to kill Hitler. However, nothing could be proven against Holm but he was demoted by a special army court in October 1944 to the rank of *Schütze* (private). He later served with the 19th Panzer Division and saw action in Silesia, rosing to the rank of *Feldwebel* in March 1945. He entered US captivity on 9 May 1945 but escaped and returned home on 10 June 1945.

Hermann KRESS

Generalleutnant

* 23 July 1895, Hassfurt, Unterfranken
+ 11 August 1943, Myžako south Novorossijsk, Soviet Union

Knight's Cross: Awarded on 20 December 1941 as *Oberst* and Commander of Mountain Jäger Regiment 99, part of the 1st Mountain Division, for his part in action near Lemberg in June 1941 and during the battle for Antonovka in the Soviet Union. During the encirclement of Antonovka *Oberst* Kress and his regiment were able to attack the enemy with great accuracy and Kress decided, on his own initative, to continue the attack while leading his men from the front. He continued to see action in the Soviet Union as part of the 1st Panzer Army during the tough battles near Kharkov until September 1942, when he was promoted to *Generalmajor*. From 26 September he attended the Mountain Artillery Firing School near the Dachstein Mountains and from 23 October he was Commander of the 4th Mountain Division. He was promoted to *Generalleutnant* in May 1943, and as part of the XXXXIX. Mountain Army Corps he led his division during the capture of Rostov and in the Caucasus campaign. Following the retreat his division was engaged in heavy fighting near Novorossiysk, where on 11 August 1943 Kress was killed.

Carl PÜCHLER

General der Infanterie

* 13 May 1894, Bad Warmbrunn, Prussia
+ 5 February 1949, Heilbronn, Baden-Württemberg

Knight's Cross: Awarded on 20 December 1941 as *Oberst* and Commander of Infantry Regiment 228 while attached to the 101st Light Infantry Division for his actions during the fighting across Kiev in the Ukraine and into southern Russia at Kharkov. From June 1942 Püchler was Commander of the 257th Infantry Division, seeing action during the Battles of the Uman and Kiev Pockets. In July he was promoted to *Generalmajor* and his division was sent to France to rest and refit. He returned to the Soviet Union in April 1943, where he was promoted to *Generalleutnant* and was heavily engaged in fighting at Dnepropetrovsk, Krivoy Rog and during the Battle of the Dnieper Bend as part of the 1st Panzer Army. From 13 November 1943 he was delegated with the leadership of the XXXIX. Panzer Corps and saw action from early 1944 in the Soviet Union, once again as part of the 4th Army in Orsha, Belarus. From March until April he was delegated with the leadership of Corps Group B and entered the Reserves until 25 September, when he was given the deputy leadership of the LXXIV. Army Corps in France as part of the 7th Army. On 28 October he was appointed Commanding General of the LXVII. Army Corps and saw action at Hürtenwald, North-Rhine Westphalia in Germany and then at Malmedy in Belgium, seeing action against Canadian troops from early November, when he was promoted to *General der Infanterie*. From 16 December he was Commanding General of the LXXIV. Army Corps, and after the Americans broke out of Normandy his Army Corps managed to escape and moved towards Belgium and then into Germany, where they took part in the Battle of Aachen. He surrendered to US troops in the Ruhr Pocket on 16 April 1945 and was held prisoner until 1947.

Siegfried RUNGE

Generalmajor

* 8 June 1884, Breslau, Silesia
+ 24 March 1945, Königstädten, Hesse

Knight's Cross: Awarded on 20 December 1941 as *Oberst* and Commander of Infantry Regiment 219, part of the 95th Infantry Division, for actions on the southern sector of the Russian Front. He took part in the fighting at Kiev and Ukraine until February 1942, until he was seriously wounded and hospitalised. He was away from front-line combat until 20 September 1942, when he returned to duty as the Commander of the 26th Infantry Replacement Regiment in the Netherlands, and within ten days his command was renamed the 26th Reserve Infantry Regiment and was attached to the 156th Reserve Division on the Channel coast. By February 1943 his regiment was located at Calais, and by late 1943 it was reported to be a fully fledged combat division.

On 16 April Runge was transferred and became Battle Commandant of Mainz and Wiesbaden in Western Germany, seeing action against the American 317th Infantry Regiment. On 1 October 1944 Runge was promoted to *Generalmajor* and continued to see heavy action against the Americans. In early 1945 he was named Commander of the Rhine and his headquarters had been moved to the basement of the Waldhaus near Königstädten. On 24 March, as he left his basement headquarters after an American artillery raid to see the damage and what the shells had hit, a shell hit a tree just behind him and exploded. Runge was struck by the shrapnel, and fell down and died. Runge was a recipient of the First World War decoration the Pour le Mérite.

Otto Hans Friedrich SCHÜNEMANN

Generalleutnant

* 6 October 1891, Doberan, Mecklenburg-Schwerin
+ 29 June 1944 Pagost, about 12 miles east of Beresino, Belarus

Otto Schünemann volunteered for the Army in October 1906, trained as an NCO and was attached to the 3rd Foot Guard Regiment from October 1910. He served with this regiment throughout the First World War and was promoted to an officer candidate in September 1915, being awarded the Iron Cross 1st and 2nd Classes. When the war was over he joined the police, rising to the rank of *Polizei-Major* in December 1933, and he entered the Army in March 1936. From October he was Commander of II. Battalion of Infantry Regiment 77 with the rank of *Major*. He was promoted to *Oberstleutnant* in January 1938 and from August 1939 he was Commander of Infantry Regiment 184. (*Deutsches Wehrkundearchiv*)

Knight's Cross: Awarded on 20 December 1941 as *Oberst* and Commander of Infantry Regiment 184 while attached to 86th infantry Division for his outstanding leadership of his regiment, which enabled the city of Polotsk to be taken by an air strike on 15 July 1941. Schünemann went on to distinguish himself in the fierce fighting near Smolensk in October and took part in the attack on Moscow. His regiment advanced towards the Volga before being pushed back by the Soviet winter offensive, and from October 1942 he was given the leadership of the 337th Infantry Division. He was promoted to *Generalmajor* in November 1942 and his command was confirmed. He continued to see heavy action during the defensive fighting near Rzhev on the Volga River. From March 1943 Schünemann saw action once again near Smolensk and in May was promoted to *Generalleutnant*.

Knight's Cross with Oakleaves: He became the 339th recipient on 28 November 1943 as *Generalleutnant* and Commander of 337th Infantry Division while attached to the XXXIX. Panzer Corps for his excellent leadership during the defensive battles south of the Dnieper. During October and November he led his division during the fighting around Rzhev and during the withdrawal from Yelnya, Smolensk and Orscha, where his command was decimated during the Soviet summer offensive of 1944. On 22 June Schünemann was delegated with the leadership of the XXXIX. Panzer Corps after *General der Artillerie* Robert Martinek had been killed. Just seven days later Schünemann was himself killed by an aircraft while on the street near Pagost in Belarus.

Bibliography

Angolia, John R., *On the Field of Honor: A History of the Knight's Cross Bearers* Volume 1, San Jose, California, Roger James Bender, 1979.

Angolia, John R., *On the Field of Honor: A History of the Knight's Cross Bearers* Volume 2, San Jose, California, Roger James Bender, 1980.

Barnett, Correlli, edited by, *Hitler's Generals*, Weidenfeld & Nicholson, 1989.

Beevor, Antony, *Ardennes 1944: Hitler's Last Gamble*, Viking Press, 2015.

Beevor, Antony, *Arnhem. The Battle for the Bridges*, 1944, Viking, 2018.

Beevor, Antony, *Stalingrad*, Viking Press, 1998.

Binns, Stewart, *Barbarossa and the Bloodiest War in History,* Wildfire, 2021.

Bouysse, Grégory & Mark Spencer, *Encyclopaedia of the New Order. Knight's Cross of the Iron Cross Holders Part 1 September 1939–May 1940*, Author Publisher, 2021.

Bradley, Dermot, Karl-Friedrich Hildebrand & Markus Rövekamp, *Die Generale des Heeres 1921–1945 Band: 1–7*, Osnabrück, Bibili-Verlg, 1993–2004.

Brett-Smith, Richard, *Hitler's Generals*, Osprey, 1976.

Buttar, Prit, *Retribution. The Soviet Reconquest of Central Ukraine, 1943*, Osprey, 2019.

Buttar, Prit, *The Reckoning. The Defeat of Army Group South, 1944*, Osprey, 2020.

Caddick-Adams, Peter, *Monte Cassino. Ten Armies in Hell*, Arrow, 2013.

Chales De Beaulieu, W., *General Erich Hoepner. A Military Biography*, Casemate, 2021.

Clark, Alan, Barbarossa, *The Russian-German Conflict 1941–45*, Hutchinson, 1965.

Clark, Lloyd, *Blitzkrieg. Myth Reality and Hitler's Lightning War – France, 1940*, Atlantic Books, 2016.

Carruthers, Bob Edited, *Hitler's Wartime Orders. The Complete Führer Directives 1939–1945*, Pen & Sword, 2018.

Cooper, Matthew, *The German Army 1933–1945. Its Political and Military Failure*, Macdonald & Janes, 1978.

Dimbleby, Jonathan, *Barbarossa. How Hitler Lost the War*, Viking, 2021.

Dixon, Jeremy, *The Knight's Cross with Oakleaves 1940–1945. Biographies and Images of the 889 Recipients Vols 1+2*, Schiffer Ltd, 2012.

Ellis, Frank, *The Stalingrad Cauldron. Inside the Encirclement and Destruction of the 6th Army*, University Press of Kansas, 2013.

Erickson, John, *The Road to Berlin*, Weidenfeld & Nicolson, 1983.

Erickson, John, *The Road to Stalingrad*, Weidenfeld & Nicolson, 1977.

Forczyk, Robert, *Case Red: The Collapse of France*, Osprey Publishing, 2017.

Forczyk, Robert, *Case White: The Invasion of Poland 1939*, Osprey Publishing, 2019.

Forczyk, Robert, *Where the Iron Crosses Grow. The Crimea 1941–44*, Osprey, 2014

Fraser, David, *Knight's Cross. A Life of Field Marshal Erwin Rommel*, Harper Collins, 1993.

Gerbet, Klaus Editor, *Generalfeldmarschall Fedor von Bock. The War Diary 1939–1945*, Schiffer, 1996.

Giziowski, Richard, *The Enigma of General Blaskowitz*, Leo Cooper, 1997.

Glantz, David M., *To the Gates of Stalingrad. Soviet–German Combat Operations, April–August 1942. The Stalingrad Trilogy, Volume 1*, University Press of Kansas, 2009.
Glantz, David M., *Armageddon in Stalingrad September–November 1942. The Stalingrad Trilogy, Volume 2*, University Press of Kansas, 2009.
Glantz, David M., *Endgame at Stalingrad Book One: November 1942. The Stalingrad Trilogy, Volume 3*, University Press of Kansas, 2014.
Glantz, David M., *Endgame at Stalingrad Book Two: December 1942–February 1943. The Stalingrad Trilogy, Volume 3*, University Press of Kansas, 2014.
Glantz, David M., *The Battle for Leningrad 1941–1944*, University Press of Kansas, 2002.
Glantz, David M. & Jonathan M. House, *The Battle of Kursk*, Ian Allan, 1999.
Goeritz, Walter, *Paulus and Stalingrad*, Methuen & Co. Ltd, 1963.
Goralski, Robert, *World War II Almanac 1931–1945. A Political and Military Record*, London: Hamish Hamilton, 1981.
Hargreaves, Richard, *Blitzkrieg Unleashed. The German Invasion of Poland 1939*, Pen & Sword, 2008.
Hargreaves, Richard, *The Germans in Normandy*, Pen & Sword, 2006.
Hastings, Max, Overlord. *D-Day and the Battle for Normandy 1944*, Michael Joseph, 1984.
Hébert, Valerie G., *Hitler's Generals on Trial. The Last War Crimes Tribunal at Nuremberg*, University Press of Kansas, 2010.
Holland, James, *Normandy '44. D-Day and the Battle for France*, Bantam Press, 2019.
Holland, James, *Sicily '43. The First Assault on Fortress Europe*, Bantam Press, 2020.
Holland, James, *The War in the West. A New History Germany Ascendant 1939–1941*, Bantam Press, 2015.
Holland, James, *The War in the West. A New History. The Allies Fight Back 1941–1943*, Bantam Press, 2017.
Irving, David, *The Trail of the Fox. The Search for the true Field Marshal Rommel*, E.P. Dutton, 1977.
Isaev, Alexey, *Hitler's Fortresses in the East. The Sieges if Ternopol, Kovel, Poznan & Breslau 1944–1945*, Pen & Sword, 2021.
Jacobsen, Hans-Adolf, *Dunkirk. German Operations in France 1940*, Casemate Publishers, 2019.
Kursietis, Andris J., *The Fallen Generals: The Destruction of the German Officer Corps in World War II and its aftermath*, Netherlands, Andris J. Kursietis, 2015.
Lucas, James, *Hitler's Commanders. German Bravery in the Field 1939–1945*, Cassell & Co., 2000.
Luther, Craig W.H. and David Stahel, *Soldiers of Barbarossa. Combat, Genocide, and Everyday Experiences on the Eastern Front, June–December 1941*, Stackpole Books, 2020.
MacLean, French L., *Quiet Flows the Rhine. German General Officer Casualties in World War II*, J.J. Fedorowicz Publishing, 1996.
Mallett, Derek R., *Hitler's Generals in America. Nazi POWs and Allied Military Intelligence*, University Press of Kentucky, 2013.
Manstein, Erich von, *Lost Victories.* Henry Regnery Company, 1958.
Marshall, Charles F., *The Rommel Murder. The Life and Death of the Desert Fox*, Stackpole Books, 1994.
May, Ernest R., *Strange Victory. Hitler's Conquest of France.* I.B. Tauris, 2000.
McCroden, William T. & Thomas E. Nutter, *German Ground Forces of World War II. Complete Orders of Battle for Army Groups, Armies, Army Corps & other Commands of the Wehrmacht*, Savas Beatie, 2019.
Melvin, Mungo, *Manstein. Hitler's Greatest General*, Weidenfeld & Nicholson, 2010.

Messenger, Charles, *The Last Prussian. A Biography of Field Marshal Gerd von Rundstedt 1875–1953*, Brasseys, 1991.

Mitcham, Samuel W., *Blitzkrieg No Longer. The German Wehrmacht in Battle, 1943*, Pen & Sword, 2010.

Mitcham, Samuel W., *Defenders of Fortress Europe. The Untold Story of the German Officers during the Allied Invasion*, Washington DC: Potomac Books, Inc., 2009.

Mitcham, Samuel W, *The German Defeat in the East* 1944–45, Stackpole, 2007.

Mitcham, Samuel W., *German Order of Battle. Volume One: 1st–290th Infantry Divisions in WWII.* Stackpole Books, 2007.

Mitcham, Samuel W., *German Order of Battle. Volume Two: 291st–999th Infantry Divisions, Named Infantry Divisions, and Special Divisions WWII*, Stackpole Books, 2007.

Mitcham, Samuel W., *German Order of Battle. Volume Three: Panzer, Panzer Grenadier, and Waffen-SS Divisions in WWII*, Stackpole Books, 2007.

Mitcham, Samuel W., *Hitler's Field Marshals and their Battles*, Guild Publishing, 1988.

Mitcham, Samuel W., *The Men of Barbarossa. Commanders of the German Invasion of Russia, 1941*, Casemate Publishers, 2009.

Mitcham, Samuel W., Panzer Commanders of the Western Front. German Tank Generals in WWII, Stackpole, 2008.

Mitcham, Samuel W., *Panzers in Winter. Hitler's Army and the Battle of the Bulge*, Praeger Security International, 2006.

Mitcham, Samuel W., *Rommel's Lieutenants. The Men who Served the Desert Fox, France, 1940*, Stackpole, 2007.

Mitcham, Samuel W & Gene Mueller, *Hitler's Commanders.* Leo Cooper, 1992.

Möbus, Ingo, *Die Sächsischen Ritterkreuzträger 1939–1945 Band 1: Ahnert-Haude*, Westermann Druck Zwickau GmbH, 2021.

Moorhouse, Roger, *Poland 1939. The Outbreak of World War II*, Basic Books, 2020.

Müller, Rolf-Dieter, *Enemy in the East. Hitler's Secret Plans to Invade the Soviet Union*, I.B. Tauris, 2015.

Nafziger, George F., *The German Order of Battle. Infantry in World War II*, London: Greenhill Books, 2000.

Nafziger, George F., *The German Order of Battle. Panzers and Artillery in World War II*, London: Greenhill Books, 1999.

Newton, Steven H., *Hitler's Commander. Field Marshal Walther Model – Hitler's Favorite General*, Da Capo Press, 2006.

Paget, R.T., *Manstein. His Campaigns and his Trial*, Collins, 1951.

Parker, Danny S., ed. *The Battle of the Bulge. The German View*, Greenhill Books, 1999.

Sadarananda, Dana v., *Beyond Stalingrad. Manstein and the Operations of Army Group Don*, Stackpole Books, 1990.

Scherzer, Veit, *Deustche Truppen im Zweiten Weltkrieg: Die Divisionen* Band 2–7. Scherzers Militaer Verlag, 2007–2011.

Scherzer, Veit, *Ritterkreuzträger 1939–1945*, Scherzers Militaer-Verlag Ranis, 2007.

Seaton, Albert, *The German Army 1933–1945*, Weidenfeld & Nicholson, 1982.

Shepherd, Ben H., *Hitler's Soldiers. The German Army in the Third Reich*, Yale University Press, 2016.

Stein, Marcel, *A Flawed Genius. Field Marshal Walter Model. A Critical Biography*, Helion & Company, 2010.

Stockert, Peter, *Die Eichenlaubträger 1940–1945 Band: 1–4*, Verlag Friedrichshaller Rundblick, 1997.

Taylor, Brian, *Barbarossa to Berlin: A Chronology of the Campaigns on the Eastern Front 1941 to 1945*, two volumes, Spellmount, 2003 & 2004.

Thomas, Franz & Günter Wegmann, *Die Ritterkreuzträger der Deutschen Wehrmacht 1939–1945 Band: 1–7* Osnabrück, Biblio-Verlag 1987–2010.

Thomas, Franz & Günter Wegmann, *Die Ritterkreuzträger der Gebirgstruppe Band: 1–2* Osnabrück, Biblio-Verlag 1993–1994.

Trig, Jonathan, *Barbarossa Through German Eyes. The biggest invasion in history*, Amberley, 2021.

Tucker-Jones, Anthony, *Hitler's Panzers. The Complete History 1933–1945*, Pen & Sword, 2020.

Turney, Alfred, *Disaster at Moscow. Von Bock's Campaigns 1941–42*, Cassell, 1970.

Wegmann, Günter, *Die Ritterkreuzträger der Panzertruppe Band: 1–2* Bissendorf, Biblio-Verlag, 2004–2009.

Williamson, Gordon, *Knight's Cross and Oakleaves Recipients 1939–40*, Osprey, 2004.

Williamson, Gordon, *Knight's Cross and Oakleaves Recipients 1941–45*, Osprey, 2005.

Williamson, Gordon, *Knight's Cross, Oakleaves and Swords Recipients 1941–45*, Osprey, 2005.

Williamson, Gordon, *Knight's Cross with Diamonds Recipients*, Osprey, 2006.

Yerger, Mark C. & Leslie K. Fiorenza, *Honoring Those They Led. Decorated Field Commanders of the Third Reich: Command Authorities, Award Parameters, and Ranks*. Helion & Co., 2016.

Zetterling, Niklas & Anders Frankson, *The Korsun Pocket. The Encirclement and Breakout of a Germany Army in the East, 1944*, Casemate Publishers, 2008.

Ziemke, Earl F., *Stalingrad to Berlin. The German Defeat in the East*, US Army Center of Military History, 1968.

Ziemke, Earl F. and Magna E. Bauer, *Moscow to Stalingrad. Decision in the East*, Military Heritage Press, 1988.